SPELL BOUND

E. E. ROBENS

To Harley,

My One and Only

Beware of the devil that'll kiss you goodnight,

Then crawl inside your head and mystify your sight.

PROLOGUE

I snapped my eyes open as ambulance sirens grew nearer by the second. The world hung belly up as rain drops clashed on the windshield and the gloom pressed on my soul. I unbuckled the seat belt, dropped and turned slow as a serpent until my eyes aligned with the horizon. I tilted my head in the cracked rear view mirror, my face purple and bloody. Specks of raw flesh on my arms shone in the dark and only then, my body ached with every inch.

I kicked the car door open and comminuted windows crumbled to the ground. I crawled out and away, chasing the fumes of a pickup truck rolled on its cheek with the windshield shattered and the wheels gyrating like French roulette. And the closer I loomed, the more I trembled with fear. Fear I dreaded to fear. His chin was dunked into his chest, his body belted into the seat.

I extended my hand, shaky and mortal through the windshield frame and brushed the dashboard to flip his hair away. Away from his forehead, away from his face. As my fingertips swam through, my chest rose out of composure and my pulse hastened in fright. I tucked the hazelnut strands behind his ear and gasped in anguish. Tiny pieces of broken glass slithered from his locks as he craned his head up with blood dripping down his temples and one eye swollen shut.

I cupped his head in my hands. "Stay still. Stay still. Help is on the way . . ." I choked on my words and tears mixed with a tint of revenge.

PART ONE

SPELLBOUND IN C

CHAPTER

1

I reclined in the coffee shop and sipped on a fresh latte while the rain drenched the windows, a dripping façade of haze. A booklet nestled on the table, baby green and bright, waiting to be claimed, rescued by a hominid. I drew it closer and scouted the room. Humans scattered with laptops were engrossed in their own reality. I flipped it open to one of those programs where infinite amounts of applicants compete for a handful of seats and impossible to squeeze through acceptance. I'd strutted home from college with the big G once, diploma in hands, booster to the morale, family pride. My father set up a small trust with enough to pay a good chunk of an average college tuition. Average my ass — if you count private college fees — but okay, whatever, I did it.

I glimpsed at my phone for the time, downed the last sip of latte and rushed out of the café.

"Glad you're here. I can go home and dote on my son," Heather said as I strolled inside The Beauty Bar.

"Race it." I planted my tote on the glass counter top and fished out my handheld mirror.

"College?" she asked toward the course guide sticking out of my tote.

"No, not again," I said, mending my lip gloss.

"Then why are you carrying a college booklet?"

"Someone left it in a coffee shop."

"And —"

"And nothing. How far is Brenton City anyway?"

Heather picked up her purse on her way to the door. "About a forty-minute drive, northbound. See you at home."

At dusk, I sat in bed with the booklet on my lap, parted in half, pages open and daring. Maybe I'll ask my tormenting questions, find out the program is way over my head and leave it at that.

Eight o'clock in the a.m., I cruised to Brenton City, sizzling drive-thru coffee in hand. Brimley College unfolded its logo in front of my eyes before I hopped onto the highway off-ramp. I never entertained the idea of community college and yet, here I was swaying into campus on this crisp January morning.

I parked by the meters outside the library and when I stepped into the lobby, I froze in awe. Students marched in every direction, gigantic stairs lead to the upper floors and an impressive library on the right shone in all its glory. Music played by the library entrance, the atmosphere upbeat. So, this is the vibe of a community college. The private college I attended had a classroom and a spa room for practice. End of story.

I tucked my reticence in my back pocket and ambled to the information desk.

"I'd like to inquire about the Paramedic Program admission process."

"Your name?"

I half-opened my mouth, then seized a pen from the clerk's desk and jotted my name on a piece of paper, eyeing my own cursive with a bucket of vanity, saving me practice for Spelling Bee. She peeped at my last name, a scarce appellation and instead of handing me a college application, she sent me to a counselor's office. I tracked the directions in a daze, uncertain of my need for counselor advice.

"I suggest enrolling in Pre-Health Sciences," the counselor said.

"Uhm, can't I just write the Paramedic Exam?"

"No. How long ago have you graduated from high school?"

"Five years ago," I murmured, as if I'd committed a sin.

"Which is why you need to complete a preliminary program to make you eligible to write the exam."

"I had no idea it'd be this complicated."

"Plus, to be accepted for the introductory program and at the college altogether, you'd have to pass an entrance exam for English and Math."

"Doesn't my high school transcript count?"

"No. You've graduated more than a year ago."

"What about the private college I attended before this?"

"Not in the least."

My breath wedged in my throat. "So, I'd have to register for a program before taking *the* program? And before that, I have to pass two tests?"

"Basically, yes. Rules toughen every year. It would be wise to apply now and not wait until later."

I finally understood the need for counselor's advice. It came in order after this conversation.

"Now what?" Leave the college, buy a coffee, head to work.

"Let's see," she said, scrolling on the computer. "I can book you for English and Math tomorrow."

"No," I shouted, then I caught myself. "Sorry, not tomorrow."

"Thursday?" Thursday as in the day after tomorrow? I nodded, swallowing hard. "All right, you're booked. Good luck."

I sauntered out of the office dejected and fiddled through the day at work just the same. Never mind the Paramedic test, I feared Math. My lowest marks in high school were at Math. I only passed because my best friend fed it into me on supplemental hours.

After I prepared for two nights — scarcely enough for two crucial tests — I debated whether to show up at the college or not until the moment I coasted through the campus gates. I tried to counsel my own nerves. What's the worst it could happen? I fail, I go home.

I crept inside the testing room with shivery skin. Then I rolled through the test with shaky hands and gasping for air. Post-test, I reassured myself I had nothing to lose. Except for a greater future.

When the testing lady strode in with the result paper in hand, I stared at her the way I did at the vaccinating nurse in childhood.

"Congratulations and welcome to Brimley College."

I lunged at her for joy as she hugged me loose with obvious discomfort. Then I raced to the counselor's office to boast the news, paper in hand.

"Well done. Classes started a week ago but wait . . .," she said and picked up the phone. A short conversation later, "I squeezed you in. I hope you're ready. It's going to be a long and difficult road."

I dismissed her words for the moment to relish my triumph. I marched to the Office of the Registrar and when I held my student card, my excitement amplified tenfold. I navigated through the corridors with blood rushing to my cheeks, adrenaline kicking in and holy crap, I was officially a college student. Again. I eased onto a bench next to the library to take it all in and unconsciously prepare for the greatest ride of my life.

CHAPTER

2

The first day at school, I lost my way around the hallways in search for the lockers and the classrooms, mouthing questions of anxiety. Will I fit in? Will I make it through the day? Will I come out alive after the first week?

I stepped into the first lecture hall, wishing I could turn into a fly. The door opened from the back of the auditorium. No one turned and I liked my classmates already. I tiptoed to an aisle seat.

"All textbooks away. I'll be passing the test shortly," said the math professor. What? No. Someone help me. He dropped the paper test on my desk and I scanned it with a sudden urge to bolt. No way will I make it through the day. I won't even make it through this class.

I handed the test over with a disconsolate heart and stumbled to the bookstore next to the Registrar's, as if I'd escaped from the torture room. Despite the horrific textbook prices, my pulse normalized and I ventured to the library with goosebumps on my arms. It came as a glimmering state-of-the-art with towering stacks, brand new computers and floor-to-ceiling windows. At the back of the library, couches soft as feathers faced the fireplace, a cozy corner for book reading or socializing students.

I attended the leftover classes with brightened countenance. I did survive the first day and drove home with a shard of optimism. But my enthusiasm turned to full blown anxiety when my brain shifted into overdrive, much like starting a car that hadn't been running for years and pressing the pedal to the floor. Mounting curriculum. Rivers of demand. I squirmed in a miasma of self-doubt.

When I received my test grade for Math at fifty five percent, I sighed with relief. Yay, I passed. It took me ten hours to write my first biology lab report and it still came out horribly wrong. Countless pages waited to be memorized but my brain failed to retain. The pressure pushed on my sanity. Unreal, terrifying. And no matter how much effort I shoved into my studies, it didn't make a difference. My grades came back low and ugly.

"It's stressful but it's good stress," Heather said one evening, when she found me in a trance with my head on the kitchen counter.

I moved in with Heather right off the steps of Pearson after I indulged in European air for a year and a half.

"Had enough?" she asked at the arrivals.

"Never."

"You can take the top floor. Carl and I will hang out on the first. It's easier with the baby until he grows a bit more."

"It's temporary until I'll find my own place."

"You can stay as long as you like. I need someone I trust to take over the spa during my maternity leave. Besides, Carl bought a transport truck and he's mostly on the road these days."

I befriended my classmates, a cool gang. We'd been assigned in pairs and groups to work on projects. We loathed it at first — forced interaction, yikes — but it worked like a charm and soon enough, I conquered the hallways in giggles next to my peers.

"Let's go to the bar," said a classmate from the group after class.

"There's a bar inside the college?" I asked.

Chuckles in unison. "Two bars and a restaurant."

"Really? Can we bring our homework?"

"We're going to the bar for beers not homework."

I brought my homework anyway. The guys gulped on beer while us girls talked academics, then we bounced to Physics with virtuous vibes. And bang, I was hooked on school. I couldn't wait for the weekend to pass, just so I'd gallop to school again. On break periods, I hung out at the library, the ambiance soothing like the wind on a hot summer day. And sometimes, I didn't want to leave school at all.

I called my mom to give her the news.

"You started college for two weeks and I'm finding out now?"

"Mom, congratulations would be nice."

"How could you not call me the minute you made such an important decision?"

"I had to pass two tests. I didn't say anything, in case I failed. I held a student card before I even digested the notion of community college. It happened at the speed of light."

"Congratulations but make sure you keep me up with the current events in your life."

"That's what I'm doing, Mom."

"I mean, sooner than soon," she said. "How do you like your new school?"

"It's different than private, which was awesome too but I adore Brimley. My classmates are friendly and the teachers are amazing."

My mother paused in astonishment. Then, "What profession?"

"Paramedic."

"Paramedic? That's a noble career but I never pictured you in the medical field."

"Mom, I work in aesthetics. Many concepts cross over from medical. But thanks for your support."

"I meant to say good luck. I'm sure you'll do well."

One morning at school, the perfect picture student grazed my shoulder with locking eyes as we passed each other in the library. Tall, slender with chestnut hair and prominent cheekbones, well dressed. He was the model type, the hottest one in school.

"Hey, what's your name?" he asked, when we stumbled upon each other at the parking office later in the week.

I checked my invisible watch, "Hi, I have to go," and raced down the hall.

"Nice to meet you, I Have To Go," he yelled from behind.

Two days later, I lingered with homework at the library. When I hit the cafeteria for a coffee break, the fashion model swerved in my direction.

"Hi, I'm Marcus."

"Alexa . . . short for Alexandra. Sorry about the other day. I had to run to class."

"What are you taking?"

"Pre-Health."

"Pre? It sounds like you're preparing for something."

"The Paramedic Program," I said, straightening my posture.

"Wow, paramedic. Maybe you'll save *me* one day. I'm in Business Management."

"Figures," I muttered under my breath. "On your way to class?"

"Yeah, I have a late one. But I'll give you my number, if you want to chat sometime."

I marked his number in my phone and dialed it back before he blew a kiss and wandered back to the hallway. Hours later, Marcus tapped a goodnight text while I still chewed my homework dry at the library.

I'd picked my locker close to my classes and a stone throw from where I parked my car. And every Tuesday morning, the same dude paddled through the college doors and down the hall, mere seconds after I would, his locker five down to mine.

The first time at his locker, I caught him peeking sideways. Forget it dude, it ain't gonna happen. The next morning, shy guy made his entrance like clockwork, moments after I did and I huffed. Loud. When he fiddled through his locker, a water bottle fell on the floor and rolled to my feet. His profile clouded with panic. I picked it up and handed it to him. He nodded a thank you with his eyes on the invisible bottle impression on the floor.

The following morning, locker boy took a lifetime to gather his textbooks, inches away from me. Okay bud, stop lingering around your locker, take your shit, go to class and give me my space already. But he didn't, so I slammed my locker door shut and rushed to class instead.

"Hi. Is it still snowing outside?" he asked a week later, rushing down the hallway in my direction.

You just came in, shithead. "No, not anymore," I sneered.

"Have a good day," he said and strayed away, eyes to the floor.

But on our next encounter, my sensitivity chip kicked in. The poor guy tried to be sociable to a fellow student and instead, I let out my inner bitch for granted.

"How are you?"

His face brightened. "I'm good and you?"

I held out my hand. "Alexandra but my friends call me Alexa. We see each other every day. We might as well know our names."

"Good idea." He shook my hand, unable to hold eye contact for long. "Ezekiel."

"Ezekiel? It's a beautiful name. What's the story behind it?"

"It's from a TV show my mom watched religiously when she was pregnant with me. And my friends call me Zeke."

"Zeke it is. Have a good class." I brushed his face with my ponytail and gunned it to class.

The next time Zeke found me by the lockers, I hadn't heard from Marcus since our late evening texting in the library and I wasn't in the mood to talk but locker boy was.

"How was your weekend?"

"Exhausting . . . so much to study."

"What, your boyfriend didn't make you breakfast in bed?"

Does that line even work anymore? "I don't have time for a boyfriend right now." I tossed my textbooks in my tote. "I'm busy with school and everything else in my life."

"All right. Good luck with school," he murmured and the moment he stepped away, I sighed. Why did I have to be such a bitch? I brushed my fingers through my hair in contempt of my morose.

Marcus texted with an invite to his house for drinks. I frowned at the nerve and didn't reply but when my phone vibrated again, I snapped it to my ear.

"Your house?"

"No, it's . . . it's not what you're thinking."

"What am I thinking?"

"My mom and my sister will be at home. It's strictly socializing to break away from school. I thought it would be more relaxing and comfortable at the same time." He paused. Then, "When would it be good for you?"

"I don't know right now." I hung up the phone, shifting my eyes from nothing to nothing.

I retreated to the library for more homework until kickout time, zombie tired and in need to glue the brims of my eyelids to my eyebrows to keep my eyes open. And as my head drifted downward before I could stop it, a human breeze woke me to cognizance. Zeke clicked the mouse on the monitor on my left side.

"I'm studying at the table behind you," he said, when I turned my head his way.

I spun my chair to his textbooks scattered on the table, my words too heavy to articulate. He roamed back to his table and I gyrated now and again to check on him — not that I cared, only to be polite — and I caught his sparkling stare every time.

When I pushed my chair behind to pack my textbooks, another chair scratched the floor behind.

"I'm done with homework too," Zeke said, zipping up his knapsack. He pointed to the aisle. "After you."

I stepped along with a faded smile toward the library exit. "What time is it? I lost track."

"Close to eleven. They're closing in a few minutes."

"That late?"

"Do you have a test tomorrow?"

"I always have tests," I said.

"So . . . do you do anything else besides school? Do you work?"

I shuffled down the hall beyond tired for an interview but I tried. "Yes, a friend of mine owns a mini-spa. I'm an aesthetician. I work four days a week, now that I'm in school."

"Ah, it explains why you're so gorgeous." An awkward silence cut through our flow. "It must be nice to work with a friend."

"I work for her but you're right, it doesn't feel like she's my boss. We met in cosmetic school and have been friends ever since."

At the lockers, we slipped our jackets on and flung our textbooks on the shelves. No energy to carry them home.

"I cannot believe you don't have a boyfriend."

"I told you, I don't have time."

I carried down the hall and peeked over my shoulder. He trailed behind with glistening eyes. I opened the exit door and the parking lot shone an immaculate coat of winter.

"Where did you park?" I asked.

"I don't have a car. I'm poor."

"You're not poor. You just don't have a car." His face caught my eye sideways. "Wait, are you even old enough to drive?"

"I'm twenty. I wouldn't be in college if I didn't have the driving license age."

"You're right but then again, there are those geniuses who make it to college before the college age. Not that you don't look the college age." This was my brain on crutches sputtering out senseless words.

Zeke's cheeks flushed while we stood outside the door, the winter breeze burning our faces. He rubbed his hands together as he faced the parking lot.

"How far do you live?" I almost offered him a ride home before my potential date with Marcus popped in my head.

"The next street over."

"I'm going the opposite way, to the highway."

"Sleep tight," he said and stumbled away in the snow.

In the a.m., Zeke waited for me by the lockers to wish me good luck with my test of the day. The next day, I did. He switched from a stroll to a strut, the moment he spotted me at the locker.

"Good morning," he said.

"What program are you taking?"

"Environmental Technology."

"Are you good at Chemistry?"

"I think so."

"No time for modesty. Are you good at chemistry or not? I need a graph drawn."

"Let me see." He leaned over the notes in my hands.

"Can I show you later? I have to run to class."

"So do I and since both our classes finish at the same time . . . why don't I wait for you after class?

"Where?"

"Meet me at the library?"

"See you then," I said, before I veered around the corner.

Three hours later, Zeke waved from a table at the back of the library, then cleared his throat as I scattered my notes on the table.

"How was class?"

"Great." I slid the graph in front of him. "This is it."

He shifted his gaze late onto the paper. "Ah, that's easy. Give me a pencil." His magic hand drew the graph in one single motion. "You never told me what program you're taking."

"Pre-Health Sciences." He scratched his cheek. "Does nobody know about this program?" I dropped my tone as *sorry* flashed across his face. "I'm taking it as a preliminary to Paramedic."

"Paramedic? I heard it's difficult to get in," he said and I gave him the death stare. "But I'm sure you'll get in just fine."

"I have to run."

"Class again?"

"Yes. Thanks for the graph." I swiped it from under his hand.

"You're welcome," he said, still in his seat. "Let me know if you need anything else."

The day I was set to meet Marcus, I ambled to the library after my last class of the day and after I slouched into a seat, he called.

"I didn't drive to school today. Can we take your car?"

"Sure."

"Where do I meet you?"

"B building by the lockers," I said with a trace of regret. The locker area had become hallowed ground for Zeke and me. I bumped into Marcus as I rounded the corner next to my locker. "I'll be two seconds."

"Take your time," he said.

I tossed the textbooks in my tote, slid my winter coat on and shut the door. We hopped in my car in giggles. And as soon as I peeled away from campus, GQ boy leaned over to kiss me.

"Relax. I have to drive."

"I don't care. I want to kiss you," he said, pushing against my cheeks.

"You should care. You're in the car too." I pressed him into his seat. "Directions please."

He guided me to a cul-de-sac in a high end area of Brenton City with million dollar mansions. Handsome and rich, how cliché. I parked my little black Toyota on his driveway, leaped out and shock-whistled in my mind.

He wrenched the door open and invited me into the foyer. A stunning Italian woman with chocolate hair and infinite legs shook my hand in introduction. Mrs Leni Pellini, his mother. Even her name echoed a Hollywood movie star. Two steps behind, a bald stocky man invited us into the brick-walled living room.

"Meet my uncle, Joe. He's funny, you'll like him," Marcus said and I hoped my crinkled face didn't betray my bewilderment. The sibling physical resemblance was missing.

"Make yourself comfortable," Mrs Pellini pointed to the couch.

"I'll bring drinks for us. I make some mean cocktails," Uncle Joe said.

"Would you like to meet my sister? I think she's in her room with a cold," Marcus said. I nodded, although not really. I suck at meeting people.

We climbed upstairs to one of the bedrooms. Marcus' sister poked her head from under the mountain of covers, high school textbooks at the foot of the bed. She groaned her name.

"Nice to meet you. We'll let you study. Get better," I said before I closed the door.

When we descended to the living room, bar-like citrus cocktails glimmered on the chess-patterned coffee table.

"Wow, you're good with cocktails," I said to Uncle Joe.

"I'm good at many things."

"Don't mind my uncle's dark humour. He's harmless," Marcus whispered in my ear. "Should we order pizza?"

"Yes."

Marcus called for pizza, then pointed the remote to the home theatre system next to a projector TV. Across from the couch, a massive backyard sprawled behind the floor-to-ceiling windows.

We chatted and giggled at the uncle's riddles, who sat in an armchair across from us. When my bid to brush off his lingering eyeballing fizzled to pieces, I tried to extinguish my annoyance with Marcus' *harmless* connotation.

The exquisite mother strutted to the living room. "I'm leaving for The Bahamas at two in the morning. I'd like you guys to turn the music on low and be discreet. I'm hoping to catch a few hours of sleep before I head to the airport." As Marcus turned down the volume, the bell sang at the door. "Your pizza is here. Enjoy and goodnight," she said, padding up the stairs with a ballerina's grace.

Pizza indulgence conveyed to silence but once finished, Marcus tapped my knee.

"Do you want to see my room?" And before I could answer, he yanked my hand to the basement. The boy of the house always scores the basement, even in a mansion. I scooted to the bathroom to freshen up.

"Don't use the toilet. It's broken," Marcus said, outside the door.

"I wasn't planning on it."

An array of expensive cologne and hair styling products aligned the shelves. I tried to pinpoint the amount of hours he spent in front of the mirror, combing his mane to perfection.

I roamed a door down to a modern and masculine bedroom with too many textbooks still sealed in their original bookstore wrap. Without wasting time, he cupped my neck and lodged a vicious kiss on my lips. Then he pushed my body toward the bed but I regained my balance.

"Slow down. I don't like what you're doing."

"You're fucking hot and I want you." What?

I stiffened my posture. "I didn't come here for this. I thought we'd relax and talk, shake off the studying jitters."

He reached for my hand. "Okay. Let's go back upstairs."

I ripped my hand away, pranced out the door and up to the living room with a scorned Marcus in tow.

He raised my glass off the coffee table. "I'll fill this for you."

"No, thanks. I have to drive home."

"Come on, you need to relax," he said, en route to the kitchen. "You can take my bed. I'll take the couch," he added, coming back.

"I'm not sleeping here tonight."

He laced an arm on my shoulder. "You're in college. Live it up."

"I am, by studying not drinking."

He planted the glass on the coffee table but I'd made up my mind that I wouldn't touch it.

"Do you know Ezekiel O'Connor?" he asked.

"Zeke? Yes. I had no idea you two knew each other. What about him?"

"I told him you were coming over tonight."

"What? Why would you do that?" A loud breath came out of my throat. "Did you two talk about me?"

He rubbed the nape of his neck. "He asked me if I thought you were hot and I said, 'yeah, she's hot' and he said, 'her locker is right next to mine, I'm talking to her.' I said, 'I'm talking to her too' and that you were coming over for drinks."

"So you talked about me." Maybe I did need a sip of cocktail but just one more. I'd told Zeke I had no time to see anyone outside of school, meanwhile, I sure made time to swing by Marcus' home at first invitation. I jolted upwards. "I have to go."

"You're not going anywhere. You can't drive."

"What? I drank maybe a glass in total."

"My uncle makes them strong. You shouldn't drive right now."

Uncle Joe barged into the room. "I heard my name. Who wants me?"

"What is up with your uncle?" I whispered.

"Nothing. Let's go to my room where it's peace and quiet."

I shadowed Marcus back to his room to escape the dreadful uncle. After he shut the door, his eyes raked down my body. He drew me into an avalanche of smooches. His charm abounded, no doubt about it and his tongue tasted like cotton candy.

"I want you." He moaned in my ear and tugged at my zipper. As I held on to his belt loops, my head spun into vertigo and I fell on the bed. "Are you okay?"

"No, I don't think I am."

He cupped my chin to kiss me but I shoved his hands away. Then I shimmied out of bed and crashed on the floor. The door flung open and Marcus' voice squealed out.

"Mooom."

Before I could breathe again, a spasm of nausea tumbled in my gut and my poor attempt to make it to the bathroom scored me a puking gig on the carpet, thick as moss. I lifted my body off the floor and stumbled up the stairs, more and more stairs, holding on to the bannister. I charged into the second floor bathroom with my stomach in a rumble and attempted to lift the toilet lid. When it wouldn't budge, I christened the bathtub with an angry cocktail with the chubby uncle's special signature on it. Then I slid on the floor with my head in my hands, dying of embarrassment.

Marcus dashed in. "What happened?"

"I don't know."

"Let me help you."

He laced an arm around my waist and hauled me up and onto a truncated wooden counter. But I slid off like water, hit my head on a potpourri basket and crumpled on the floor. My eyes closed against my will and Marcus yelled for his mom again. Steps closed in until the door opened.

"Did she hit her head?" Mrs Pellini asked with a shaky voice.

"I don't think so."

Two fingertips pressed on my radial pulse.

"Squeeze my hand if you can hear me," she said. I did. I was awake but not alert. "Are you going to be okay?" I half-nodded. "Should I call an ambulance?" I gave a mere shake of the head. "How many drinks did you give her?" she scolded Marcus.

"Mom, she only had a glass. I don't know what happened."

"Take her somewhere comfortable where she can rest until the morning."

Marcus picked me up and after he descended a million stairs, he deposited me on a bed. The clunk of the door shut startled me into semi-awareness. I was alone in his bedroom with the ceiling light burning my pupils like the sun. I rolled on my side and closed my eyes.

Minutes or hours later, when the door creaked, I flicked my eyes open. "Hello. Hello. Hello." The uncle's grunt disturbed my peace. I shut my eyes and lay still. "Alexa. Alexa." Get lost. After he called my name a dozen times, he stopped. I hoped he'd disappear — possibly forever — but instead, his short steady steps loomed toward the bed. His body weight dipped into the mattress and I froze into my wits, fully awake now with my skin crawling with bugs. He nudged my back and I envisioned my fist swatting into his morbid face but I stood still as a statue. He slid his hand down my spine in a rub and flipped his palm under my jeans.

I jolted up like burned. "What are you doing? How dare you touch me? Where is Marcus?"

I levered out of bed in abrupt sobriety, stormed upstairs to the foyer and parked my behind on the second step of the staircase to put my shoes on.

Marcus raced out of the den, next to the foyer. "Alexa, what happened?"

"Why did you leave me alone? Your uncle came to your room and tried to fondle me."

"What?"

"Did you plan this? I'm out of here."

"I'm so sorry. I had no idea. I should've never left you alone."

I threw my coat on my back, snatched my tote and banged out the front door with Marcus chasing my footsteps.

"Come on, you cannot possibly think I knew this would happen. I wanted to give you space and let you sleep."

I tramped through the deep snow and unlocked the door to my car. Before I could open it, Marcus shoved his body against it and barricaded the driver seat.

"Let me get in my car." My howl echoed to the neighbours.

"No. You can't drive right now."

"You brought me to your house. You were supposed to look out for me." I pushed him to the side and swung the car door open.

"What is going on?" Mrs Pellini rushed outside in a satin house-coat, gorgeous and lush against the angry rockets in the snow.

Uncle Joe leaned against a family collection deluxe SUV in the driveway. "I didn't do anything. I tried to make sure she was all right. She's drunk. She doesn't know what she's talking about."

"You liar. You're a fucking pervert."

I dove into the driver seat but Marcus held the door open. He bent inside my car. "Come on, you have to believe me."

I tugged on the car door to close it. "Let go of my door now."

"Please, believe me."

Mrs Pellini hovered over her son. "Marcus, take her keys away."

He faced his mother. "But she doesn't believe me."

"Hold the door," she told him. She squeezed in front of him, shoved her torso inside my car and stretched for my right hand. "Give them up," she said while the uncle still yelled out his innocence in the background.

I swung the keys in the air with tears gushing out of my eyes. "No, I'm not going back in that house."

Mrs Pellini mobilized my arm and seized the keys, my hand like jelly. Then she paddled toward the house without a word, car keys squeezed tight in her fist.

"Can you please come inside? It's freezing out here," Marcus said, holding out his hand for mine. I finally hurdled out of the car. He towed me to the house and on the way, I evil-eyed the uncle who puffed on a cigarette with eyes on the ground.

Once in the living room, I made a beeline for the couch where I curled into a ball. Marcus produced a blanket and covered me up.

"I promise you that my uncle won't come anywhere near you again," he said.

Then I closed my eyes.

"Do you want to sleep in my room?" Marcus nudged me awake.

"How long have I been asleep?"

"A couple of hours. Don't worry, I'll be there beside you. And the bed is more comfortable than the couch."

I shadowed him toward the descending stairs but stopped in my tracks when Mrs Pellini's voice echoed on the phone upstairs. I climbed up to the stunning mother in her bedroom, bent over a suitcase opened on the bed. When I stepped on the landing, she turned on her heels and met me in the hallway.

"I'd like to apologize. I'm sorry about the noise and I feel awful about the circus," I said. "Thank you for taking my car keys away and also for being such a good sport."

"Don't worry about it. I'm glad you're okay now," she said and drew me into a hug.

I wasn't planning on driving away. In my dread over the uncle, I would've slept in my car without considering the chance of turning into an ice sculpture by morning. I owed Mrs Pellini my life.

I tiptoed inside Marcus' room to find him in bed watching TV he didn't care about. The moment I crawled next to him, he rolled my way and lanced for my lips with eyes glimmering like two stars on a clear night. I shook my head.

"You don't want to?"

"No, not after what happened tonight." I said it with sorrow in my voice and rested my head on his chest.

When the alarm buzzed at ten a.m., we crawled out of bed with the energy level of a newborn baby. The bathroom mirror down the hall reflected my face ravaged, my mascara smudged, my tresses — typically wavy and shoulder length — now frizzy and disheveled at the top of my head. I refreshed my face but lost interest after five seconds, then dragged my feet out and up the stairs behind Marcus. My car keys waited for me on a tallboy in the foyer.

"I'll lead you out to the highway," he said.

I half-nodded and after we struggled with the shoes, we ambled out in the snow.

"I'm sorry again about last night. I never meant for any of it to happen," Marcus said, before he broke away to his car.

"I believe you," I muttered.

"Are we cool?"

"We're cool."

"Come here." He pulled me into a hug, a bit more violent than he should after a night of uproar.

I tailed his car to the main road while I admired his striking face glowing in his left side mirror. His perfect facial features stood out, even with the hood on and the grimace from the morning sun.

I'd never step foot in his house again and I wouldn't point fingers to the theory that someone — and I have a good guess who — spiked my drink. I'd rather blame my nocturnal derail on low alcohol tolerance and student fatigue.

CHAPTER
3

D ays after the experiment of a student's body and alcohol mixture pathetic turn out at Marcus' house, neither of us attempted to communicate. I needed time to digest the events, not to mention the embarrassment of vomiting and falling all over the place at his house. I hardly found the strength to go to school the following Tuesday. I had no desire to face anyone, not even Zeke. I took the back hallways to class.

When Zeke's head popped from behind a library computer next to the windows, I hunched my back and took to the opposite side. I sprinkled my textbooks and notes on the desk without an ounce of concentration. My body craved an extra-large coffee, as long as the line at the cafeteria wasn't a hundred miles long. I dragged my boots to the center aisle on my way to the exit.

"Alexa," called a voice from behind. I pretended not to hear but the sound of my name hovered over my shoulder. Zeke rushed to catch up. "Alexa, how are you?"

"I'm fine. You?" I turned my stroll to a strut.

"Same. So, how do you like living in Brenton City?" he asked with a trembling voice.

"What?" I asked as he dared a smile. "I live in Newrock."

"That's like forty minutes south, right?" I didn't answer. "How was your weekend?" The tremble in his voice intensified.

"I don't want to talk about my weekend. Are you heading to class?" I hoped he'd say yes.

"No, I'm following you. Alexa, do you want to hang out sometimes, like, outside of school?" He fished his phone out for my number.

"I don't know what to say right now, Zeke. You always ask so many questions. I have to go."

"Can I at least get a hug?"

"No."

On Valentine's Day, I showed up for the Paramedic test at school, a brutal examination. Quick thinking and mastering anatomy came in order and a month of school served me no justice. I waddled out of the exam room dejected and drove to work on my day off. I refused to go home and sulk. I helped Heather at the spa, a busy Saturday and at closing time, I discovered a missed call and a text from hours before with Marcus' name on it. I hadn't seen him at school since the house visit. I doubted he attended often. He'd sent a text too. "Would you be my Valentine and spend the day with me?" I didn't call back. The day had seized and I'd exhausted my emotions. Hot mint tea, my warm pajamas and my comfortable bed sounded like the perfect way to end the day.

When my senses refreshed, I craved the collegiate interaction but neither Zeke nor Marcus crossed my path, as if they both vanished from school. Day by day, I drifted in loneliness but the minute I forgot my phone in the locker before class, I missed another text from Marcus. I'd swerved my mind into giving it another go, maybe, if we stayed away from his libidinous uncle. My reply was left unanswered.

A week later at the library, I debated on dialing Marcus' number but held back, hoping to bump into him in the corridors. But when I approached the locker area, I stopped in my heels at the sight of Zeke. He gazed at me with a grin plastered on his face, next to the water fountain while he zipped up his knapsack.

"Zeke." I rushed his way and threw myself in his arms, fighting my anguish for secretly missing Marcus.

Zeke dreamed a big future and bore more drive than anyone I'd ever known. But somehow, I pictured him as the type of guy a girl would take on as a friend and do homework with, which I did. He was the kind of friend who would comfort a girl when she'd have her heart broken by someone like Marcus Pellini.

I almost confided in him but my words would've hurt him. Nonetheless, I found his friendship soothing. I hugged him tight but when I let go, our hands intersected halfway. We sauntered to the lockers holding hands and moments later, we freed our fingers with neither of us giving it much thought.

I rummaged through my locker for textbooks while Zeke gabbed about his courses, hobbies and passions leaned against the lockers.

"You know what I'd like to do? Travel with someone close to me."

I glimpsed at him, "Yeah?" then back at my notes.

"Have you been anywhere? Like, somewhere far away?"

"I've seen a good chunk of Europe and the usual Caribbean vacation with parents. I returned from overseas a couple of months before I started school."

"Really? Tell me about Europe. I'm half-Irish."

I closed my locker and rounded the corner with Zeke next to me. "There's so much to tell, every country is different. But maybe one day, I'll tell you some stories."

We stopped at the top of the stairs before he left for class.

"Alexa, you're so pretty all the time. You don't even have to say anything, just smile." I gave him a smile with blushed cheeks. "You feel like doing homework together after class?"

I blinked in approval. "I'm done with classes for the day but I'll wait for you at the library. I'll be there working on an assignment anyway."

Zeke waved with a beaming face and strutted down the hall. I descended to the library and settled at a computer by the windows. The natural light brightened my brain and my entire existence. I spread my textbooks on the desk, still bearing Marcus in mind. My focus was off again, which is what happens when boy-play in college interferes with academic responsibility.

I toyed with my phone, tossing it in my bag and digging it out again. I typed a hey and deleted it. I typed it again and pressed sent with a crinkled face. Within a short minute, Marcus called.

"I'm leaving campus. Flying to Mexico tomorrow. Do you want to come for a drive?"

"Right now?" I almost jumped off my chair.

"Yes, right now. Meet me at the roundabout in two minutes."

I logged off, raced to the lobby and through the front doors. Marcus waited for me with the car door open. I skipped through the snow and hopped in his car. He leaned close and planted a kiss on my lips. We squealed out of the parking lot with locked lips and giggly as hell, Marcus peeping sideways at the road while he cupped my knee with his right hand.

He parked in a commercial lot a couple of streets away. As soon as he turned off the engine, he loomed in my seat and kissed me with vigor. Then he dove into the back seat, took off his jeans and his sweater.

"What —" and before I finished my question, he yanked me in the back. He attacked my lips and tugged at my clothes. "What are you doing?"

"I'm undressing you."

"No, you're not."

"Why not?"

"Because, no."

He panted. "Please."

"Are you aware that we're in a corporate parking lot?"

He scouted around and shrugged his shoulders. "Yeah. So?"

"I get it. You're the live-in-the-moment type of guy but come on. Look, someone's walking to their car."

"So what? Maybe they can learn something." He pressed his body against mine for a kiss and an expectant quickie before Mexico.

I pushed him away. "I'm trying to become a paramedic. What I don't want to learn is how it feels to be arrested."

He puckered his lips. "Oh, baby. I need to save you."

"From what?"

"From yourself," he groan-whispered in my ear.

"That's it. Let's go." I jumped out and into the front seat.

"Oh, come on. You're no fun," he whined, still in his white shorts with neon tennis balls and a wifebeater.

"Glad to disappoint you. Let's go."

He slipped his clothes back on and stepped out in a mumble. He slouched into the driver seat, then steered away in silence.

"I'll text you from Mexico," he said at the roundabout, unsure, then leaned in for an unreturned goodbye kiss.

"Enjoy your vacation." I hopped out without looking back.

I scampered through the front doors and jetted to my locker where I tossed the leftover textbooks in my school tote. Then I zipped to my car, ignoring my library date with Zeke. I had to bounce out of school. I had an acrid taste in my mouth.

CHAPTER

4

Reading week rolled in, a well-deserved week off school half-way through the semester. Intended for studying purposes, used for Caribbean travels, family visits and friend get-togethers. I passed the days at The Beauty Bar with my brain spiking the Zeke-Marcus marathon to a ten-to-one ratio.

The first morning at school, I waited for Zeke at the locker in vain, then shuffled to class in gloom. I stumbled upon Marcus at every corner.

"Where are you going?" he asked after the third time I brushed him off.

"Class." I stopped a distance away, ready for takeoff.

"And you can't stop to say hello?"

"Hello . . . how was Mexico?"

"Awesome. Sorry I didn't text you."

"That's fine. I have to go. I don't like to be late for class." I left him with a suspicious expression on his face.

I'd set myself on a quest to find Zeke and I searched for him everywhere at school, including our sitting spot at the library. No sight of him. I'd contemplated asking Marcus about Zeke's where-abouts. How comical would that have been? "Hey, Marcus. Have you seen Zeke?" Boy, it would have curved down his ego. Big time.

On Wednesday, I brainstormed with a classmate the essential points of an upcoming presentation at the college bar on the first floor. When we finished our work, we skimmed to the library as Zeke strolled in the opposite direction with another student. He continued his walk with a blank stare. I smiled with chilled enthusiasm.

A week later, I wrote, "Z, where are you?" on a note. I folded it and pushed it in my pocket, then after the lecture, I squeezed it halfway through the vent of his locker. The next morning, the note tail disappeared and when I unlocked mine, it landed on the floor. It was blank, except for my words but it was meaningful.

On break period, I deviated to the library on my way to the cafeteria and tore through the entrance with a hunch. I angled toward the window aisle but something made me swirl my head to the left and there he was, coming on his way out, earbuds in his ears, baseball cap on and hood over the cap.

"Z."

He snapped the earbuds off and I galloped straight into his arms, tipping him off his feet.

"Hi, Alexa," he said with me still glued to him. He wrapped his arms around me in confusion.

I leaned back. "Zee, where have you been? I looked for you everywhere."

He beamed. "I've been here."

I dragged him by the hand, away from the library traffic and next to the staircase in the lobby that lead to the second floor.

"I thought you were mad at me," I said.

"Why would I be mad at you?"

"That day before reading week . . . did you wait for me at the library?" He was about to open his mouth. "Never mind. We should exchange numbers. Now."

His eyes twinkled. "I'd like that." He rooted for his phone and this time, with his mouth curved into a smile.

"I missed you."

"You did? I'm surprised," he said with reddening cheeks. I pulled him close to me. His hands trembled on my spine.

In-crowd students lingered at the front of the library and nudged elbows as they glared at us. The classmate with whom I'd produced the presentation introduced me to them at the college bar. The likes of Marcus considered Zee a loner, a misunderstood youngster who didn't belong with me. But the kid with the hoodie was smarter than all of them combined. And besides, I've always sided with the underdog and I wasn't about to change that for a flimsy status with the intangible mob. At least Zee's compliments were genuine.

Zee glimpsed at the spectators, then back at me.

"Ignore them." I wriggled my hand into his.

"I don't care," he said, then dropped his eyes to the floor.

I pinched his chin. "I'm up here. Take my number."

"Yes-yes." His voice revived and reiterated my number three times. "I have class now," he said with a pout.

I drew him close, almost violently and hugged him one more time. "Go, we'll talk later."

I strutted passed the ogling clique inside the library and up to the second floor. I tiptoed into the quiet study and scattered the notes for my next class on a desk. My phone chimed with a text. I muted it and read the message with a sparkle in my heart. "It was good to see you today." I giggled before someone shushed me from one of the study carrels. "I feel the same way," I replied. "You're so damn pretty, I'm still smiling," he keyed back. "Would you get out of my head? I'm trying to study." We texted during my studying session, in Biology class and during dinner at home about whatever came to our minds.

Zee's first call found me nestled in bed with my nose buried in textbooks.

"Hi, gorgeous." The sound of his voice was deep but topped with warmth and curiosity.

"Hi, Zee."

"I like your nickname for me."

"You do?"

"I started thinking about you before we ever exchanged a word."

"Really?" I lied.

"Alexa, I never saw anyone as pretty as you, the first time I saw you by your locker." He paused and blood rushed to my cheeks. "I had a strange feeling the moment I laid eyes on you. In a good way, like, I felt drawn to you."

"It's all about the vibes. By the way, what zodiac are you?"

"Gemini. Do you believe in this stuff?"

The crepuscule refracted through the window. "'Believe' is an overstatement but I like to read about it. There are some consistencies with signs."

"What sign are you?"

"Libra, which happens to get along great with Gemini. We're both air signs. That said, we're far from airy."

"No clue what an air sign means but I'm like you and you're like me. We have a solid connection."

"See? We already agree on everything."

"No, you don't understand. You make me melt. Every time I see you, my heart beats so fast." I victory danced in my mind as I slid in bed and glanced at the ceiling. "Don't you have something to say to this?" he asked.

"Maybe I'm enjoying it in silence."

"I've never been close to anyone who knew me well. Have you?" I let his question hang in the air. "The wind is blowing against my window. It's so lonely here and I wish you were in my arms," he whispered and my forearms prickled with goosebumps.

"Where is *here*?"

"In my room. I'm sitting in the dark, talking to you," he said and a sensual vibe traveled from his mouth to my ears in a frightening way.

"I should go back to studying. I have a Chem test tomorrow."

"OK, I'll let you study."

"Goodnight."

"Goodnight, gorgeous and good luck."

The door crackle interrupted my post-conversation giggles. Heather popped her head in to confirm my work schedule for the upcoming weekend. Then she caught my smile again.

"School's going well for you?"

"Like you wouldn't believe it," I said as ear-splitting cries boasted from downstairs.

"My son woke up. Goodnight."

In the morning, I rubbed my eyes open and reached for the phone. "Good morning sunshine," I typed away. "Be careful driving, the highway is windy and I want you here in one piece. See you at school," Zee wrote. I cruised to school with a warm glow bouncing in my gut, despite the minus gazillion degrees.

On break period, Zee waited for me at the back of the library, where he drew my chemistry graph two months ago. I made my way with two coffees and an oatmeal raisin cookie for him on a tray.

"How did the test go?"

I dropped the tray on the table. "Good. You know I love Chem."

"I thought you loved Bio."

"I do, both."

"And you're not even sarcastic. Thanks for the snack."

I spread my notes on the table. "You're welcome. By the way, I got perfect on the chemistry graph. And I have another one for you . . . last one, I promise." I pushed the paper his way.

He inspected the note. "No problem."

I admired his crafty fingers as they drew the graph while I sipped on coffee. My right hand rested on my leg under the table when his left hand brushed on top of mine above my knee. I shifted my eyes from his drawing fingers to his face but he wouldn't dare to look at me, he just let his hand do the dance. I flipped my hand and our palms kissed and our digits weaved. He glimpsed at me with a red face as his pencil slid along its route without grazing off the charting paper.

"When's your next class?" he asked, eyes still on the graph.

"Fifteen minutes. Healthcare in Canada. Guest speaker today."

"Uh, boring."

"Yeah but otherwise it's my favourite class. It's the prof who makes it that way. His sense of humour keeps it fresh."

He tore his hand away as he slid the graph to me. "Done."

"Thanks, I should go. I like to sit at the front."

"That should be no problem. No one sits at the front."

We strode out of the library bumping arms and rubbing elbows. My class ran on the first floor, a mere distance away. Outside the classroom, he gripped my pinky with his thumb and index finger.

"I'll wait at the library until you finish class," he said, hopeful.

"Aren't you going to be bored?"

"Waiting for you? Never. Besides," he glanced over the shoulder at his knapsack, "I can always do my homework."

I pulled him into a hug, pushed him back and blew him a kiss. He caught it and puffed it back. "I miss you already," he texted as soon as I slid into my front row seat.

Zee proved right about the guest speaker. Some do turn out engaging, even entertaining. But this one spoke for three hours straight. Not only did he steal our class break but he kept the same tonality in his voice. It took enormous strength to stay awake. The class lasted ten years long.

I rushed to the library. "Are you bored, yet?" He shook his head with flat eyes. He was bored. "Walk with me. I have to drop off my chemistry report."

"You mean, the graph?" he asked as he gathered his textbooks.

"That's part of it."

"You could've left it with me. I would've taken my time with it."

"I didn't know you'd wait for me."

"Don't I always?" he said as he inspected my hair.

We ambled out of the library and a strike of guilt stung my conscience like paper cut over his forbearance for my standing him up. After I slipped my report along with the graph into the professor's mailbox, we headed to the lockers and out of school. We lurked outside the door, a déjà vu of the bone chilling January night, except for the snow and the awkward conversation.

"Can I give you a ride home?"

"All right."

On the drive, we concealed our trouble finding the right words with smiles. He rubbed his hands together as he uttered directions, the only words grasped until we rolled into his neighbourhood.

The old part of town bore one brick house after another, two storeys high, a crimson drape hemming the lake and shamrock picket fences to boot. This little city snuck under my skin along with the swanky college and the baby-faced hip hopper next to me.

Zee pointed to one of the houses and I pulled into a metered spot across the street.

"I live with my mom and my two little brothers . . . it's not the best looking house but it's better than nothing."

"It's a beautiful house and a lovely neighbourhood with the lake nearby. It's picturesque."

"You're being polite. These houses are old." He scanned the row until the line of houses vanished into the horizon.

"It's called vintage not old and vintage is expensive."

He shifted his eyes to me. "You lift me up, you know that?" His gaze pulled us close. Our lips tested into a soft-soft kiss. "Thanks for the ride." I nodded with a smile and he leaped out of the car.

At home, I marched into a lonely house with a crushing desire to share my enthusiasm. Instead, I prepared a spinach salad with chickpeas and olive oil, next to the mail on the kitchen counter. I leaned over and eyeballed the letters up close. One envelope stuck its head out from under the pile, bearing the Brimley logo, green and blue on the corner. I scooped it up with shaky hands and reluctant to open it. I slammed my food bowl on the counter and called Zee.

"I received the Paramedic result but I'm scared to open it alone."

"Go ahead," he said with a smiling voice. I gasped for air and tore the envelope with a grimace, then covered my eyes with one hand. "Did you open it?"

"Yes but I didn't read it yet."

"Come on, I'll catch you if you fall."

"This isn't funny, Zee."

"I'm trying to loosen you up."

"Here we go." I peeked through my fingers, then lowered my clammy palm. "Oh . . ."

"What?"

"I'm on the waiting list."

"Is that a good thing?"

"It depends on how you look at it," I said, deflated. "It means I passed the exam but failed to obtain a high enough grade to secure a seat in the program."

"That's better than failing."

"But I'm still not in."

"How many applicants?"

"Almost two thousand over sixty seats."

"Then what do you expect? You've had a whole month of biology and chemistry behind you. Like I said, admission is tough. And besides, there's still hope," he said.

"Not at number thirty three, there isn't."

"You didn't fail, think about that. And think what you can do next year, if that's what you want to do."

"I'm not giving up."

"Good. Now stop torturing yourself and get some sleep."

"Thanks for being there for me."

"Sweet dreams, gorgeous."

I woke up with a clear head. Zee had a point about keeping focus on the bright side. It perked up my soul. I drove to the spa while he attended Friday school and texted with him after work while I studied in my bedroom. I'd attached my phone to the hip. I took it with me everywhere in the house, just in case he called.

"Do you want to get together this weekend?" he asked before bedtime.

"I have to work at the beauty salon and I'm loaded with homework. But I'm off next Saturday for a hair appointment. We can go see a movie or something, after I'm done."

"That should work."

Before our goodbyes for the night, we made plans to spend the summer together, despite my last semester in Pre-Health and my job. He had the summer off school and planned to work full time but we promised ourselves to make it work.

Only one text from Zee made its way into my phone over the weekend, to wish me sweet dreams. I held back too, I didn't want to hover. But late Sunday, I gave in and tapped "sleep well" his way. No response and I reasoned that he was busy studying.

By the start of the week, my phone slipped into a coma. I drove to work with a confused face and hardly kept my concentration at the spa. At dusk, I signed on Skype to his active status. "Not sleeping yet?" Nothing came back and by now, a dozen questions tormented my brain.

On Tuesday morning, Zee zipped up his knapsack by the lockers as I ambled over.

"Hey," he said, leaning close for a superficial hug.

"How was your weekend?"

He grazed a hand through his hair. "Good, I guess . . ."

"I texted you."

"Yeah, but . . ." He angled toward his locker and closed the door. "Do you want to go out for drinks for St. Patrick's Day?"

"Today?"

"Yes, after school. The Irish in me wants to celebrate. Do you have homework?"

"I always have homework but we can arrange that."

"Are you walking to class?"

"Yes. Let me take my textbooks out of the locker."

Zee waved me ahead, an after-you gesture as I flung my school tote over my shoulder. He sauntered in a daze, close enough to chat but far enough to keep from bumping shoulders.

"I might take off to Alberta for my co-op this summer," he said.

I stumbled to a halt. "But I thought we made plans to spend the summer together."

"Yeah but you've been to all these places and I've never been any-where. It'd be good for me and I'd get school credits."

I could hardly set my feet in motion and up a short set of stairs closer to my classroom as the echo of his words carved at my heart.

He rubbed his face. "I don't know for sure if I'm going but it's something I have in mind." I angled away, speechless. "You okay?"

"I have to go."

In Math, I couldn't make a word of the lecture, as if the professor spoke an alien language. It poured outside and the classroom air was gloomy, adding to my misery. I stooped in my chair with arms crossed, then shuffled though classes in a stupor.

I still waited for Zee to text me about our plan to go out for drinks. I figured we'd leave the school together and if anything, he'd be the one to fear that I'd change my mind, wait in anxiety for the moment we'd finally go out together.

I texted him from my last class of the day, twice before he answered. "Alexa, what's up?" "Are you still at school?" I buttoned. "No, I left." You left? "But I thought you wanted to go out for drinks," I tapped. "I had to leave. I have things to do." My stomach dropped and holy crap, he stood me up. He stood me up and someone might as well have hit me over the head with a baseball bat.

I shot another text, sitting in my car. "Zee, is everything all right?" I turned the key in the ignition. "Everything is fine. It's just so hard to get everything done." *Things to do. Get everything done.* How vague and unless there was a fire or a family emergency, what else could be more important than me?

My impulsion to call frayed at the edges upon the demise of my phone battery. I lay in bed, staring at the walls, then I sat up like charred. I remembered the landline in the kitchen. I took the portable, dialed his number and cleared my throat.

"Who is this?"

"Hi, it's Alexa. I called you from the home phone. I just put my cell to charge but it's still dead for now."

"Oh, okay." His chilled tone hurt worse than an axe through my skull.

"You know we could talk about anything, right?" I said, the conversation vibe unnerving. "Is there something wrong?"

"No, everything is fine. I'm hanging out with my friends. I'll call you later."

"That's all right. See you at school." I hung up with a groan. I'm sorry I called, I yelled at the phone. Then I crawled in bed and folded under the covers in pure apathy.

I didn't run into Zee at school for the rest of the week, nor did I receive a message from him. On break periods, I retrieved to the library with homework. I'd become creative in finding excuses to decline my classmates' repeated invitations to join their study groups for all-nighters at a twenty-four-hour Tim Hortons.

On Saturday, I texted Zee as soon as I stepped out of the hairdresser with Jennifer Aniston's layered haircut from mid-series *Friends* and a sandy blonde hue, locks swinging in the air, ready for the summer, only a hundred and fifty seven months away. No answer to my text. I drove to work on my day off again. Where else would I go? I couldn't bear the solitaire of the house and Heather couldn't be happier for the extra quality time with her son.

By Monday evening, my eyes shifted from my textbooks to my phone like a pendulum. I slipped a text away before my rationale forbade it. "There is a change in you. This isn't the Zee I've met." And my heart pounded for an answer in vain.

Late at night, I lay under the covers in the dark and delineated Zee's face through the opaque room. When my phone rumbled, I took in a sharp breath. "What's up?" wrote Zee. I rose up in bed and called him with the lights off, only a temporary glow bouncing off my phone display.

"Hello?" I muttered.

"Hi."

"H-how are you?" Minute droplets of unnerving sweat trickled down my temples.

"Alexa, I haven't been with a woman for some time. I need you to come over, take my clothes off and have your way with me."

"What? Where is this coming from?"

"Wanna get coffee?"

"Right now? It's almost one in the morning."

"Right now."

"Zee, it takes me forty minutes to drive to Brenton City. I have an early class tomorrow."

"True."

"So, tell me — why the change in you? Let's have coffee tomorrow and talk about it."

"I'm going to bed. Goodnight."

"Zee, don't go . . ." He hung up and I glared at my phone, as if it deserved punishment. I slid under the duvet at a snail's pace and closed my eyes in disbelief.

I pranced to school with heart palpitations and an extra-large green tea in hand. Zee cut my path on my way to Math. He'd climbed the staircase from the lobby and took the landing in my direction.

"You know, I don't get you. I thought you wanted to hang out. And I don't mean at one a.m.," I said.

"And it would be nice to do that when I have some time . . . Look, I lost my head in the clouds and right now I have to concentrate on school because I need to make sure I'm still here next year," spoken by the genius who knew everything under the sun, his face beet red.

I held his gaze. He bore the deepest eyes I'd ever seen, the laser of his vision digging through my heart like piranhas. And he brimmed with emotion, the very notion he feared most.

"Come on, Zee." I hurled myself in his arms, beset to keep my blistering tea from spilling, my body glued to his, a perfect fit.

He gently wrapped his arms around me. "I'm not worth it."

I leaned back and grabbed his hand. "You're worth it to me."

"Well, I don't think I am." He angled away with glossy eyes.

I yanked him back. "Zee." He ripped his hand away but stayed still to listen.

"Something you said last night — 'come take my clothes off' — what's up with that?"

"A joke. Don't worry about it."

I pulled him in my arms fighting back my own tears. The second floor was the busiest in the a.m., hardly an ideal setting for an emotional spill but I didn't care. I refused to let go of him. I feared I'd lose him forever. I squeezed my eyes to take in his scent, spun on my heels and raced to class.

I took my lunch in the cafeteria alone, which sucked and sent him a message. "I'm sorry if I overstepped my boundaries. I'd much rather you concentrate on school. Your future is most important." My phone spat out a text. "Thanks for understanding. Have a good day, gorgeous." Yeah, sure. I'll give it a try. He'd pierced traces of his contagious persona deep in my senses and snubbed the will to depart my soul. How have I come to this point and how could I escape this hole in my stomach?

The next day at the library, Zee's ascension to the upper floor stole my focus away from the textbooks. Dressed in black, he climbed the stairs in the lobby in all his poise. Up on the landing, he swirled his head, as if he sensed my gawk at the nape of his neck. He met my eyes in the air through the library glass wall and sent shivers down my spine. Then he wandered into the school.

I rearranged my thoughts — although with more difficulty than I imagined — and dove into the creation of a global warming assignment for Communication. When I raised my head from the monitor for an eye rub, the nightfall spurred me back to reality. Almost eight o'clock, three hours away from closing time.

I shifted my line of vision back to the monitor when Zee's frame popped in the corner of my eye. He'd settled at a computer several rows across, nose buried in homework. I dared to key a text, pay-back for picking a seat in my radar. "Don't look so serious."

I jittered in my seat, waiting for his reply. He retorted with his head still hovered over the desk. "I have a huge presentation on Monday. I have to be." Then he shot me a glimpse. Of course he didn't scan the library for me. He'd spotted me before he picked the computer seat, wanting me to see him. And he wanted me to want to see him while he played cool as fuck.

Another text flew my way. "How are you?" My heart startled and I hoped the meaning behind his text counted more than mere courtesy. We exchanged a couple of texts on schoolwork and shared student exhaustion. It would've been nice for him to navigate to my desk for a mini-conversation, friendly and light but sprinkled with a personal touch but I guess that was too much to expect at this point. "Going home to sleep. I'm tired," he texted on his way out without so much as a glance my way or the hint of a gracious goodnight.

Saturday night, I toiled over a lab report with an assigned partner from Biology. We divided the assignment into equal sections, composed them and shared them with each other on Skype for corroboration.

Late into the night, at a time when somewhere on a mountain a wolf might howl at the moon, my Bio partner and I called it quits. A second and a half before I was about to sign off, the notification sound of Zee's sign-in had my heart skip a beat.

When he dropped a hello, my heart skipped two beats. Then, "Let's get together," and I froze in my chair. When the phone rumbled, I unfroze by the third ring.

"Hi, gorgeous. You studying?"

"I . . . I just finished an assignment." I ran my fingers through my hair, as if to wipe my exhaustion.

"Do you want to get together? I miss you."

"It's after midnight and the lab report drained me out of the last bit of energy."

He sighed. "Okay, goodni —"

"Wait. You miss me?"

"Will you drive?" His soft tone buttered my sentiments.

I paused to digest my foolish decision. "I'll drive."

I shunned my fatigue and charged out the door. The itch to find out the truth about his changed behaviour propelled me straight to the highway to meet in private with Zee for the first time.

I trailed the directions he texted to Grant Street. Downtown Brenton City gleamed with bar music in surround sound and the occasional group of drunks, who defied the chilly weather. I rolled to a stop at a red light and scouted for Zee through the intersection. He snapped the door open and hopped in.

"You scared me," I said with my fingers splayed on my chest.

"I had to be quick before the light changed. Straight ahead."

He wore a red and white windbreaker with one of his collection caps, some baseball team I'd never heard of — not The Blue Jays, I knew them — and admired me drive with his million dollar smile, contagious and yummy.

"U-turn it into that spot," he said.

I parked and stepped out of the car. Zee sashayed to my side and reached for my hand. He led the way to a destination only he knew but he could've booked a VIP room in purgatory and I would've followed faithfully.

"Can you tell me what happened?"

He stopped and turned to me. "I don't mean to hurt your feelings, I just . . ." His eyes sparkled under the lamppost. The bony edges of his face sharped a statuesque shade in a way I hadn't noticed before. He leaned close for a kiss but I stepped back.

"And I don't mean to push myself on you. I just want us to be friends again," I said. "I mean, friends first, right?"

He marched ahead in silence gripping tighter on my hand. We crossed an empty parking lot — the kind where bad stuff happens in movies — and squeezed between two buildings into a narrow alley back toward Grant Street.

"Don't be scared," he said.

"I'm with you. Why would I be?"

"I don't know. It might be a bit ghetto for you."

We wandered inside a brick building and climbed a spiral staircase to the top, then continued our way to an obscured door at the end of a dim lit corridor. I feared nada. Because if I was to die, I'd die happy with Zee attached to my hand.

A brief struggle with the lock later, we shuffled inside an apartment that resembled a maze. Several small rooms, each auxiliary to another.

"It's a friend of mine's recording studio. We hang out here sometimes." He pointed toward the couch in the main room, an improvised lounge. "Make yourself comfortable. We keep bottled water in the fridge. Can I offer you one?"

"I'm fine," I said and he scooted on the couch for what would be a kiss. "Wait, we need to talk." He frowned. "You know we need to talk. Please tell me what's wrong."

"Nothing." He tossed his baseball cap on the couch and stroked his honeyed hair into a cowlick.

I ruffled it out. "You have such cute hair. Why do you always wear a cap?"

"I don't know. It's my style. I have a collection of them."

He drew in again and this time, he stole a kiss. Then he rubbed his thumb over my bottom lip and I kissed it in goosebumps.

"Alexa, what would you say if I told you I haven't been with too many girls?"

"I'd say, I believe you."

"Shut up." He swatted his hand playfully into my shoulder, slanting my spine against the back of the couch.

I soared up in giggles and sprinted to the labyrinth. He chased my tail amused as ever. I hid in the soundproof room while he searched for me around the apartment. I glued my body against the wall behind the open door with a racing pulse while his footsteps grew nearer. And when the tiptoes came to a standstill, so did my heart.

He bolted inside the room, wearing nothing except black boxers with arms wide open as I screamed unconsciously loud. And maybe if he was fully clothed, the tension in my heart might have lasted a bit longer. I scanned his toned legs unfolding from his boxers as he shut the soundproof room door.

"Aren't you cocky?" I said.

"Well, my dear Alexa," he whispered in my ear, "you can scream all you want. No one's going to hear you." He cupped my neck with one hand, spun me around and pinned my chest against the wall. Then he pasted his body against my spine — happy to see me and all — and slid the other hand to undo my zipper, then inside my panties finger down my stripe. And the drive of his touch stirred tepid vibes inside my belly. "You're so fucking tight." His lips brushed against my hair and over my ear lobe.

I snapped his hand away, swirled around and zipped up my jeans. "Maybe I don't want anyone to hear me."

"Then why d'you push my hand away?" He pinched my chin and tested my lips.

I kissed him back breathlessly and embraced the waistband of his boxers, lazy on his hips. He tugged at my zipper and in a moment of mental distraction, I escaped his ambuscade and dashed out the door to the main room.

"Cock-tease," he yelled from behind.

I wasn't trying to be. I didn't want to be. I'd come to talk before anything else but his gaze and his touch drifted my mind away from the original purpose. Never in my wildest dreams, or when I woke up this morning, have I imagined I'd be pinned against the wall by a boxered Zeke in a soundproof room by the end of today.

He raced behind, caught up with me and fell on the couch, pulling me on top of him.

"I could be with you every day forever and I'd never get bored."

"I feel the same way about you," I said as his eyes begged me to let him slide my jeans off. "Zee, it's not a good idea. Not right now anyway. It could ruin our friendship."

"No. If anything, it will draw me closer."

"I'm telling you that there will be tension between us at school and I don't mean the good kind. I don't want us to get to the point where we're avoiding each other, just because of one night of sex. It's not worth it. Our friendship is much more important to me."

"No. It's the closeness we need."

He glided his index against the Cupid's bow of my lip as blood rushed to my head. He planted a gentle kiss and rubbed the inside of my mouth with his tongue. He shifted on top of me, took my jeans off and tossed them on the floor. Bad idea. Bad idea. The rest of our clothes came off as we kissed uncontrollably, our hands exploring our bodies, his touch spinning me dizzy.

He slid inside me in a chasm of passion and took me to a place where dreams are made of moments like these. His body fell comatose after two pumps but the closeness of our spirits mattered more to me than a climax. I grazed my fingers through his hair as he rested his head on my chest, exhausted from the long-needed orgasm.

"Your heart's beating so fast," he said.

"That's because I'm with you."

He levered to the sitting position and scouted for his clothes. "Here's a candy for you." He handed me one from an impression of a coffee table while he picked his T-shirt off the floor.

"I'm not into sweets but thanks."

Once dressed up, he stood tall with arms crossed and watched me slip into my tee and jeans. I lifted on my tippy-toes to steal a kiss. He stepped back and I dropped on my heels.

"Don't get close to me," he said. "Don't try to get close to me. I'm a loner and I don't do well with getting close to people."

I gasped in pain. No girl in the world wants to hear these words from the guy she has just been intimate with, let alone one she cares about and admires to death.

"But I'm not *people*. I'm your friend."

I fell on the couch with my tongue tangled in my mouth. He dropped next to me and cupped his head in his hands.

"What is it, Zee?"

He lifted his head. "Oh, you won't like what I'm about to say."

The angst in my stomach deepened. "Tell me, tell me everything."

"My friend left me," he said with a trembling voice, gaping at the floor. "I had a friend who left me and moved to Alberta."

"What kind of friend?"

"A girl."

I clenched my teeth. "Girlfriend?"

"No, friend. We've known each other for a long time."

"I thought you said you've never been close to anyone before."

"I'm not now since I'm not talking to this person anymore."

"You said you've *never* been close to anyone. And why are you telling me this now? Why didn't you say something when we met? Or any other time up to the moment we screwed on this couch, like ten minutes ago, you ass."

"Because I'm feeling this way now and I want my friend back and I don't care about anything else." His voice betrayed a cascade of tears waiting to burst from behind his eyeballs.

My stomach churned with nausea and my knees weakened in temporary paralysis. My brain rebuffed the new impersonation of Zee, as if I'd talked to someone else.

"Why did you chase after me in the beginning?"

"I don't know. Why the fuck do you have to ask so many questions? Leave me alone," he said, his face cupped in his hands again.

Anger looped up my legs and I reclaimed my strength. I stood up in indignation and away from his sullen pose.

"Asshole." I slammed the door behind me as hard as I could.

I careened to the car and once in the driver seat, I burst into a bawling concert with my head on the steering wheel and my forehead honking the horn.

Minutes later, I rattled the key in the ignition and stomped on the accelerator back to the highway. I cried silent tears of anger and frustration. I'd been such a fool all along. I couldn't make sense of the reason why he tried so hard to win me over at school. I stood him up, I blew him off, I avoided him and he still stood by my side. But as soon as I opened my heart, he turned the page into a jerk. Classic.

Heather cracked my bedroom door open with an invitation to join her for freshly brewed morning coffee in the kitchen before work. I declined and asked if she'd work the spa instead. Carl was at home, he could stay with the baby.

"No worries. Get some rest."

The next time she opened my door, she found me in the same sleeping position she'd left me.

"Okay, get up. Let's go."

"What day is it?"

"It's Sunday. You couldn't work, remember?"

"Oh, yeah." I sat up and covered my eyes until the head rush faded away.

"I'll wait for you in the kitchen. First, you'll eat, then you'll tell me about it over tea."

Food restored my strength and girl talk lifted the rocks in my heart. Before bed, I called my sidekick from my most puerile days for a heart-to-heart. Maureen Chastain, Miss Congeniality in high school. We took the same courses, sat together in class and talked about everything girls couldn't tell their parents. Her optimistic vibe boosted my spirits to the sky. And as I lay under the covers, I envisioned my friends in a relay race where Heather handed the baton to Maureen.

The next day, my phone hummed with a text as I studied in bed after work. "I'm not interested in falling in love," wrote Zee and my heart took the plunge again. The tone hurt more than the meaning. I dialed his number with a shaky hand.

"Are you insane? Who said anything about falling in love?"

"Great. Then we understand each other," he said, his tone sharp.

"Who are you? I don't even know who I'm talking to right now." I swallowed my tears.

"That's right, you don't. Let's keep it that way," he said, then his voice flatlined.

"Why did you say you've never been close to anyone before?"

"I never thought I was until I tried again. I'm sorry."

I hung up and dropped the phone on my bed, gasping for air, my body immobile like stone.

CHAPTER
5

The day I received my graded chemistry report with the graph Zee drew while he held my hand under the library table, my brain fell prey to melancholy. On break, I fidgeted in my chair troubled by my own hands searching for the phone in my school tote. I couldn't stop my fingers from buttoning the letter keys. "Somehow, you snuck under my skin and I don't know how it happened. I'm trying hard to forget you but I'm not doing a good job. I reminisce about the way you used to look at me, so adoringly. They say everything happens for a reason but I wonder why we felt such a strong connection, if it was meant to end?" And what in the world possessed me to type that away? His reply shot like a rifle. "Try harder. I'm no one to get close to. Yeah, it was meant to end." Cut and dry. Bang-bang, my heart dead.

How could he be so wintry? Yet, no matter how many daggers he twisted in my belly, my sentiments stayed the same. So untypical of me, the reason why my ability to give Zee a cold shoulder shut down stretched beyond my own comprehension.

I lingered at the library late into the evening when I moved to a desk at the back and typed a goodbye letter in tears. I bawled my eyes off. And once I finished it, I sat back and exhaled.

On my way to the lockers, Marcus saluted me with raised eyebrows, as if to say, you look like crap, what happened to you? I wore a hoodie to school — Zee's style rubbed on me — and covered my head with the hood as I picked up the speed. Too embarrassed to stop and talk. I drove home a wreck and cried myself to sleep.

In the morning, I half-smiled at the letter before I squeezed it through the vent of Zee's locker. And when he found it, it read like this:

"Hey Zee,
I wanted to tell you in person but then I thought, it'd be better if I wrote it. I want you to know that I respect your wishes and I understand you. Nobody ever said anything about love, so I don't know how you got that idea. I confirmed on Saturday night our friend status but maybe we came a little too close for comfort. I just hope that no one else will call you Zee again because that's my nickname for you and I own the rights to that shit. I don't regret anything that happened between us. We did have a solid connection and knowing you was a good experience. You don't get to share that with just anyone and I will cherish the moments we spent together. Good luck with school and I hope you achieve your goals. If you're happy, I'm happy. I will always care about you, don't ever forget that.
Alexa."

I dove into my studies and despite my stomped-on heart, my grades improved. The emotional pain drove me in the arms of learning. Professors praised my essays and reports. I prepared a remarkable presentation on global warming in Communication, a tie-in with the assignment. I'd started the semester with the lowest average in class, unsure I'd even finish the damn thing and approached the end in good academic standing.

One given day at school, I rounded the corner to my locker and stumbled upon Zee. I wobbled to a halt, trying to decide if I should delve with the lock or spin around and race down the hall.

He broke the ice. "How is it going, Alexa?"

"I'm okay. You?" I muttered, still hugging the corner.

He opened his posture. "I had a horrible weekend. Nothing but bad things happened to me."

"That's because I'm not in your life anymore." I stepped closer.

"I read your letter . . ." I nodded in my wait for a more elaborate statement but he dug through his locker. Then, "Do you like my new basketball shoes?" He held them up for me to see.

"They're nice."

He tossed the shoes in his locker while I took out textbooks for my next class. He plowed a hand through his hair, a master at crafting an unintentional cowlick, which had me giggle inside. "You see, I . . ." His words faded to a blur while I pretended to be absorbed by the story but in my mind, I pinned him against the lockers and smooched him to death. "Anyway, see you around," he said and trotted away, leaving me hanging by a thread.

The last week of the semester, I ventured to the library for a printout and passed by Zee in a group of classmates at the top of the stairs. We locked eyes for a split moment and my skin tingled. Moments later, I made my way out of the library and up the stairs on my way to class. He waited alone next to the bannister. We greeted each other and he brushed his arm against mine as a signal for me to stop.

"You're always so pretty, Alexa."

"It doesn't do anything to you though," I said as butterflies flapped their wings against the lining of my gut.

"That's because I'm a cold motherfucker."

"That's not true. I've met the other side of you, remember?"

"Yeah, well. That's exactly what scares me."

"Zee," I threw myself in his arms, "I miss my friend in you."

He laced his arms around me, surprisingly tighter than usual. "I'm here. I'm not going anywhere."

I flopped my head on his shoulder and kissed the side of his neck. He dropped his posture and tightened his grip on me even more. Then he gently broke away.

"I have class."

"No." I pulled him back. "I'm not letting you go." He leaned back with a grin on his face. We angled away from each other, holding hands until our fingers couldn't touch anymore.

The last day of the semester, I cut my way to the library flanked by two peers. We planned to study for our last test in Healthcare but we yapped away with open textbooks on the table. I'd memorized the material to death, at home in bed, under the April rainstorms and between my erratic cries for Zee. But today, my classmates and I — three girls with good dispositions — flaunted our way out of the semester. My hard work paid off and I beamed with satisfaction over my incoming final grades.

Zee made his presence at the library, dressed in black, eyes sparkling like stars in the midst of my laughter. As he neared my table, he bowed his head and I winked. He carried to a desk and dipped into a seat facing me. Zee kept a straight face through my giggles with my peers as he swotted over drawings with a classmate. By the end of the week, he'd put a cap on his freshman year, a freshman who'd grown so much into his skin.

I rose up from the table, having no idea if I'd see him again. I still had a semester to go in the summer while he'd allegedly take off to Alberta and my return to school in September remained undecided, courtesy of the Paramedic Program waiting list.

I sauntered to Healthcare with my classmates and after handing in my final test, I made my way to the locker area. I stood still, except for my eyes shifting between my locker and Zee's. I took a deep breath. This was where it all began. I fished out a Sharpie and drew a heart on his locker. Then wrote "U 4 ever" inside the heart, my way of confessing my feelings for him.

I zoned out to the road on my way home. With no homework and nothing to study, I already missed my beloved college and counted the days until my return.

CHAPTER

6

One evening during my short May vacation from school, I came home from work and signed online for shits and grins. Zee's active status on a Friday night while out of school for the summer came as predictable as daylight. "Hey you," he typed and I read it with a hesitant mind and a pounding heart. A few days of spa work took my mind off Zee and I feared being suckered back in his trap. A new phone number popped on the screen, the temptation now impossible to resist. "Is this new?" I replied and the phone rang in the next split second.

"If you're ever in town."

"I thought you were leaving for Alberta."

"Change of plans. I took a job in Ottawa for the summer."

"Oh." Same difference.

"Could you swing by my place? I have a few things to say before I leave in a few days."

"I'm not in town."

"Yeah but the highway will help you with that." His tone grew into a smile.

"I have to work tomorrow."

"Come on, it's Friday night and we don't get together every day. I moved into a new place and I'd like to show it off to you," he said, his tone dulcet. I paused in disbelief. "It's most important that I see you before I go."

"Text me the address."

I raced out the door and drove with an occasional burst with a dry laugh in my quest to discover the mysteries of this young soul named Zeke and also grasping the unmysterious fact that I did miss him and was dying to see his face.

He waited like a delivered plant on the doorsteps of a house in a newly molded residential neighbourhood. He traced my steps with his gaze as I hopped out of the car and shambled toward him.

"Come here." He drew me close and hugged me tight. I shut my eyes to inhale his scent. I'd missed it so much.

He led me by the hand inside the house, brand new and modern.

"It's my friend's family home. I'm renting out a room," he said and hauled me upstairs.

"I liked where you lived before. The lake was nearby."

Up on the landing, he pointed to the second room on the right.

"Yeah but I wanted to be on my own." He opened the door. "I mean, I'll be twenty one soon." I tittered and stepped in. "What?" he asked and I shook my head. "You're laughing at me?"

"No." I shielded my giggles and the bottom half of my face with my sweater's neckline as we entered his room.

A mattress rested on the floor and a desk was cornered on the opposite side of the room. Clothes erupted from the closet and textbooks were scattered along the edges of the floor.

I stepped to the window across the door while he attempted to tidy up. But soon, he roamed next to me, opened the window and filed behind me, embracing my waist.

"Look, this is what I wake up to every morning."

I took the fresh air into my lungs. "You have the lake here too. Only it's outside your window now." It hid behind the house.

"I can see the pond and hear the birds sing every morning."

We relished the nightfall in comfortable silence and watched the moonshine in the glimmering water.

He spun my shoulders around and cupped my head. "I haven't been treating you very nice lately. I want us to be friends again. I missed you." His eyes bubbled and my butterflies quivered. He pressed his lips on mine, a savoury kiss. I browsed my palm on his chest and he carved his fingers through my hair.

He moved to the mattress, sank in and tapped it with his palm. "Come, sit beside me. This is me improvising until I get a bed."

"It looks like you don't have much of a choice."

"Look who's getting smart ass on me." He shifted closer and hugged my neck.

"I never thought I'd see you again," I said, staring into the room. Leave it to me to ruin a chummy vibe.

"I wasn't happy with myself and I couldn't appreciate your friendship. I'm a lot better now."

"I'm glad." I glimpsed at him and away again.

He pinched my chin to face him. "I'll be in Ottawa during the week and here on the weekends. We'll see each other over the summer, like we said we would."

"What makes you so sure?" I said and he raised his eyebrows. "I'm kidding. So, did you keep your locker?"

"No, I don't need a locker until September. It's empty now. You can have it." He pulled himself up on the mattress and turned the TV on to a random channel.

I climbed up too. "But Zee, your locker has my scribbles on it. It has history now. You should've kept it."

"I gave it back. I took a picture of it though."

"You took a picture?"

He reached for his phone on the night table and showed me.

"Do you remember that time when . . .?" And he pulled me into the magic world of reminiscing our finest moments as we sat on the mattress with our backs against the wall, like two good friends who bonded with laughter. But he cared to make a point about the times I stood him up and blew him off. "But that's okay, I forgive you. Do you forgive me?"

I turned my head to cartoon Batman on TV, my mind in a relaxed state, happy to sit next to his warm body, safe as if nothing else mattered. He radiated an incredible energy and I was drawn to him like a magnet.

I angled my face toward him. "I —," and he kissed me before I could finish my sentence. He leaned back and wetted his lips as our mouths played the testing game. He fumbled with my blouse.

"You know it's a bad idea, right?" I said, half-lipped as we kissed.

"What?"

"This."

"It's a very bad idea," he said as he undressed me.

I snagged my blouse back. "I mean it. Remember what happened the last time?" He threw my blouse across the room.

"This is different." His clothes followed my blouse.

"Different how?"

He threaded his fingers through his hair. "You're killing me. I told you, I'm different now." He peeled my jeans off but left my socks on, then yanked me on top of him. "I love your body so much. Your skin's so soft," he said and glided his fingertips down my back giving me goosebumps.

"And I love your body and your soft skin."

"Kiss me from head to toes." What?

His request came as a bit daring but there was something attractive about the strength of his words and it wasn't like I wouldn't have done it anyway. I kissed his smooth hair and brushed my lips against his cheekbones. I glided my mouth down his neck as he moaned. He tightened his grip on my spine, then loosened it. I slithered my lips across his chest and stomach, skipping over the underwear. I scooted down and nibbled on his toned legs from the thighs to the ankles. Then I stopped.

"You have the cutest toes, you know that?" Neither bony nor plump, clean and anatomically uniform. I worked my way back up on his legs when a wet surprise magically appeared on the surface of his underwear like a lagoon.

"You've got to be kidding me," I said, before I could stop myself.

"See what you do to me?" he said, his face red like a tomato.

We burst with laughter, two semi-naked fools collapsed on the mattress, laughing so hard until my gut muscles hurt and he broke into a cough. I shook myself into emotional sobriety, rolled off the bed, collected my clothes and asked for the bathroom.

"Down the hall, to your left."

I popped my head out of Zee's room, checked both ways as if I'd broken an entry and dashed to the bathroom in my bra and panties, clothes dangling in hand. I still chortled under my breath as I slipped my garments on. I fixed my hair in the mirror and roamed back to the corridor. Someone's angry footsteps tramped downstairs. I leaned over the bannister. A masculine shadow jittered about the unfamiliar Toyota in the driveway that stole his spot and who would dare such sacrilege?

I rushed to Zee's room. "Someone in the house is livid about me taking their parking spot. I have to go."

"Don't worry about it," he said, fully dressed now.

"I don't want to get you in trouble. Let's go."

"You won't, relax."

By the time we descended the stairs, the person vanished from the living room but he'd blocked my car in the driveway. I kissed Zee in the doorway and leaped in my car. When my engine revved to life, the house exterior lights flickered on and a head peeked from behind the curtain. I swerved onto the grass, backed my car onto the sidewalk, dropped it on the pavement and straightened it on the road. I pumped on the gas pedal in laughing hysteria and without looking back. "You're crazy," he texted on my way home.

The next sundown, Zee called — I guessed — to check in after the last night's events.

"Did I get you in trouble last night?" I asked before he could breathe out a word.

"No, I told you it was fine. Listen, I thought maybe we could get together on Monday for driving lessons?"

"Sure. Let's meet at school."

"That's right, you're starting your second semester. Uh, summer school. I feel for you."

"Believe it or not, I'm looking forward to it."

"You can't be serious."

"Dead serious. I'm done class at eleven. Meet me then."

I beamed the entire Sunday at work, at home through dinner and during a movie I watched with Heather while her son was asleep in his room.

"I'm not even going to ask," she said before we split for bed. "But I'm sure it's good news. Goodnight."

Monday morning, I rounded my car into the college grounds with bells on for my new semester but my delight turned sour at the forsaken décor. The campus was hollow with parking spots galore, a far cry from the routine morning battle for a parking spot close to the entrance.

Zee's former locker stood tall and available. My engravings on it bore through the teeth of general cleaning. I placed a lock on it and sprinted to the bookstore to pay for it before class. That way, his locker would be next to mine again in September, if I returned to school.

The college was stripped of the morning rush and its vacant hallways turned it into a ghostly mansion. Students popped up scarce at the library, the atmosphere dead silent. I missed the busy corridors, the crowded library where the search for an available computer transpired to mission impossible at times. I longed to see students hanging out or sleeping on the couches. I yearned for a jammed packed cafeteria where I sometimes had my coffee at the standing counter. The ambiance so demoralizing, I could hardly handle it. I finally understood the true meaning of summer school.

Only when I strode into Psychology class, I was certain summer classes did, in fact, take place. The professor, a well-spoken lady with a warm face and soothing voice delivered thought provoking stories that made even an intro class stimulating but I had trouble concentrating on the lecture. I couldn't escape the fear of Zee pulling one of his stunts again. I fiddled in my seat and half-smiled at the classmates next to me during forced interaction.

I set my phone on class silent but checked it every minute. The longer I waited for a word from him, the deeper the hammer drilled a hole in my stomach. On class break, I texted him with the pretext to let him know I saved his locker. "Thanks. I'm taking off to Ottawa in half an hour." My damn gut instinct. "I'm leaving my phone here to focus on work. Do you have Facebook?" Shivers blazed down my spine. Yeah, I have Facebook and you can't be my friend. I left his question dangle in the air.

After class, I raced home and crept into bed in pure daylight to numb the pain of his lies with sleep. But I tossed and turned while my brain consumed itself into a single nerve cell.

Three days later, he tapped an arid "back home" my way, as if I was supposed to jump for joy while grabbing my own ass. But I wrestled my hands off the phone and in the end, his magnet vacuumed my shadow of a will into retorting. "Can you help me with chemistry?" I did need help as it turned out Chem II bore graphs as well but I should've bitten my tongue before asking. "A graph?" "Yes, I'll scan it and send it over." We signed in and I sent him the scan. "Aren't you going to ask me about Ottawa?" I didn't particularly sense a crushing curiosity to ask but I did it to humour him. "I'll get back to you in a few minutes," he wrote without even answering my forcibly induced question.

An hour later, his status was still active but too busy for me. Ten minutes after I signed off without a word, he texted my phone. "Still need help?" I turned off my phone and curled under the duvet. Fuck you and your help. I've had enough.

CHAPTER

7

On June 9th and Zee's twenty first birthday, something on his lock caught my attention before my first class of the day. The hexagonal plastic locket attached to the lock and bearing the rental code had been moved from its position, as if someone nudged it walking by. Now, as a proud titleholder of OCD and therefore, extreme particularity about things and arrangements, an eye disturbance as such stood out on my radar. The blood rushed to my head and beyond my imagination and wishful thinking, I sensed his aura from a mile away. I guess, I haven't had enough.

I pondered in the morning over the decision to send him a birthday message. I settled in the library with homework scattered across my desk and ended my inner turmoil with a text. "Happy birthday, Zeke." I wanted to keep a neutral tone, no dearest vibes. No reply, not even a thank you, which pushed me to grasp the meaning of letting go. I missed the old me. The strong, confident girl who strutted her way to class and I wanted me back. But no matter the efforts, I couldn't bring me back. On the surface, I kept my head above water but deep down inside, I drowned in heartbreak.

On reading week, I savaged the days with work at the spa and slew the nights with stares in the dark. The loneliness pressed on my soul and I could hardly breathe. I buried my nose in textbooks. After I studied, I slept. After I slept, I worked. After I worked, I studied.

When I returned to class post-reading week, I dove into the core of school chatter with classmates. I'd missed the ambiance and connections. School, the only notion that made sense in my life, became my survival rope. I could hardly wait for the next assignment, the next presentation. My grades catapulted, my academic confidence blew through the roof and I'd come to consider grades below eighty percent unacceptable.

On Tuesday, my longest school day of the semester, I paddled to Science Fiction class. I took it as a General Education course for kicks along with Introduction to Psychology. Depending on the semester, one or two Gen-Eds were required, the student's choice from a list of courses aside from the mandatories and not linked to the domain in the current program. Colleges practice it to expand students' horizons on various academic topics and outside one's professional interest.

The course captivated my interest from the start and I counted the minutes until class time. Held in one of the two college theatres, we watched science fiction movies and wrote assignments about it. In college, it doesn't get any better than that.

I paraded into the theatre straight to the top. I'd claimed a seat, up in the nosebleeds where I could slouch in a chair with my feet up and no shame on the days when fatigue hit like a wrecking ball.

A soothing collective murmur flowed in the air in the wait for the professor as students strolled in one by one, laptops under the arms, knapsacks on the backs. A peer in particular took a seat a dozen rows below to the left, then swirled his head to salute me. And if I didn't sit in the last row, I'd have glanced over my shoulder in suspicion that his greeting wasn't meant for me. But it was.

His name was Ethan Webster from attendance, not that I cared any more than I did about the others. Up to reading week, he brushed by in the corridor adjacent to class with an occasional hello while I half-nodded with a blank expression but an intentional greeting came as an eyebrow raiser.

I lounged in my seat and sipped on extra-large green tea as Professor Hawthorne, a man with silver hair and cooler than life, played *Equilibrium* on the big screen. The film, powerful and intense, absorbed my mind like ink on blotting paper and how could this not be my favourite class?

On break, I descended out of the theatre for a stretch.

"Hey," a voice echoed from behind as I strode down the hall. This time, I did peer over my shoulder as none other than Ethan, a first class nerd with rectangular glasses, rushed to catch up.

I rolled my eyes. "Hi."

"What's your name?"

"I guess you don't pay attention to attendance."

"Sometimes my friends talk my ear off. I'm Ethan."

"Alexandra." I decided to go for the full dramatic first name and kept my initial pace down the hall.

"How do you like the course so far?"

"It's great."

"Are you walking to the caf?"

"No, the restroom. Do you mind?"

I barged into the washroom and wasted the break reading nonsense on my phone. When I bustled back to class, the latter half of *Equilibrium* had started. I tiptoed in the dark up to my seat while Ethan's gaze at my shadow struck like laser light. He kept twisting his head my way and when I gave him the evil eye, he gave up.

After class, I raced down the stairs and to the lockers. The idea of making another friend at school didn't scare me. Being burned did. And I had no desire for another male student friendship crap.

At the lockers, I put my hand on Zee's with my fingers spread, as if I'd want to draw the edge of my palm. I deciphered the lock and tossed it in my bag with my stomach in a knot. Then I closed mine and dashed out the doors.

CHAPTER

8

Monday morning nine o'clock on the dot, I rushed to Psychology with scorching coffee in hand, my first class of the week, a breath of fresh air. Hidden in a binder under my arm, an assignment on depth perception dissected in academic style in *The Sacrament of the Last Supper* by Salvador Dali awaited a trade-in for a top mark on the title page. I'd discovered my passion for psychology and studied the material with as much interest as I did sci-fi and biology and chemistry and sometimes I asked myself, which one was my favourite course and then I decided they all were because the college was my favourite place in the universe.

My second floor corridor strut took a hit on the speed when a ghost in the body of Zee slithered about a hundred feet down the hall. My mind played tricks on me before where I'd do a double take at a hooded student, who turned out a stranger.

Now I frowned in concentration. As the apparition grew nearer, it shaped up into the real Zee. Nobody else at the college wore a black and yellow Wu-Tang Clan anorak. His glinting eyes shifted between me and the hallway like strobe light and his glances spiked my breathing into tachypnea.

He reached the staircase leading to the library below before we'd brush each other's air.

"Hi, Alexa," he said as he plunged on the first step. My heart skipped a beat as I glided along the bannister.

"Hey," I said, then huffed with regret.

I promised myself to ignore him but I couldn't put it into practice. I suspected there might come a time in September — and by now I'd made up my mind that I'd return to school — when we'd unavoidably face each other. But I didn't think it'd be today.

I scribbled ideas for my next assignment at the library in my wait for my cherished Tuesday evening Science Fiction class. We were set to watch *Blade Runner*, my favourite classic. Exhausted from nights of three hours of sleep, I couldn't wait to snag an extra-large green tea, bounce to class, put my feet up and watch the film. My treat after hardcore studying and I wouldn't miss it for the world.

I sauntered to the auditorium and up to my seat in the last row. Then classmate Ethan hobbled in not-so-fashionably-late after Professor Hawthorne. He slipped into a chair and twirled his head with a smiling hello. I didn't flinch. He turned his head dejected. A minute later, he glanced up again with a maybe-contagious grin on his face. I half-smiled.

"Okay, kids. As we're approaching the end of the semester, I thought we owed it to ourselves, science fiction lovers, to watch one of the greatest movies of all times, *Blade Runner*. Enjoy class," Professor Hawthorne said and switched off the lights.

Ethan gazed up again, almost in desperation, pleading with his eyes for me to join his nerdy club. I wondered if he feared I'd kicked him out of my row, should he dare climb up next to me. Okay, Ethan. You want it, you got it.

I pouted as I parted ways with my top row seat and descended to Ethan's row, tea paper cup in hand. I scooted in the available seat next to him, perhaps left on purpose, nobody minded.

He straightened his posture and curved his mouth into a smile. "Hi."

"You already said hi today," I said, my eyes on the big screen.

He leaned closer, eyes on me. "Welcome then."

"I figured it's much better to watch it in two."

"I agree," he whispered. "I haven't seen it in ages."

"Same here. It's my favourite movie and soundtrack ever."

"Mine too." He unfolded the tray table between our seats. He placed a coffee on it that I didn't know he had, then tapped it to put my tea on it. We slouched in our chairs with our elbows grazing when he pulled out a chocolate egg the size of a coin.

"It's not Easter, is it?" I asked, startled.

"No but they're good energy boosters when you're tired at school. You want it?"

"Where the hell do you get Easter chocolate eggs in July?"

"Bulk Barn," he whispered.

I love Bulk Barn. "I'll take half." I snatched it from his hand.

"No, it's okay. You eat it."

"No, come on. We'll share."

"You have it."

"I said we'll share . . . sorry, I'm tired."

He took the egg back, unwrapped it, broke it in pieces and used his hand as a platter while we snacked on the chocolate bits. And all this with flying cars and Harrison Ford in the background.

On break, I moseyed to the cafeteria for another tea and by the time I returned, Professor Hawthorne restarted the movie. I hunched and ascended the stairs. Ethan shot me a will-you-sit-with-me-again look and when I reclaimed the seat beside him, he sighed with relief. As if we hadn't just talked about seeing *Blade Runner* before, he leaned close to describe the scenes I'd missed. We reached for our cups at the same time with our eyes on the screen and broke into faded giggles, much to the professor's dismay. I must admit, after the fiasco with Zee, Ethan kicked a whiff of oxygen in my disposition.

He came tall as a tree and thin as a rod and sported dark brown hair, his locks probably as straight as his high school A grades. He belonged to a clique of geeks who stayed true to itself and shortly after I joined the crowd, the entertainment ignited. His friends leaned over to glimpse at the miracle of a blonde sitting next to Ethan. They nudged elbows and gossiped into their palms. When a chocolate egg landed on the tray table and rolled in my lap, I slanted my head and raised an eyebrow farther down the row.

"They mean well," Ethan said.

"It's fine."

"My friend couldn't reach over this far. It's a welcoming gesture," he said, rubbing his leg.

I smiled at the tittering crowd, then at Ethan. "Easter chocolate eggs must be like a group entity or something."

"Like I said, they're good for energy and they taste good," he murmured, brushing my hair with his lips.

"Let's watch the movie, shall we?"

When the second egg bounced off my arm, Ethan turned to the giggling crowd.

"Hey guys, time to stop." Then he turned to me. "Sorry." And when he did a double take, we burst with laughter and covered our mouths a second too late before the professor darted devil stares at us.

I turned away to regain control of my emotions. Then, "Shhh, our prof is going to kill us."

"No, he won't. He's too cool for that."

Professor Hawthorne was a science fiction magician, who worshiped Isaac Asimov. He'd created the Science Fiction course himself and had it approved by the college. On our first class, he fished a miniature airplane out of his pocket and confessed that he still plays with it when no one's around. He filled our classes with virtuous humour and stimulating curriculum. Nothing in the world could ever convince me to skip any one of his classes.

At the end of class, I whipped it down to the professor's desk before anyone beat me to it. I sought clarification on the upcoming assignment on a sci-fi movie of choice. I picked *Aliens*.

"Great choice. Ask away," Professor Hawthorne said.

After he cleared my neurotic muddle with his magic wand, I darted out of class. I sped through the college buildings on my way to the lockers. No one followed and I decelerated my pace. But I couldn't wipe the smirk off my face on the way home.

In the morning, I skipped through the school doors. I'd slaved over a presentation on vegetarianism with two classmates from

Humanities and I couldn't wait to show off the end result. The professor advised we dress as elegant as we can bear when presenting. I wore black Capri pants, a black mixed with grey tunic top and black wedges, my hair blow-dried in layers, mascara and clear lip gloss to boot. My partners and I presented our work next to the projector screen, bouncing the words off one another. We high-fived each other on our way to our seats after scoring a hard-earned ninety five percent.

I shrugged off the post-presentation jitters at the library. As I waited for the computer to log me in, Zee strolled by the circulation desk. I leaned forward with bulging eyes. He lingered by the main printer, then exited the library with papers in hand. I wished he stayed around long enough to see me dressed.

A week later, I staggered to Science Fiction with sore eyes and tingling skin. I'd sweated my wits over my last psychology assignment, a fifteen-page paper on the *Little Albert Experiment*, a controversial study led by John B. Watson on a baby evoking classical and operant conditioning in humans. I'd slept for an hour the night before. But Science Fiction had become my therapy and delight class of the week and skipping didn't count as an option.

On my way to the top row, I passed Ethan's empty seat. I fell into my chair, struggling to stay awake. When Ethan tumbled in late, he rushed up the stairs and up to my row. I stiffened my posture as he stood at the end of the row, waiting for approval. After a two-second wait, my reflections dead slow, he skipped the consent and shimmied beside me.

"Hi," he said as he gazed into the auditorium.

"Hey."

He tossed his knapsack on the floor, then bent his elbow on his knee and lodged his chin on his knuckles. He was the cool, calm and collected type, my total opposite. He placed a piece of paper on the tray table. "Tired?" I took the pen from his hand. "An hour of sleep last night." He retrieved his pen. "What program?" "Pre-

Health Sciences. You?" He brushed my hand with his fingers. "Whatever that is, I'm sure you'll explain later. Computer Technologies." "Gee, I wouldn't have guessed." He nudged my elbow, then shifted his eyes to the professor. We absorbed the lecture in silence and took turns to sneak peek sideways.

On break, I stood up and stretched. "I'm going to the caf."

"Can I come with you?" he asked and took it as a yes when I descended the stairs.

"Alexandra —"

"Alexa but Alexandra is fine too."

"Alexa, what made you take Science Fiction?" he asked in the hallway.

"Why? Don't I fit the type?" He shook his head. "It was the next most interesting option after Psychology on the Gen-Ed list. I'm glad I did, it's my favourite class." A smile flashed across his face. "What type do I fit into?"

"Oh, I don't know, a girl who has a closet full of clothes but thinks she has nothing to wear."

"FYI, I play video games . . . played. I don't have time anymore."

"I don't believe you."

"Believe."

"Name one," he said and aligned himself behind me in lineup.

I bought a much needed coffee and waited to the side for Ethan.

"*Medal of Honor*," I said as he joined me back to class.

He wiped the coffee drips off his fingers with a napkin. "Sorry, what?"

"I've played many games but MOH is my favourite. I used to be part of a video gaming clan for a while. We kicked ass."

He parted his lips. "Wow, I've gained a whole new respect for you." I bumped his arm. "Ouch," he yelped from the coffee spill burning his fingers.

We crept into class and reclaimed our seats on mute until the movie culmination.

"See you next week," I said as I rose up.

"Where did you park?"

"B building. My locker and most of my classes were there during my first semester."

"I parked there too. I'll walk with you," he said and I swallowed hard. The walking part reminded me of Zee. "Are you coming back in September?"

"Yes, I am. You?"

"Yeap. How long is your program?"

"I'm graduating at the end of this semester," I said. He tilted his head. "It's a preliminary program to the one I'm targeting." Head tilt again. "I'm on the Paramedic waiting list but I'll be back in September anyway. I'll complete the leftover Gen-Eds required for Paramedic and maybe a higher level Biology. Then if I don't make it in this year, I'll give the Paramedic exam another try next year."

"So, you're a former video game player, you like Science Fiction and you want to be a Paramedic. You amaze me." I slipped a lop-sided grin. "I have to take Gen-Eds in the fall too. Maybe we could take them together?"

"You and me to agree on the same courses other than Sci-Fi?"

"What could be odder than meeting you in Science Fiction?"

"My locker is around the corner. I have to stop by the restroom first. Carry on without me," I said.

"It's okay. I'll wait."

"No, go ahead."

"I'll wait."

I banged into the washroom, hoping he'd leave like the first time. I wasted ten minutes reading crap on my phone and five more ruffling my tired hair.

"You're still here," I said as I came out in the hallway.

"Can I have your email?" he asked on the way to my locker.

"Because phone numbers are outdated in 2009?"

He handed me the paper from class. "I'm okay with that too."

I jotted my email address and shoved the paper into his hand. Then I zipped my school tote and locked my locker. I stepped away, thankful about the love notes on my locker gone unnoticed or unasked about. We navigated down the hall and out to the parking lot.

"Goodnight. See you next week," I said.

"I'll follow you on the highway."

"No. You won't."

"Why not?"

"Because I'll leave you in the dust."

He tailed my car out of campus. On the highway, I gunned the engine about twenty K over but spec boy clung at the back, like I'd predicted. I decelerated until he caught up with a grateful smile. We drove back and forth and around each other, shooting off grins and funny faces. Then he waved and split on the off-ramp.

When I dropped my school tote and textbooks on my desk at home, an email with a new number popped on the display. "Want to skype for a bit?" I signed in despite the fatigue and yapped and laughed with Ethan until four in the morning, at which point my body transformed into a carcass of numbness.

The rumble on my phone woke me to life. "Good morning. Are you at school?" Ethan texted. I checked for the time. "Morning. No, I slept in," and the phone rang.

"How come you didn't make it to school today? You didn't miss any tests, did you?" he asked from the library. The background chatter gave it away.

"No, just lectures. And I wonder if it's because I went to bed at four a.m. after an hour of sleep the night before."

"Sorry. I'll be more vigilant next time."

"I'm joking. You didn't put a gun to my head. I had fun too."

"I'm heading to class now but . . . call you later?"

"Call me later. I have projects to work on too."

Ethan's lack of push for personal questions and answers rubbed me the right way. He let me come around on my own, to tell him whatever and whenever I wanted to tell, unlike Zeke, who drilled me with an interview as soon as we exchanged more than awkward glances and a couple of stiff words. Ethan's personality was unruffled and everything came easy with him. I liked it and I finally smiled again. I loitered in bed with homework until dusk when Ethan and I shared a casual phone call and goodnight texts.

Early in the a.m., he tapped another text my way to make sure I'd make it to school. "Good morning. I'll be at the library if you have time." I'd been up and on my way.

I swaggered to the library half an hour before class and scouted for a slender dude with glasses on the beak. A lengthy arm flapped in the air from behind a computer. Ethan cooked up a presentation with classmates, the same gang from Sci-Fi, which made them my classmates too, only this presentation was for a different course.

"Hey, we're taking a break. Join us for breakfast?"

I glanced at the nodding heads next to Ethan. "All right, I have some time before my first class."

Ethan and I navigated to the cafeteria with geek squad in tow, dissecting our timetables for the day. We plunked our boots in line and when his dilated pupils bore into my face, I dropped my eyes to the floor and jiggled my foot in pretend maladroit. He pulled me into claim and kissed me without caring about potential spectators. I gave him props for that. I'd never been a fan of public display of affection but I recognize a true pair of balls when it dangles in front of my eyes. Zee would not kiss me on school grounds in a million years from now and then counting backwards.

We gathered around a table in a cluster of overstudied brains to devour breakfast and yakked about science fiction movies. I enjoyed being myself for a change. I didn't have to care about what I'd say or do because no matter what I said or did, they slurped it alive along with their breakfast. They reminded me of how awesome nerds could be.

After we scattered to class, I texted with Ethan and met up on breaks, even the short ones to chat about academics or just to say hi. Before Biology, my last class of the day, I slumped into a booth in the cafeteria with my nose buried in my two hundred dollars and change textbook while he sat across from me. His stare poked my eyelids but I tried to focus on my Neuro chapter instead.

"Stop eyeballing me. I'm trying to study." When he ignored my request, I glimpsed at him with scolding eyebrows, then back at the pages.

"I love you."

I held my breath in my throat and my face in the book as it took me moments to process his words. Then I flirted with the options of either pretending I didn't hear or asking him again to make sure I heard him right.

"Did you hear me? I love you."

I shot him the look of doubt. "Don't say that."

"Why not? I do."

"No, you don't."

"Yes, I do. You don't believe me?"

"It's not that I don't believe you, it's just . . .," way too soon. "I have class."

I shimmied out of the booth, snagged my tote and marched out of the cafeteria. He chased after me down the hall and matched up my steps on my way to the Science Building.

"Look, I'm sorry. I had no idea it would make you uncomfortable," he said, his voice shaky. "I should've kept it to myself."

I waned my strut as we approached the Biology Lab. "I have to go." I spun on my heels and veered inside.

The class ran short and I considered jetting home without a word but I didn't have the heart to give him the cold shoulder. "Meet me at the library," I texted him.

We dipped into the couches at the back of the library and next to the fireplace, which despite being shut off for the summer, it still made for a lavish décor. The vibe had shifted and we found it next to impossible to crop a conversation after the I-love-you bomb blasted on the cafeteria table and fizzled next to my Bio textbook.

"Do you have plans for the long weekend?" he asked.

"I'm working at my friend's beauty salon."

"My family's going to my aunt's house but I don't know if I want to go. It's going to be a drinking party and I can't drink."

"I wasn't aware other kinds of parties exist. And why not?"

"I just can't." I narrowed my eyes and he rubbed the nape of his neck. "I take medication."

"What kind of medication?"

"Antidepressants." He stared into the library.

"Why? You're happy all the time."

"That's because I take the meds."

"Please do explain."

"I was a mess after I broke up with my ex. She cheated on me and I tried to kill myself."

"What? I'm so sorry. How?"

He bumped his glasses up his nose. "Booze and pills."

"I'm speechless, honestly." This info turned out a bigger bomb than I love you. "How long ago?"

"April."

"This year April? Like, three months ago? Don't you think you needed a breather before jumping into another . . . another —"

"Relationship?"

"Yeah."

"No. I'm fine now."

Ethan came from a well-to-do family, whose parents provided him with everything a twenty-two-year-old required for college. A car, paid tuition, paid textbooks, free rent, pocket money. But this seemingly peaceful guy was more troubled inside than I could've ever imagined.

"Time for my class now," said Ethan. "Walk with me?"

I escorted him to the third floor, neither of us saying much on the way. By the classroom, he leaned in for a kiss. I stepped back.

"I don't want this to be some kind of rebound for you. I'm not interested in that. And besides, I have my own emotions to re-arrange. It's all too much right now."

"I am as sure of my feelings for you as I am that my name is Ethan Webster."

"I need to think this through. It's probably better if we don't talk for a while. Sorry."

CHAPTER

9

On long weekend Monday, the college held no classes and the beauty salon was closed for Civic Holiday. Heather and Carl left for a picnic by the lake with their son but not before they invited me to tag along. I declined in favour of their need for family time after he'd returned from the road the day before. But the August sun shone bright and a gripping desire to enjoy the outdoors pushed my fingers onto the phone keys. I texted Ethan. He called in thirty seconds.

"Studying?" I asked.

"On this gorgeous day? No way. Let's get together."

"What do you have in mind?"

"Movie and a walk in the park?"

"It sounds good. I'll see you soon."

I hopped on the highway to Brenton City and met him at the movie theatre. He waited for me on the platform with the same frantic library wave, tickets flapping high in the sky. I squeezed through the parked cars and climbed the steps in his direction.

"I bought the tickets."

"You decided on a movie?"

He laced an arm around my shoulder as we pressed against the theatre front doors. "You trust me?"

"Not really but I'll buy the popcorn."

He cuddled me in lineup for snacks and during the movie, a constant rub on my leg, a pull under his arm, a search for my hand. After the movie, which turned out half-decent, we stumbled in the parking lot at midpoint between our cars.

"Let's drive to the beach. It's beautiful this time of year," he said.

"The beach?"

"I live close to the lake. We'll take my car."

We drove to Clearlake, a town just south of Brenton City, first exit off the highway and through a residential area. Clearlake Park, equally rich in grass and sand, resembled a bucolic remote island. The occasional bicycle rider passed by or someone walking a dog. And it exuded serenity like Ethan.

After a dozen steps on the boardwalk, he yanked me on a picnic bench in the grass, our butts on the table, our feet on the sitting pew. The trees swooshed their smaragdine mane against the breeze on one side and the lake rippled smooth waves on the other.

"I love you," he said and I glanced away. "I mean it." He loomed close and kissed me with delicate lips. They tasted like berries and my skin prickled with goosebumps under my clothes.

I slid off the picnic table. "We should go."

"Why? You don't like it here?"

"It's lovely but let's go. We have school tomorrow."

"I'll bring you back here. Just so you know." I dragged Ethan toward the parking lot. "Why are you so sensitive about those three words? Words don't bite."

"They're words with weight," I said as we leaped into his car.

"I have a friend my age who has three kids."

"Seriously? Good thing you're not him. He probably envies your freedom." I dug through my tote for the lip gloss.

"No, I envy him."

My fingers stopped the lip gloss halfway across my bottom lip. "Why? Would you want to have three kids right now?"

"Maybe not three but one."

I folded down the visor mirror, speechless. This dude meant business. He wanted the whole nine yards of a relationship.

"Thanks for today," I said in the theatre parking lot, one step out the door and toward my car.

"No kiss goodbye?"

"Goodnight, Ethan."

*

Ethan arrived at school early to work on a project with classmates. So after my Psychology class, which spread over Mondays and Wednesdays, I skipped to the library and snuck behind a standing Ethan. I held my index across my lips to his friends. Then I covered his eyes and his gang turned to mush. He spun around and splashed a kiss on my lips.

"What's with the giggles?" he asked.

I handed him the assignment on the *Little Albert Experiment*. "Remember when I only slept for an hour?"

"A hundred percent. Kudos to you."

The nerd squad applauded in unison. "Great job."

I bowed. "Thank you very much. I slaved over it. I bled too."

"My brilliant Alexa." He wrapped his elongated arms around my waist and gave me a boost in the air.

"Let's keep it grounded, shall we? We're at the school library," I said, flipping my toes off the floor.

He lowered me down, gently as ever and I dropped into a chair next to him. I sprinkled my homework across the desk. He angled away to work on the project with partners but held on to my hand.

"Ethan, I need both hands to type."

"Mmm, okay."

He turned to stamp a kiss on my cheek from time to time and that meant every minute. I crinkled my face every time but I didn't have the heart to burst his swollen enthusiasm. He'd changed his Facebook status from *single* to *in a relationship* and left the screen on for me to see. I'd deleted my account, one night in a paralyzing rage over Zee, so he wouldn't find me and left it at that.

"Who are you in a relationship with?"

"There's this girl at my school and her name is Alexa."

"And . . . is she your girlfriend or . . . ?"

"Yeap, she's my girlfriend all right." I dreaded and cheered at the same time. A boyfriend? Yikes, I used to think. "Can I take my girlfriend to the mall for lunch? It'll be just you and me."

"I parked in a good spot this morning, close to the entrance."

"We can take my car."

"Let's go then."

The idea of lunch with my newly acquired boyfriend between classes buttered my senses more than I thought it would. Ethan wasn't the best looking guy but he was definitely the nicest.

We enjoyed a quiet lunch at a table for two at the food court, the mall a five-minute drive from campus. Then we raced back to Science Fiction class, ten fingers kissing at the fingertips.

I wore a pink T-shirt with a stylish blonde in a pinker dress holding hands with a dark haired boy donning glasses, a blue garb and a tie. *I only date nerds* were scribbled at the bottom.

Professor Hawthorne, who dawdled next to the theatre door, held still to read my T-shirt.

"Miss Avadani, does he qualify, though?"

"Big time." I tugged Ethan up to our seats, next to his friends.

We watched two episodes of *Star Trek* while Ethan and I shot melancholic glances to one another in the dark. It was our last lecture before the final test of the course next week.

At home, we spoke again on Skype for hours, mostly about our beloved Sci-Fi class until we couldn't keep our eyes open anymore and kissed one another through the screen off to bed.

Late morning, I meandered to the library after my only class of the day. Two unpolished fifteen page assignments for Biology and Physics weighed my guilt and nerves to the ground. I'd been slacking off homework since I'd met Ethan — I usually finished them a week before the due date — and I had to catch up.

I sweated over the bio report with my lab partner when Ethan made an appearance and dashed hopeful glances my way every minute. By the afternoon, I glided to his desk.

"I'm about to go to class. I hoped you'd be done sooner."

"Sorry, we had to finish it. It's due tomorrow," I said as I sat next to him.

"Are you going home?"

"No, I'll be here after your class too. I have another paper, also due tomorrow."

He pouted, then he rose off the chair, kissed my cheek and vanished to class. I staggered back to my desk and dug my wits deep into my homework. The next time I raised my head up for air, Ethan rolled in after class and inquisitive about my progress.

"Still working on it."

He pouted again. "Torque, angular momentum. What is this?"

"Physics. A paper on a topic of choice that involves physics, which is pretty much everything that comes to mind, including you leaning forward and gawking at the computer right now."

He peeked at his posture and back at the monitor. "And what are you writing yours on?"

"Gymnastics. The physics of gymnastics."

"Plenty of physics there, I imagine. Should I wait for you?"

"No. It'll take a few more hours and I don't like to rush."

"Fine, I'll go home." He grumbled standing up and drifted out of the library but not before the faithful peck on the cheek.

I stayed at the library and typed away like a robot, revised and edited, racing against time. I hadn't digested my school year coming to an end until the drive home. My existence without Brimley — my creative missile — didn't make sense anymore. I loved everything about it. Handpicked professors, good natured peers, cozy atmosphere. I found it excruciatingly difficult to break away, even for a short time.

I handed in my physics and biology assignments with pride and dark circles under my eyes. Staying awake was a challenge on repeat. Students slept on couches at the library again and sometimes napped in class with their heads slanted on the desks.

The Physics lecture flew by but Biology dreaded on brutally slow, as the teacher shoved new material down our throats before the final test next week. A pounding headache split my head in half but I refused to bustle out of class. My classmates and I texted our farewells fighting back our tears.

I united with Ethan at the library in mid-afternoon. We'd planned to study for our Science Fiction final test, then movie and the beach. After I organized a list of studying material for an hour while Ethan flipped through the textbook like nobody's business, I scraped the chair back and arched my spine into a stretch.

"I'm going to the caf for a green tea. You want something?"

"Medium double-double."

I ventured to the cafeteria for hot drinks. On the way back, I abated in the second floor hallway above the library when a flash-back hit like a truck, the wheels trampling over my heart back and forth. Not many months ago, Zee and I locked eyes in this section of the corridor and he told me how pretty I was. I leaned my fore-arms against the bannister, facing the library below in nostalgia, paper tray held tight in my hands. It must have been a case of the end-of-the-semester blues that set off my memories, still alive like they happened yesterday. And I couldn't escape the flutters in my stomach.

Ethan's nose remained buried in the textbook, despite my slam-ming his coffee on the desk. Zee sensed my inner troubles from miles away but with Ethan, I'd undergo five different gut turning emotions and he'd have no clue about it.

I drowned in lingering memories in front of the monitor. When my eyes shifted to the library entrance with a mind of their own, I froze in my seat. I swore I could feel my pupils dilate when Zee ambled in, my untimely butterflies explained. I squeezed my eyes shut for a moment to shake the imaginary ghost but when I opened them again, the apparition unveiled in real dimensions. Zee himself strode down the middle corridor in the flesh. I stooped in my chair with a pounding heart and my head hid behind the monitor. The telepathy I shared with this guy was unreal.

I raised my forehead above the monitor with my breath caught in my throat. Dressed in summery blue, he settled at a desk in plain view. As the computer logged him in, he threw a one-eighty scan around the library and I ducked. When I poked one eye out of the left side, Zee's glittery eyes and hefty smile jangled every nerve cell in my body. He waved hello, then moved his knapsack from the chair next to him to the floor and jerked his head, as if to invite me to sit beside him. My butt almost lifted itself off the chair. It took mystical powers to fight the urge to race to his desk and take in his scent.

Ethan nudged my elbow. "Do you think we should study these definitions?"

"What?"

"Should we study these?" He pointed to a row of senseless words in the textbook.

"I don't know."

"What do you mean? You organized the study list."

"I said I don't know." He crinkled his face, tracing back to the definitions and I couldn't believe the amount of fog someone could hold inside their head.

Zee meandered to the printer and back to his seat with papers in hand. He tossed them in a folder, then the folder in the knapsack and gaped at me again. I shuffled my eyes back to my monitor. I feared he'd make his way over and then I'd have to crawl under the desk and let the two of them figure it out. After Zee set a pair of sunglasses on, he moseyed out of the library, school bag over his shoulder. I thanked the skies above that he took off before Ethan decided it'd been too long since his last kiss on my cheek.

"Ready to go?" he asked. "It's nice out and I don't feel like studying anymore."

"Yeah." Neither did I.

"Follow my car?" he asked in the parking lot. I nodded with a lack of interest even a blind man could see but not Ethan.

I tailed his car in a daze to Cherry Avenue. I drifted through the heavy traffic into the centered lane with an equally heavy heart when Zee popped on the sidewalk, strolling with earphones on. I bounced my head up and down like an owl through the moving cars, partially blocking my view from the inside lane and waved my hand in a frantic to catch Zee's attention. Ethan smiled and waved back, then frowned in confusion at the look of death I shot his way.

The stream of traffic shot down my attempt to change lanes closer to Zee and didn't allow so much as an inch of quick maneuver. The mass of cars pushed me ahead in the middle lane as he strutted to the music in my right side mirror. I pictured pulling my car over, beckoning Zee, him jumping in and me driving away. A terrible thought in respect to Ethan but I couldn't shake the pleasure of it.

At the intersection, Ethan swerved to the left and I followed with a giant pout on my face while the shadow of Zee diminished behind. We rounded into the first plaza where Ethan's mother worked as an insurance broker. We'd planned to drop his car off at his mother's work and head to the movies in mine.

He leaped out of the car and bent down to my window. "I have to drop the car keys off. Wish to come with? Meet my mom?"

"Maybe some other time? I'll wait here for now."

As he sauntered away with his mouth curved into a sulk — you're not the only one pouting here, dude — I stepped out of the car for open space to breathe. I wasn't in the mood for meet-the-mom moment. Unless his mom was a carbon copy of Mrs Leni Pellini, in which case I'd spill the beans on my emotional troubles over coffee and she'd listen and give good advice, no thank you, not today.

I leaned against the trunk of my car when Ethan made his way back with a mountain of a woman in tow.

"She wants to meet you," he said.

"Hello, I'm Alexa."

"Right. Are you going to the movies?" she said and her unkempt hair sliced through my sight more than her thick specs.

"Yes."

"I came out here to make sure you'll give him a ride home after the movie." As compared to dropping him in a ditch somewhere?

I glimpsed at Ethan, then back at his mother. "That's the plan."

"Make sure she gives you a ride, okay?" she told her son with her index pointing at his face. He nodded and dropped his eyes to the ground. She narrowed her eyes at us, spun around and waddled back to the plaza.

"What the fuck was that all about?" I asked as we stepped into my car.

"She wants to make sure nothing happens to me."

"Ethan, you're twenty two not twelve."

I guessed she only wanted to meet me for a mental portrait, in case she had to describe my facial features to the police, if her son went missing.

"Do you want to go to the mall for a bite before the movie?" he asked. No, not really.

I drove to the mall without a word and I didn't know why I couldn't excuse myself and go home. Waiting in line for food, he hovered and kissed me and suffocated my senses beyond belief.

"Ethan, you know I'm not a big fan of PDA."

"Is this about my mother?"

"No, this is about kissing in public."

We carried our trays to a table and I prayed to eat in silence. I wanted to drift into my own bubble but he wouldn't allow it. He reached for my hand and I snapped it back.

"Why won't you give me your hand?"

"Because I need to eat."

"You only need one hand to eat."

I raised my left hand. "Fork." I lifted my right. "Knife. See? I need both."

He grumbled under his breath and we finally ate in peace as I scrutinized his eating habits. He licked the French fry grease off his fingers.

At the movies, I slumped in my chair away from Ethan.

"You look like there's something on your mind. You okay?" he whispered.

"No and yes."

"Are you sure?"

"Watch the movie."

After the film, we shambled to my car when he wrapped an arm around my shoulder.

"What should we do now?"

"I'm taking you home."

"But we said we'd go to the beach."

"Don't you have a curfew?" I pictured his mother waiting behind the door with a baseball bat in her hand, a minute late into his curfew.

"I do not."

"By the looks of it, you do," I said as I climbed in the driver seat.

I took the Clearlake exit off the highway. "Directions please."

"Come on, you can't possibly believe I have a curfew." He pointed his finger to the left.

"Maybe you don't but I don't particularly desire to see mugshot sketches of my face on every tree in your neighbourhood, in case you're an hour too late for your mother's taste."

He chewed on his bottom lip. "You're exaggerating." He pointed to the right after a stop sign, another left and a driveway on the right side of the street.

I shifted the car into park. "Delivered at home safe and sound."

"Would you like to come in and meet both my parents?"

"No, thanks. Maybe another time."

He groaned while he leaned in for a kiss and I turned my cheek sideways. "Goodnight."

I heaved out of bed refreshed and sprinted to work for half a shift. Early afternoon, when Heather popped in to cut me loose, I pounced on the highway toward Ethan's house. He forgot his phone in my car last night and I tapped an email in the morning that I'd deliver it after work. He shot back from his home computer with a proposition to study together for Science Fiction at his place. He had the house to himself.

I swerved off the highway straight into Clearlake and hit the first Tim Hortons drive-thru for two large coffees, the main ingredient for studying. When I lost my way in the residential maze, I emailed Ethan with a cry for help but nothing came back. I wandered around his area for more than half an hour and by the time I discovered his house, I hurdled on the door step with a crimson face and flaring nostrils.

He screeched the door open, as much as his body fitted through the crevice.

"You gave me the wrong directions to your house."

"No, I didn't."

"I got lost and emailed you. It didn't dawn on you to check it?"

"Why didn't you call my landline?"

"You never gave me your house number."

He scratched the nape of his neck. "I thought I did." You fucking airhead.

"Your coffee, your phone." He took them, eager.

"Are you going to school today?"

"Going to school? Why would I go to school today? When did I ever have classes on Friday?"

"No, I mean to study," he stuttered.

I clenched my teeth. "I thought we planned to study together at your house." He gawked at me, as if I spoke a foreign language. "I have to go."

"Wait, Alexa."

By the time I slammed my bedroom door shut, my phone pinged with sixteen missing calls and another one on the way.

"What do you want?"

"Come on, I'm sorry. I thought you didn't want to come in the house because you were mad. Also, my parents didn't leave town as planned."

"You should have been up front about it, instead of playing dumb."

"I'm sorry."

"Goodbye."

My phone rumbled well into the night and also bright and early the next day. I checked the time before I answered. Seven o'clock.

"Isn't it a bit early for you on a weekend?"

"I wasn't trying to hide you from my parents. I'd love nothing more than for you to meet my family."

I rubbed my eyes. "You're missing the point here. Your parents' change of plans didn't bother me. You hiding behind your finger did."

"I'm going out of town with my parents to visit my aunt."

"And you're telling me this at seven a.m. on a Saturday morning because . . .?"

"Aren't you getting up for work anyway?"

"You're missing the point again."

"I want to make it up to you when I come back, if you'll let me."

"I have to get ready. Have a good trip."

I raced to work and when I checked my phone on break, I grouched at the blank display. Someone was having a good time at the aunt's. At dusk, I shrugged the no-phone-call smudge of irritation off my face and slipped into bed with school reading material. Five final tests were pending in the upcoming week and I had infinite textbook pages to read.

An hour into chewing the book pages raw, a striking thunder broke across the sky. Within seconds, a torrent of rain soaked the atmosphere, cutting out the power.

Heather barged into my room. "I brought candles. You okay?"

"Yeah, thanks. The three of you?"

"Yes, they said the storm left several towns without electricity."

"Looks like I'm going to study over candlelight."

"We'll be in the kitchen, if you want the company."

I left the bedroom door open and moved my textbooks to the desk, next to the flickering candles. The phone whirred with a text from Ethan and my face brightened with delight. "I'm still on the road heading home." "Be careful on this stormy drive." "In the back seat of parents' car, thinking of you."

I studied and texted with Ethan through the downpour. After the storm, I opened the windows and the hot, humid air saturated my skin with a veil of moisture. By the time Ethan reached home, our texts turned from friendly to flirty to sexy and I blamed the décor. The candle lighting my room, the wind ruffling the trees and the moon smiling its shine spun a romantic mood, exhilarating my senses along with my sentiments for Ethan.

I stumbled out of Psychology with a sigh of relief and a trace of sorrow at the same time. One final test down, four more to go. But I relished this class with a passion and I'd miss it dearly, my perfumed delight on Monday mornings.

At the library, Ethan's wavy hand caught my attention.

"Ready to study for Sci-Fi?" he asked.

We dunked into the fat armchairs at the back of the library, face to face with our feet up on each other's cushion. I handed him copies of our study notes and buried my eyes in the papers but when I glimpsed up, Ethan's deep blue gaze almost blinded me.

"You're supposed to study," I said.

"Let's go to my house. My parents are at work right now."

"What? No. We need to study for our final tomorrow."

I zoomed in on my notes when a group of boisterous students crashed next to us. I gave them the evil eye without result.

"Come on. Let's go. It's quiet at my house and we *will* study."

"Do you honestly think we'll study there?"

"You're disciplined. I'm sure you'll keep it under control."

A wave of background laughter flipped in the air.

"Let's go."

We booked it to Ethan's house in separate cars, parked in his driveway and descended the stairs. He'd turned the entire basement into his bedroom. Video game posters hung on the walls, a bookshelf was filled with science fiction books and films, a computer sat on a cluttered desk and a bed lined the wall with the window.

I pointed to a poster. "I played this one."

He paced closer and cupped my neck. "And you liked it?"

"Yeah." I glimpsed at his mouth with a tingling spine and he tested my lips.

Ethan took pride in being a certified geek but the strangest thing was that he was a geek who turned me on.

"Studying, remember?"

"Oh, yeah. I forgot." He angled away to his school bag. "See? I said you'll keep us on the right track."

I glided out of his room where a vintage couch nestled in a rectangular vestibule. "Let's study here."

He approached holding on to his notes and we leaned against the backrest of the couch, our arms glued to one another. His breathing waves drifted from his slanted head into my ear lobe with a sweet draft of innocence.

"Stop it," I said.

"What?"

"You're breathing in my ear, instead of reading your notes."

"Does it bother you?"

"It ruins my concentration."

"That's the plan."

"You promised."

"I did no such thing," he said and mushed my lips.

He undressed the nerdy appearance into a sensual kisser with a soft touch and a hidden charm.

"Do you realize our final test in Sci-Fi is tomorrow?" I said. "I should go. You know we won't study, if I stay."

"No, don't. I'll be good. Promise."

"No, I'll go. We're a distraction to each other."

"Would you at least stay for dinner? Meet both my parents?"

"Ethan, we have to study. Final test. Tomorrow."

I scurried to his bedroom to retrieve my tote and when I spun around, Ethan's lips lunged at mine. I slung my arms around him and we tiptoed to his bed, our clothes slipping off piece by piece. We smooched buck naked on his bed, his body lean and long, exuding warmth and comfort.

A tick went off outside his window, mounted high on the wall.

"What was that?"

"It's probably my neighbour," he said and kissed me.

I pushed him off. "Are you sure? Why don't you have blinds?"

"I'm sure and nobody ever looks down in here."

"I should go. I need to study anyway," I said and he whined.

I levered out of bed and slipped into my clothes. No way I'd let myself get caught, naked on his bed, joystick inside. And besides, I wasn't ready for the next step in our relationship.

"Let's go," I said as I roamed halfway up the stairs. He followed with a pout. I winked on my way out. "Good luck studying."

He hugged the front door. "Kind of hard now but you too."

I braced myself as the week of hell stood about to begin. After the final test in Chem class, I paddled to the quiet study, opened my Science Fiction textbook and dove into the pages. I'd forbidden Ethan to make contact until class time, so I could absorb the test material distraction-free.

Hours later, I strode inside the college theatre for my last Sci-Fi session, my treasured course and matchmaker class for Ethan and me. He rushed in, late as usual and joined me up in the nosebleeds, right before our professor passed on the tests.

"Good luck guys and try to keep your hands off each other during the test please," Professor Hawthorne said. My cheeks blushed and Ethan smirked.

He finished the test first but waited in his seat until I wrapped up mine. We descended together to hand them in.

"I enjoyed your course so much," I said to Professor Hawthorne.

"Have a great future, both of you," he said with a jovial smile.

We shared a post-test breather in the hallway — another test behind us — when Ethan's phone vibrated in his pocket.

"Is it your mom? It buzzed during the entire test."

He fished it out as I leaned close. "I love you," read a message.

"I sure didn't send it and I doubt your mom did." He scratched his head and I gunned it down the hall.

"Alexa, stop. I honestly don't know what the message is about," he said, catching up.

"I don't care."

"Can you give me time to find out?"

"If you have someone else on the side, you need to leave me alone." I paced to the main building above the library, on my way to the lockers.

"That's ridiculous. I only love you and I only want you," he said, his voice shaky. "Stop running." He jumped in front of me and draped his arms around my waist with eyes welled up.

"Can you let me go?" I shook my body to free myself from his trap. "Please?"

He unfolded his arms with a blanched face. I raced to my locker and to the parking lot. By the time I veered out of my spot, he shoved the college door open, panting for air.

Twenty three missed calls and a text message later, I barged into the house. "The I-love-you message was a Facebook generated script, the kind that people send in bulk. Nothing to do with me." I still had his hollow face painted on my mind. I called him up.

"I believe you."

"I'm glad you do."

"It's the exhaustion and the stress from the tests and the end of the semester emotions that brought out the worst in me today. Sorry."

"You should rest."

I fell on the bed. "I think I will."

*

I meandered to the library after Humanities to study for Biology. Ethan had aligned with classmates at a row of computers to work on a presentation. The library thumped with unruly chatter. Drained students shuddered about imminent final tests, due presentations and unfinished projects. In late mornings, computers at the library and seats in the cafeteria kicked off perpetual battles after all, even in the summer semester. Insanity floated everywhere at school.

I slithered by Ethan's desk to exchange a few units of language but the crowd swallowed our words intact. The noise had elevated to piercing levels and we had to yell at each other to make ourselves heard.

"I'm going to the quiet study."

"It's full. My classmate checked for his girlfriend."

"Then I'll venture up to the floors. Maybe I can find an empty classroom."

"I'll come and find you later."

I hiked up to the third floor in the K building, searching for tranquillity. I settled at a wooden table in the hallway, next to the outer glass wall and across from the midsection of classrooms. I sprinkled my notes on the table and drifted in the material with my brain sapped from too much information.

An hour later, Ethan streamed around the corner with a smile.

"Did you finish the presentation?"

"Not yet but I had to see you before I went home," he said, lounging in the seat next to me.

"I have to study for my test."

He leaned in for a kiss. "Just for a few minutes."

I pushed him away. "You're aware we're at school, right?"

He scanned the corridor, then he stood up. "Leave your stuff here."

"Why?"

"You'll see."

He unglued me from my seat and dragged me to the first class-room. He turned the doorknob and it opened, empty inside. I trailed behind inside the classroom. He took off his glasses and placed them on a nearby desk. He cupped my head against the wall with seductive eyes, clear blue as the summer sky. I clasped my fingers in the waistband of his jeans. He pushed his chest against mine, gently and slightly, enough for his manly scent to sneak down my throat. He brushed his lips against mine soft and tender, then deeper and stronger, his signature kiss. And as our quivering breaths broadcast the whiplash of our kiss, his phone rattled in his back pocket.

"It's my brother. He's picking me up."

"And I find out now that you have a brother?"

"I don't know, it never came up. He's three years younger." He pushed his glasses back on. "I have to go." He opened the class-room door and arched his arm above my head.

"I guess I'll go back to my notes."

His phone buzzed again.

"On my way downstairs," he yelled at the display and hung up. "Have fun with your studies." His whisper came out like a leftover pant. He planted a kiss on my lips before he rushed away, leaving me wanting more.

I tossed my school papers in my tote and descended to an empty classroom on the second floor. The thought of losing myself in a classroom, perhaps being locked inside the school overnight by mistake and crashing on a couch until dawn, crossed my mind with exhilaration. The college bore everything I needed — vending machines with snacks, water fountains, washrooms galore. I kept a spare toothbrush and toothpaste in my locker to freshen up on long days and a fleece blanket for study marathons at the library. I even had two theatres at my discretion, just turn on the computer and play whatever movie I desired. I mean, what was the point of going home anyway? I had class the next day, first thing in the morning.

I slammed my textbooks on a desk but first, I roamed to the blackboard, pure black as onyx. I squeezed the chalk between my fingers and wrote *I love Brimley* on it and drew hearts all around it for added tinsel. I propped back to venerate the meaning of my artwork, my sentiments conveyed in cursive armour, then grabbed my belongings and hurtled home. I wanted my soft bed after all.

Ethan waited for me at the front of the library and passed me a morning coffee before I pranced to Physics. An hour after I handed in my final test, I sauntered to Biology with my brain skipping like a broken record. When I scrambled out of class, I shut the door behind me and tipped my body against the wall. I kneeled down and cupped my head in my hands.

"You okay?" a peer asked, squeezing out behind me.

I stretched my legs in the standing position. "Yeah, glad it's over. I mean, the tests not the academic year."

"That too. Good luck."

"Same to you. I'll miss you all," I said with swallowed tears but nobody heard me. She'd wandered farther into the building.

I rummaged through my locker and packed my textbooks away before fighting a sudden urge to smear my old notes off Zee's former locker, wipe the door clean. I stopped my fingers an inch away. Then I closed mine and headed down the hall, expecting the director of a college TV show season finale to yell cut.

I cruised on the highway with my eyes at a standstill from the semester finale nostalgia. At home, I dropped my school tote in my room and hit the rinsing chamber.

"Someone's in better spirits," Heather said, peeking from the doorway biting on an apple.

"It's quite the opposite," I said, facing my closet fresh out of the shower, towel wrapped around. I glanced at her, then back at the row of I-have-nothing-to-wear. "You're home early. Who's working the spa?"

"Inventory day. I hired a professional. I couldn't be bothered with it."

"That's right." I held up a dark pink blouse. "What do you think about this?"

"It suits the colour of your hair," she said, rolling the bloody-red apple in her hand. "I take it Zeke came around?"

"It's not Zee, it's . . ." I dropped the blouse on the bed. "I don't know what to wear."

"Where are you going?" She returned from the hallway without the apple core.

"Ethan's taking me to dinner to celebrate my Pre-Health Science graduation."

"Congratulations. When's the convocation?"

"Thanks. I'm not going."

"Why not? Don't you think you deserve it? And . . . Ethan?"

"I'll go to the convocation that'll give me my next career." I fell on my bed and blew out my cheeks. "Ethan's . . . nice."

"Oh, and we know what that means."

"I'm serious. He's a sweet guy who tries his hardest to make me happy. I met him in Sci-Fi."

She raised her palm. "Say no more."

I soared up and pulled my navy skinny jeans out of the wardrobe.

"He may be a self-proclaimed geek but he's also sensual and sexy when he wants to be." I threw my jeans on the bed. "I have to get dressed."

"Have fun at dinner. I'm taking my son to the park."

"Have fun at the park."

I zipped to the highway, eyeing my fresh makeup in the sun visor mirror. Then I checked the time on the dashboard — almost five o'clock. Ethan's classes were wrapped up for the day.

I pulled into the infamous plaza where we planned an encore of the car drop at his mother's work. The sun blazed against the metal of my little black Toyota, turning it into a furnace. I tottered out and leaned against the hood of my car, loitering in my own rumination. My first year of college sciences accomplished and my mouth curved into a proud smile.

Ethan's car roared into the parking lot and squeaked its tires on the pavement. He opened the car door and inclined his head.

"I have bad news." He winced. "We haven't finished the presentation for tomorrow. My classmates are still working on it at the library. Do you mind waiting with me at school until I'm done?"

I stood off the hood of my car. "What about our plans?"

"We'll go to dinner afterwards," he said, his voice stammering.

"Ethan, I'm done with school. I'm not going back there today." His eyes plummeted to the ground and his taciturn manner infuriated me even more than his academic negligence. "Why did you make dinner plans if you knew you had to stay at school?"

He let out a self-punitive breath. "I don't know. I didn't think about it."

I rubbed my temples. "Go back to school. I'm not coming." I spun around and jumped in the driver seat.

He hopped out of his seat and next to my window. "Wait, maybe I can work it out." He drew the phone to his ear. Five minutes later, he leaped into the passenger seat. "It's fine, I worked it out with my classmates. I don't have to go."

"But now I feel bad about keeping you from your school responsibilities."

"I've put in the extra work plenty of times. That's why they agreed to cover me."

We stewed in silence, gazing through the windshield, dinner date enthusiasm long gone.

"Should I drop the keys off?"

"You should go to school and do your part," I said, my tone unconvincing.

"Don't worry about it. Besides, if there's something left to do, I can do it tomorrow."

"Isn't it due tomorrow?"

"Afternoon class." We gaped at each other and I nodded. "And people tell *me* I'm square." He opened the car door. "I'll be back." He strutted away, shaking the locks of hair away from his face and returned sans human armament, halleluiah. "Are you still in the mood for dinner?"

I crooked the key in the ignition with a fragmented smile. Then I sped out of the plaza and straight to the highway. We paraded inside Basil Garden holding hands and took a table for two.

"Pasta?" he asked.

"Pasta."

When the waiter arrived, Ethan ordered for both of us with his chest puffed out. Then he handed the menus back to the waiter and raised his eyebrows at me.

"You look like you want to say something."

"No."

"So," he said, rearranging the cutlery on the table, "are you excited about graduation?"

"I'll be more excited about my admission into the Paramedic Program and that graduation."

"You're not going to the convocation? I want to cheer for you."

My mother was too far away to attend and I refused to stand out as the student without family support.

"It's an introductory program. I'm not going. What about you?"

"My program? What about it?" His foot kicked mine under the table.

I shifted the fork from the tip to the tale against the table. "I don't know why I kept thinking you were in third year but then, you mentioned coming back in September."

"Yeah . . . I . . . my class graduated in the spring."

The fork slipped out of my hand. "I'm confused."

"I am in third but I still have a handful of courses to take in order to graduate." He rested his temple against the tip of his fingers. "I couldn't handle the full program after what happened with my ex. I'm only taking two or three courses per semester." His eyes plunged to the table and even as our dinner arrived, his focus stayed still.

"Why didn't you tell me?"

"Because of how driven you are about school. I didn't want you to see me as a feeble."

"A feeble?" His lips twitched and I burst into a hysterical laugh.

"Holding up to the geek title is no easy task. Everyone thinks we're honour students. It's difficult to keep up, the pressure's insane," he said, twirling the pasta around the fork tines.

"Quit stressing about it. I'm happy we can be classmates again in the fall. Now let's eat and enjoy the rest of the day."

After we glissaded through the restaurant doors, Ethan embraced my shoulders through the parking lot.

"Feel like catching a movie?"

"No, I kind of want to go for a walk."

"Clearlake Park, here we come."

I squeezed my car into a parking spot and we made our way to the boardwalk, hand in hand. Sundown orange rays gleamed on the lake as birds chirped their offspring to sleep. The lagoon breeze ruffled the tree leaves in zephyr. Scattered timber benches awaited forlorn for whispering paramours.

Ethan yanked my hand off the boardwalk. "Let's sit here."

We patted our knees on a picnic table. He loomed close and the tender touch of his lips spread goosebumps on my back.

"I love you. We're great together," he said.

I jumped off and waded through the grass to venerate the transmuting aquatic shades as the day shifted into the night.

He rushed to my side. "Why do you always run when I say these words?"

I dropped onto the meadow. "I wanted to sit on the grass and feel the earth." He followed suit, dissecting my expression at the sky. "Look at the oncoming stars." I lay on my back against the invigorating moss. "Can you name them?"

He lay beside me. "What?"

"Can you name the stars?"

"No. Can you?" he said, gaping into the high heavens.

"I used to when I was a kid. You can hardly see them in Toronto these days."

"It's probably because of the haze."

"Look," I pointed up. "Two stars are closing in on each other. That one is me and that one is you. Did you see them?"

He propped his torso on his elbow. "Can I pretend I did?" He leaned close with a panting chest and burning desire glowing in his eyes. He grazed my lips with a delicate kiss.

I rolled to the side and inspected both ways. We were the only souls under the starry night, the lake waves rippling a dozen feet away. I pushed him on his back and climbed on top of him. He slung his arms around my back and gazed at me with wondering eyes. I removed his glasses and placed them on the grass. Then I nibbled on his neck and traced back to his welcoming mouth. He unbuckled his belt and pulled his T-shirt over his head.

"Ahhh."

"What?"

"The grass is cold on my back."

I glided my fingers down his chest. "I'll warm you up."

He drew my head into a delicate kiss, then tugged at my skin-biting jeans. "I have no clue how to take these off."

"Shut up. You're spoiling the moment."

I peeled them off my legs and checked the surroundings again, the radar clear. I hurried back on top of him and skidded my thighs into his crotch, back and forth, back and forth, panties to the side. And so we ploughed the imprint of our frames in the grass, on the bank of the lake for the very first time.

On the way to his house, we couldn't hold back our endorphin-induced giggles. He leaned in for kisses with shimmering eyes and kneaded my right leg up to his driveway. He darted out of my car at two in the morning.

"It's way past your curfew. Aren't you scared that you're going to get grounded?"

He snaked his head inside the car for a goodnight kiss. "Ha-ha, not funny. I can go home at any hour I please."

"I'm teasing. Goodnight."

"I love you." He closed the car door and wandered into the house.

On my drive home, my heart thudded like a drum against the solitude of my car. I brushed the tickles off my cheeks and my fingertips glowed in the flickering highway headlights. A fountain of tears amassed inside my skull and I let the drops trickle down until the sob source desiccated. And as I paced inside the house and snuck inside my room, only one name echoed in my head — Zee.

I preyed on school vacation to throw in more hours at work.

"When can I see you? You've been working so much," Ethan said, one night on the phone.

"Soon. But we'll still talk on the phone and Skype."

"It's not the same. You realize we haven't seen each other since the last day of school, right?"

"I do but right now, I want to take advantage of my working hours, considering they're limited when I'm in school. I'll come up next week to register."

"You're not registering for courses online?"

"I am but Advanced Biology requires special access. I have to do it in person at the Registrar's Office."

At the end of August, I jetted to Brimley to enroll as a part time student. I'd come to terms with my null chances to bounce off the Paramedic waiting list and into the program. At least individual courses would keep my feet dipped in the school vibe. I registered with Ethan online for Business Communications, which was mandatory and Social Psychology, an option as General Education.

I strutted inside the college and scanned the hallways.

"I wish you looked at me that way," Ethan said, outside of Registrar's. "You must venerate this school."

"You have no idea how much."

He frowned, then brightened his face. "We'll be classmates for two courses this semester."

"Can you handle it?"

"The question is, can you?" He tittered. "So, what's with the Advanced Bio course? You lost me on that one."

"The course is part of Nursing. You can only take it as an individual course, if your GPA is over eighty percent."

"I'm positive there's a nerd hiding under that pretty face of yours."

"I made it on the Dean's List."

"Wait, I'm confused. If you're doing so well, why do you need to take Advanced Biology?"

"Because I want to make sure I pass the Paramedic admission test next year," I said as I opened the Office door.

After registration, he took my hand on our way out of school.

"Car drop-off?"

I nodded. "And dinner's my treat today."

"Why is that?"

"You bought the last time. Plus, I sacrificed you for work lately. I want to make it up to you."

We drove to the plaza where he jogged to pass the car keys, then returned and sprang in my car.

"Let's go to a coffee shop. It's too early for dinner and I want us to sit down and just be with each other. Agree?"

"Yes," I said and cranked the ignition.

We ventured to a café where we snipped a table for two with titters in our voices and lattes on the table.

"Come here, I missed you."

I yielded to his embrace a bit coy. "I missed you too."

His phone rumbled. "Sorry," he said as he picked it up. A muscle in his jaw twitched as he listened on. "At the coffee shop around the corner from your work," he said and rested the phone on his shoulder. "My mom is asking if she can join us for lunch."

"No, no, next time. Today I want to be with you," I mouthed.

"Okay, bye." He dropped the phone on the table and swallowed hard. "She's on her way."

"What? Why?"

"She wants to know you better."

My face burned from the inside out. "But I want to be with you now. Does that matter?"

"Of course it does."

"Hello," a voice said, breathing heavily. Ethan's mother barged in like a tsunami and dropped an ugly bag on the table before we could fold in our thoughts. "I'll get a coffee," she said.

"We haven't seen each other in two weeks. Do something." But he didn't. He stooped in his chair and rubbed the nape of his neck as I fought back tears of anger.

She banged her coffee on the table. "How is your day so far?" Neither of us answered. Then her eyes flirted with the lunch box she scooped out of her bag. We watched her dig at her food with the voracity of a wolf. "Ethan, how is school?"

He straightened his posture. "Goo —"

"You better make sure you pass those courses, otherwise your father and I will be very disappointed." She licked the food off her fingers before she picked up a fork and I understood whom he inherited the habit from. "We didn't take that loan for nothing. And don't stay out late. You have a ton of chores waiting for you at home." I was right about his curfew all along.

She proceeded to dissect the family financial debts, dysfunctional relationships with relatives and everything her son ever did wrong since the day he was born. Then she snapped her head to acknowledge my existence.

"And you? Do you attend the same school?"

"Yes," I said while her son chewed a nail. "I thought Ethan might have told you by now."

"He did but I'm surprised you attend the same college." Her voice couldn't sound more condescending if she tried.

I gritted my teeth. "I'm not following."

She waved her fork in the air and bits of something that looked like vomit flew off. "Your look, your entire persona. You don't strike me as a college student, that's all."

"Mom, she's an honour student," he murmured.

I turned to Ethan. "That's okay. I'm going to go."

"No, you stay. I have to get back to work." His mother shot a darting glance at her son, then stormed out of the coffee shop.

"I'm so sorry about this whole situation."

"What is it? My blonde hair? My taste in clothes? The fact that I take care of myself?"

"No. You're perfect."

"How can she judge me based on my appearance? How can she talk about my persona? She doesn't even know me."

"That's right. She doesn't know you."

"It's one thing when she talks to you like you're a five-year-old and it's another when she offends me."

"It's because of what happened to me in the past. She wants to make sure it doesn't happen again."

"Then she should stick you in a mason jar and twist the lid on."

I blasted to the parking lot and dove in the driver seat dressed in anger. He lagged close behind and hurried inside the car.

"Oh, come on. Do we have to do this again?"

"You can thank your mommy dearest for ruining our plans and our day and our relationship."

"Why are you letting her do this to us?"

"Don't you dare put this on me." I swerved out of the parking lot. "I've never been more insulted in my life."

I drove in a hush and when I stopped in his driveway, I flashed him a killer look. He stepped out of the car in slow motion. "Grow some balls," I yelled as I peeled away from his driveway but he'd already limped inside the house. I sped off stone faced.

Hours later, countless pleas swayed my mind into driving to Clearlake Park. Ethan had parked his butt on top of a picnic table, feet away from the spot where we imprinted our bodies in the grass on a given glory night.

"I'm really sorry about what happened," he said.

"Skip to the next part. I'm over it." He swallowed hard with flooded eyes. "You're not going to cry, are you?" He burst into tears. "I thought you said we'd talk." More tears rolling down and he dropped his head in his hands. "Okay, I'm just going to sit here and . . ." He sobbed. "Come here." I pulled him close and the inner barrage broke loose, flooding my blouse. You have to be joking. "Let's go to dinner. You want to?" I asked, rubbing his back. He nodded and wiped his tears, like a three-year-old who's been handed his favourite toy that had been lost and found.

I hauled him into his car and he shadowed mine to Basil Garden for mood amendment rather than hunger.

"Let's do something drastic," I said, wrapping the pasta around the tines.

"Like what?"

"Let's go to a motel."

He dropped the fork. "Really?"

"I kind of want to be bad with you."

His eyes lit up. "Those are the most romantic words a girl has ever said to me."

We checked in at a three-star motel on Grant Street under the names of Rachael and Rick Deckard. The room had been tidied up with lavender scented baskets, freshly ironed sheets and tangerine liquid soap.

"We don't have snacks."

"Let's go get some. And you may only address me as Rachael while we're here."

I glided down the hall with Mr Deckard rushing to catch up. We hit the first convenience store for guilty pleasures and a pack of condoms.

Back in the room, we turned the TV on as we munched on Cheetos.

"I wonder if —," and the walls shuddered as the fire alarm blasted in our brains.

He inspected the courtyard commotion from the balcony as police and firefighter sirens chimed from the parking lot.

I snuck behind him. "Your mother is searching for you."

"That's it. You're grounded, young lady."

I yelped as I charged inside the room and fell on the bed. He dove beside me, cupped my head and forced a kiss on my pretending-to-be-reluctant-but-secretly-inviting lips. But the undressing game turned sour as he coveted for me to take charge with every move and every breath, the promising kiss a delusion. The ambiance switched from adventurous to jaded in seconds.

The hanky-panky came far from spectacular and worse than I expected. His passive ways tainted the mood and his bed abilities sank ocean deep. Then it dawned on me — the antidepressants but not necessarily and I realized the romantic park setting was all that made it good the first time. By the end of the night, I was disappointed and bored, so bored that all I could think of was to go to bed and catch a few hours of sleep before waking up early in the morning for work.

When he crowded me in the shower, I abandoned him under the drizzle much to his dismay.

"Do you want to watch TV before bed?" he asked, towel drying his hair.

"Sorry, I'd rather go to sleep." I trundled over and he spooned me with a huff through his teeth.

Halfway through the night, I rolled over and unbolted my eyes under his glare.

"Are you watching me?" I asked.

"No."

"You just answered me. And your eyes were wide open when I faced you."

CHAPTER

10

On a late September afternoon, I met Ethan at the movies. He waited by the front doors, rubbing his hands together.

"Finally, I get to see you after ten long days."

"Ethan, you know I have something called a job. And there's this other strange notion called responsibility."

"I have responsibilities."

"Like what? The house chores," I threw in air quotes, "that mommy says you should do but you never do them anyway? Like one of those ten days when twenty four hours passed before you realized your phone battery died? And that other day when you refilled your phone credit after two days of silence between us?"

He sighed. "I'll be more careful."

I grilled him a bit too harsh maybe but he could use a mental face-palm. After the movie, he mentioned a walk in the park.

"I'm drained. I'd rather go home and prepare for school."

"It's Labour Day Sunday. We don't even have school tomorrow."

"I've worked for ten days straight. I want to take it easy at home in my pajamas," I said, my eyes on the road.

"Are you sure you want to go home?" he asked, on his driveway.

I scanned the surroundings. "Let's go for a drive."

Brenton City limits were famous for spectacular fall backdrops with quilts of yellow leaves, hugging the russet ground and lazy tree branches preparing for hibernation. I pictured the back roads uncover a thousand shades of crimson concert under the kissing rays of sunset.

He scratched his head. "Sure but . . . what's the point?"

"The point is to see places and things, Ethan. That's the point."

"You said you were tired."

"I am but seeing places and things relaxes me."

"All right. Let's go see places and things."

I took an alley parallel to the lake and dissipated into the dusk, on a scant gravel path. When we popped on a stretch of infinite road, serpent trees lined up on its shoulders with sprawling branches like monstrous claws, draping the sky into a tunnel.

"Wow."

He ducked his head beneath the windshield, eyes up at the trees. "I haven't been on this road in years."

"It's frightening and thrilling at the same time." I pulled over and Ethan raised his eyebrows. "Don't worry. I'm not having you kidnapped."

"I'm trying to figure out what you want to do . . . aside from having me kidnapped."

I scooted in the back seat to his muddled stare. "Do I need to draw you a map?" I snagged him by the tee next to me. The outdoor setting was too perfectly scary to skip the jiggy-jiggy.

"Oh."

"You may wrap your arms around me now."

"I know what to do."

"Then, do it."

He angled toward me. "Wait, my legs are stuck." I narrowed my eyes into a death stare. "I have long legs. What can I do?"

"Sit back." I clambered on his lap and brushed my lips over his mouth, threading my fingers through his hair.

"Ouch, I banged my head against the rear." He rubbed the back of his head.

I hopped aside. "The rear window is far from your head."

"I don't know but it was something hard." I reverted to the driver seat. "Whaaat?" he whined from the back.

"We're going home."

"Whyyy?"

"The mood is gone. Let's go."

He crept in the front and I swerved the car back on the road, obscure as it was, with Ethan holding on to the granny handle. I headed in the direction we came from and absorbed the somber forest on the flanks. What a waste of a gripping setting! Only in true horror movies have I seen such daunting, yet fascinating natural décor.

Back in his driveway, I idled the car in my wait for his departure to the safe nest.

"Goodnight."

"Did I mess up again?"

"Honestly, it's not your fault," I said and he wasn't sure if he should smile or cry.

On Tuesday after Labour Day, I strutted through the college doors with tingling skin, the same way I did the first time I stepped foot inside. The school atmosphere beamed with verve but the summer semester placidity slipped under my skin so much so, I now rebuffed the crowded corridors and raucous voices.

I took a moment by the lockers to let my second year of college sink into my brain. Zee's former locker gleamed with the door ajar and my hieroglyphics still on it. I created an insane scenario with my stomach in a kink about how he picked a locker on a different floor to avoid me. Unless he hadn't shown up at school yet.

"Where are you?" Ethan's text pulled my mind back. "At my locker." Orientation Day canceled daytime classes but our evening Business Communication was still on schedule.

He beckoned me from the classroom doorstep at the end of the hall and I moseyed in his direction with my mood out of touch. In class, I escaped into my own thoughts. During attendance, he nudged my elbow, so I could retort my name out loud.

"What's with you?"

"Nothing."

After class, I mentally jumped for joy when he excused himself for having to drop his brother off somewhere. I didn't ask where.

"My brother's waiting for me in the parking lot. Do you mind?"

"No, not at all. Go ahead."

"But if you want to spend time, I could arrange for my mom to pick him up."

"No. You don't want to make your little brother wait."

"Should I come back?"

"No. I'm heading home too. Have a good night."

The next day, Ethan and I scrambled into a cafeteria booth after our morning classes.

"You're quiet this morning."

"No reason in particular." I glanced away. "I have to go to the bookstore and the parking office. I have a bit of running around to do. We'll meet at the library later on," I said, my voice monotone.

"I need to go there too. I'll come with you," he said. I gnashed my teeth.

On the way to the bookstore, I encountered my former Biology and Chemistry classmates, the highlight of my day. Their effervescent faces shot flashbacks of hard work mixed with good times. We hugged each other with tears of joy. They'd enrolled in Nursing. Had I expanded my horizons, I could've spared myself the one year wait before the second Paramedic exam and pilot my way into a career by now.

The afternoon found me sitting at the library, detached from the real world until Ethan printed a syllabus for review.

"Too many assignments," he said.

"I love writing assignments. That's my favourite part of a course."

"That's because you're good at it."

"I'm good at it because I enjoy doing it."

He reached for my hand but I ripped it back. "What's wrong?"

"Like I said before, I need both hands to type."

He flinched, then dropped his hand on my leg for a rub. I shoved his hand to the side. Two beats later, he rubbed my back while he stared at the monitor.

"Ethan, can you relax?"

"That's what I should be telling you." I gave him the look of death. "Whaaat?" There was the nasal tone again that stretched the letter *a* to a snap.

"Stop touching me all the time. It annoys me to hell."

"I have to drive my brother to the dentist. See you." I exhaled with relief.

On my way out, I tossed my freshly purchased textbooks in my locker until next week. When I glimpsed at Zee's locker — a habit I needed to break — I dropped my tote. A new lock along with a college locket glazed on it. I stepped back with prickles in my legs. A stranger wouldn't claim a locker with someone else's love notes on when plenty of available clean lockers awaited possession. I drove home in a daze, then racked my brain at work for the rest of the week, over the new lock next door to mine.

Monday morning in Social Psych, Ethan joined me moments after the teacher marched into class. He rubbed my leg as soon as he took a seat and I drew in a long breath.

After class, we ambled to the library for an early start on an assignment. I plodded to the back seats with whiny Ethan in tow.

"Why do we have to sit all the way at the back?"

"Can you stop complaining for a second of your life?"

"Do we have to start on this right now?" he asked, eyeing the papers I sprinkled on our desks.

"What would you rather do on break period?"

He threw his hands in the air. "I don't know. Something fun."

"Homework is fun."

"Only you would say that."

"You know, you're not living up to your geek profile."

"I told you, you're the queen of geeks in disguise."

"I'll take that as a compliment," I said, shifting my head to a poignant standstill.

Zee chatted with a student, his chest pushed out and inches away from our desks and my heart pounded like a drilling hammer.

"Change seats with me," I told Ethan.

"Why?"

"Just do it."

I slumped in my new chair and hid behind the human shield.

"What's going on?" Ethan bounced his head from side to side.

"Why do you have to ask so many questions all the time?"

I moved around the humanoid buffer as Zee settled at a computer in plain sight, his head sideways, uncaring. He'd grown into a bright-faced sophomore with a fresh aura. He donned a black hoodie and black jeans, always a perfect contrast to his honeyed hair and hazel eyes, along with a smile that melted the sun.

Ethan's head was glued to the monitor but his hand was sure fond of leg rubs.

"What are you doing?"

He straightened his spine, his rub pressed deeper. "What?"

"Rub my leg one more time and I'll cut your balls off."

"Why didn't you tell me you didn't like it?"

"I did. A million times over." I soared up. "I'm going to the caf and do not follow me."

I strode down the farthest corridor across from Zee with a throbbing headache and a disconcerting mind. At the cafeteria, I savoured my crisp coffee next to the windows. Freshmen frolicked with excitement in the courtyard. The exhilaration would be bitterly traded for exhaustion in the upcoming weeks. I retraced my steps to the library, the setting unchanged. I roosted next to Ethan and reopened my homework in progress. When he planted his hand on my leg, I cringed.

"Whaaat? I forgot. What about your back? Can I rub your back?"

I shot him a bullet of an eye, delved through my tote and leaped from the seat with my student card. "Where are you going?"

I rambled down the corridor on my way to the circulation desk to renew my printing credits. I liked to have my syllabi printed and folded away in my binder for class.

Across the library, Zee rose from his seat and took the corridor parallel to mine. I hid behind the arts tutoring hub and pressed my hand to my mouth. When I inspected the library exit, he'd vanished. I swung my eyes to the left of the hub and back into the library. He pranced back to his seat with his face in my direction. I gasped for air. Then I made a beeline for the circulation desk and paid for printing credits with my back at Zee's zone and much too anxious to turn around.

I rushed back to my desk and printed my notes. "Let's go."

"Where?" asked Ethan.

"Sign off and let's go. Now."

The next day, I jumped school to meet Maureen in Toronto at La Rocca, our favourite eatery downtown. I skipped for the sake of a breather from all the drama waiting to burst. And I needed one bad. A breather, that is.

"I haven't seen you in months," she said, stirring her coffee.

"Happy belated birthday."

"You wished me happy birthday two months ago on the phone."

"It's the first time I see you in person since then. I'm sorry. I'm a terrible friend."

"I've known you since junior high, long enough to know that you're not. You had homework and exams. By the way, don't you have school today?"

"I do but I needed to get away."

She took a sip. "How come? You love school."

"There's too much pressure right now and I don't mean it in an academic way."

She leaned back and flashed a comforting smile. "Tell me."

"OK and then, we'll celebrate you."

Wednesday morning, I shambled to the library for more printouts before my morning coffee, which meant I hadn't switched from zombie to human mode yet. Zee startled me with a fixed gaze in the same spot by the mouth of the library where I tipped him off his heels back in January after reading week. We faltered in unison, though we weren't sure at first.

"How is it going Alexa?" And my pulse raced like speed skating.

"Good." Our eyes danced on each other's face. "It figures. I'm walking in as you're walking out. It's always this spot."

"Indeed." He scanned my body up and down. "I like your shoes."

"My shoes are pink."

"I like the graffiti on them. Are they Chuck Taylors?"

"Ed Hardys. How was your summer?"

"Not too good."

His muscles had engorged, as if he'd been working out but I refused to step on my pride with the remark out loud. Instead, I mentally threw myself in his arms.

"What time do you have class?" he asked.

"I'm on my way. Just here to print my first lecture outline."

He drew a step closer. "Do you feel like skipping?"

"And why would I want to do that?"

"To spend time together." His voice trembled for the first time.

"You know I don't skip class."

"Sorry, I forgot how disciplined you are."

"When do you have class today?"

He stepped back and leaned against the circulation desk. "Want to see?" He rooted an agenda out of his knapsack. "I have class in an hour." He pointed at the timetables for each day of the week, as if he knew I still cared. Which I didn't. I didn't want to. But I did.

"I'm running late," I said. "Enjoy your classes."

"You too," he echoed from behind.

I picked up the speed to Business Communications with a spinning head, thanking the mighty Gods that I'd been inspired to switch classes. The night before, I dropped the evening class I shared with Ethan and registered for the morning slot, scooping the last available seat. A class without leg rubs. A spot-on heaven.

I broke the news to Ethan during lunch.

"Heya, I swapped my Communications class for this morning."

"I was wondering what class you came out of when I texted you. Why did you?"

"I like morning school."

"But Sci-Fi was evenings."

"The awesomeness of the course compensated for the timetable."

"Why didn't you tell me? I could've switched with you."

"I did it late last night. And you said that timetable suited you."

He jolted from his seat shaking his head. "You do this . . ."

"Where are you going?" I asked, without a trace of guilt.

"To see if I can switch too."

I moved camp to the library and texted Maureen for a deep analysis of my morning encounter with Zee while the computer logged me in. The more students at the library, the longer the wait. As my fingers bopped on the phone keys, a draft puffed through my hair. I spun with my chair under Ethan's stare.

"Why are you standing behind me?"

"I've been here for a second."

"Behind me. Looking at my phone."

"I didn't look, I glanced." He dropped into a seat with the usual sulk. "No more seats in the morning Business Communications class. I hope you're happy."

"Forget about class. How dare you read my texts?" I shoved my textbooks in my tote.

"I didn't. Waaait."

I stormed out of the library. Locker. Parking lot. Highway.

"I can't deal with this rollercoaster tonight," said Ethan's text hours later. I read it at my desk in my bedroom over homework. "You're right, you're not. I need some time to clear my head."

Over the weekend, I assembled my thoughts to filter my brain. While Ethan and I took an inevitable break, Zee's comeback in shining armour opened the gateway to good vibrations. Nothing compared to the intense emotional boomerang we shared.

On Monday, Ethan hunched in a chair next to me in Social Psych but no more leg rubs. In group work, I joined two peers in close proximity but inspected Ethan's banal gestures, every single one as irritating as dermatitis. He'd prop his chin on his palm and forget his mouth half-open or he'd stare at the wall with flat eyes and a crinkled face.

At the end of class, I sped out of the room to the cafeteria. I lounged by the courtyard window to savour an energizing green tea when my phone growled. I reached for it in expectation of a whiny message from Ethan. "Alexa, call me sometimes," read an email signed by Zee with his phone number attached. Before I could process the message, my name echoed from the corridor and I whipped up my head. Marcus waved a file holder in the air to catch my attention. Please don't come here, please don't come here. I waved back with a smile and he kept on his way.

I shifted my attention back to my phone with a sigh of relief to read the message again and churn the information. Then I peered over my shoulder. No one behind me. My face fractured into a smile but I held back from sending a reply. I needed space to breathe and think.

Two days later, I crossed paths with Zee in the hallway but neither of us stopped. He shot me a flirty glance as he strolled by with classmates. And when I settled in the library for homework, my mind wandered into the distance. I toyed with my phone, wrote his name in a text, then erased it four times. I'd always shout out his nickname in a text, the one I gave him — Zee — my way of initiating a conversation. The fifth time, my finger tapped a bit too hard on the send button and I regretted it the second my text flew away. He retorted and my heart banged against my ribs. We texted about school, then he wrote, "Let's get together." I tossed the phone on the desk, as if it burned my fingers. It roared again and this time, with a phone call.

"Alexa, you busy?"

"Homework at the library." I swallowed hard, his pull difficult to resist.

"Is it due tomorrow?"

"No . . . next week."

"Then it's time to take a break. Are you driving or walking?"

"Driving? You're not at school?"

"No, at my place behind the school. Grab your stuff and meet me behind the A building."

There was something tantalizing about his doze of confidence. I jostled my textbooks in my tote and raced through the hallways and building passageways with adrenaline pulsing through my veins. I charged through the exit doors with hair winging in the air. Zee popped in the distance on the road behind the parking lot in all his poise. He waved along with the irresistible smile I'd known from the beginning and my breaths quickened.

"Hi, gorgeous," he said, pulling me into a hug. I closed my eyes to inhale his scent, the familiar one that gave me wings to fly before he shot me down. Then he leaned back and held his hand for mine. "Come on." I stood still with raised eyebrows. "Relax, it's okay. We're not going to talk in the street, are we?" He wove his fingers through mine and hauled me in the direction he came from. We strolled in silence while we arranged the right words in our minds.

"So, did you have a broken heart?" he asked, gazing at me.

I snapped my hand back. "What?"

"Me too, a little bit." He pinched the air with his thumb and index while I tried to decide if his broken heart reference was tied to me or someone else.

"You? A broken heart?"

He reached for my hand again. "I know. I don't understand either." He talked emotions. Stunning. "How come you didn't call me all summer?" he asked. The smile again.

"Call you? You told me to forget you, remember?"

"Yeah but you know how it is with us."

"No, I don't. How is it?"

"Well . . ."

"Why didn't you call me?"

"Will you be mad at me, if I give you the answer?"

"Let me guess. You erased my number." He gave a guilty nod. "I figured you did when you emailed me."

At the road bifurcation, he pointed to a little white house, then up the steps and down the stairs. A basement apartment opened into a corner kitchenette and the rest of the room painted in neutral colours with a couch, a TV and a bed, a perfect fit for a student. We eased into the couch.

I cupped his biceps. "You seem . . . bigger. This may sound lame but have you been working out?"

"Yeah. I worked at the school's fitness center in the summer."

"Wait, you mean to tell me you were at the college during the summer semester?" His presence in the hallway that one morning on my way to Psychology class made sense now.

"Yeap." He dropped his hand on my leg and the touch of his fingers spread tingles through my knees like a virus.

"What about the job in Ottawa?"

"It fell through. Thanks for the birthday message. Sorry I didn't respond." Guilty smile again. "I was at school that day too. I saw you at the library."

"It's where I sent it from but I didn't see you."

He held my gaze and my insides turned to slush. He bit his bottom lip, then grazed mine with his thumb. I shook my head in slow motion but he wrapped one arm around me and yanked me on his lap in a blink of an eye. Then he kissed me violently.

I pressed his chest away. "Stop. I can't."

"Why?"

"I'm not going down this road again. You have no idea . . .," I said, then I swallowed my tears.

He cupped my face. "I'm your friend. And friends don't leave friends. I'll be here for you." And now I had to fight my tears even harder. He leaned in for another peck.

"I'm not doing it Zee. You have no idea what I've been through."

He shushed me into a rocking hug, my lips glued to his hair. "It's okay. I'm here and I'm not going anywhere." He dusted my hair and a couple of tears off my face. "You're getting hotter," he said and I half-smiled. "Ha-ha, there's a smile." I yielded to his embrace, the safest and most dangerous place at the same time.

He gently planted me on the couch, rose up and held his hand for mine. "We have unfinished business." And when I didn't give him my hand, he bent down, lifted me in his arms and carried me to the bed.

I flapped my feet in mid-air. "You know we can't do this. It'll ruin everything again."

"No, it won't. It's different this time." He set me down.

"That's what you said the last time."

"No, trust me, this time it is. Plus, I'm attracted to you and you're attracted to me. Why can't we enjoy each other?"

"I'm not attracted to you."

He chuckled, then climbed next to me and stole a kiss. "I fucking love the way you kiss me."

"And I love kissing you but . . . I have something to tell you." I rose to the sitting position. "I've been seeing someone."

He sat up too, glanced away, then back at me. "And are you seeing him still?"

"No, I mean . . . we're on a break."

"Sweet," he said, tucking my hair behind the ear. "I owe you anyway. I want to make you scream."

"You don't owe me and I don't care about that. It's not even the point of all this."

"No?" A kiss again.

"No," I said, briefly breaking our lips apart.

"No?" he asked, his voice deeper.

"No."

As our kisses deepened, we fell on the bed in a smooching ravage, the magnetism too strong to refute. He undressed me despite my semi-protest. I did want the ultimate closeness with him, the intimacy to call our own. But sex was our enemy from the start and I didn't care about it for now, not if it would break us apart again.

In the end, I welcomed him into my arms as he nibbled on my lips, my neck, then my lips again.

"Kiss me from head to toes," he said.

"No. You don't deserve it."

"I haven't asked anyone to do that since."

He flung an arm under my waist while I let his comment drift through my dissecting brain chamber. He snapped my panties with his free hand — he'd truly buffed over the summer — and when he slithered inside, our bodies burned like fire but only for a pump. One slide in, one slide out and the blaze cooled off, just like before.

"You're the only one who does this to me. I don't get it," he said as he rolled off the bed.

I think I'm the only one, period. "Don't worry about it."

"I don't understand," he said, returning from the kitchen naked, except for a pair of boxers and a carton of strawberry ice cream in hand. His stomach was flat as a board.

"I never pegged you for an ice cream dude." I dressed at the speed of light. "What don't you understand?"

He fed me a scoop. "This thing called love. It's strange and confusing at times."

"Tell me about it," I muttered under my breath.

Zee darted another scoop in my mouth, then passed the carton to me and slipped into his clothes.

We ambled back to campus, holding hands and talking school. He joked and I giggled, back to our old selves again. My heart radiated joy over a ten-mile radius.

He opened the school door. "Are you done with classes for the day?"

"Yeah, I'm going home. You?"

"Heading to class but I'll walk you to your locker."

We moseyed down the hallway, passing the library — our playground — on our way to the lockers.

"I want to write a book," he said as we bumped shoulders and elbows.

"Write a book? You never told me that."

"It's something I've thought about lately."

"I find it shockingly coincidental. I've always wanted to write a book too." At the lockers, I gave him a kiss on the cheek. "We're so much alike in so many ways."

He pulled me into a bear hug. "That, we are." He stepped back and blew a kiss my way. "Have a good day, gorgeous."

Back at the crib, I barged into my room and called Ethan to settle our status. His phone rang and rang without response. I pictured him hanging out in the living room while having left his phone in the basement for hours on end. And it was times like these, when I couldn't stand his airy character any longer.

By the time Heather swung my bedroom door open, I'd buried my nose in textbooks.

"Ready for a toast?"

"A toast?"

"Your birthday, tomorrow?"

"Right."

"Let's have a glass with Carl tonight. He's hitting the road in the morning."

I threw my books to the side and joined my friends in the kitchen for an early celebration of my twenty fourth birthday.

Heather raised a glass of red wine. "It's a day early but happy birthday. Almost a quarter of century young."

"I didn't expect this today but thank you both," I said as we exchanged hugs.

"I wanted to be the first one to wish it to you. And thank you for helping me with the spa. You came into the picture at the right time."

"I should be thankful and I am. They say business and friendship don't mix but it seems to work for us."

"I agree. Cheers."

After a morning shower and a birthday call from Mom, I rushed out the door and took to the highway, southbound lane. Maureen waited for me at La Rocca for lunch, birthday present on the table — a Juicy Couture perfume, sweet and strong, just the way I like it and my favourite book, *The Green Archer* by Edgar Wallace. My parents had a vintage copy and I read it in my teens but they sealed it away like an artifact when it came to taping the pages together. Now I could read it over and over.

Post-lunch, Maureen and I moved camp to a daytime restaurant and chatted up a storm over snacks and a light cocktail and in the end, dinner topped with a jumbo size of laughter.

By dusk, I arrived home and poured the leftover wine in a glass. I indulged while rolling through my phone list of calls and messages. Ethan called and texted earlier about the missing calls last night. He read them this morning, just the way I imagined. His birthday greeting to me translated to "I still owe you a fancy dinner." A few days back, he offered to treat me to a birthday dinner but I declined to refrain from boosting his hopes.

The rest of the list poured with birthday messages from friends to exes to acquaintances I hadn't spoken to in months. All but one whose text I craved to read the most — Zee.

Monday morning, I shadowed Ethan out of Social Psych and yanked him on a couch in the hallway.

"Can we talk?" I asked. He gazed at me with troubled eyes. "I would've preferred a birthday greeting over a dinner offer."

"I hope you had a good birthday."

"I'm sorry. I don't mean to be mean to you but —"

"Comes out that way."

"I never meant to hurt you. You're a great guy and you deserve to be happy."

"I want to be happy with you." His voice trembled.

"We wouldn't work out, Ethan. I'm particular about every detail in life, even temperamental at times and I'd torture you to death with my discipline."

He sobbed. "I loved you. I still do."

"You need someone to love you back the same way. I hope you'll find that person because it's not going to be me." His eyes watered and I spread my arms. "Give me a hug." He fell into my arms, then leaned back with manic tear drops over his cheekbones. "Good luck with school. Bye Ethan."

I rose up and ran down the hall without turning back. I'd broken his heart and surprisingly, it killed me to do it but I couldn't imprison his sentiments any longer.

CHAPTER
11

The first October weekend, I moved into a one bedroom rental in Brenton City. Time had come for a place of my own. Besides, Heather and Carl's little boy grew fast and they'd soon move back to the top floor. They helped me move and I agreed with Heather to keep working at the spa. I traded the long drives to school for six minutes in the mornings with my eyes half-lidded from studying the night before.

Basement apartments. I've always thought the worst of them but mine was a deluxe upper in a house worth more than half a mil. The owner, a business woman in winery and a sweet lady with a teenage son welcomed me with a bottle of homemade white wine. She'd decorated the rental herself. It bore vintage furniture and a separate entrance. And it worked like a charm for now.

I texted Zee my new phone number with the changed area code. "Welcome to Brenton City. Can I come by and see it?" he keyed back. "I'm drained from the move and I have a test tomorrow. Soon, I promise."

I was on my own at school for days. Zee had gone on a field trip to Algonquin Provincial Park for his major and Ethan had traveled to Denver for a cousin's engagement party. A month prior, he asked me to join him but I declined. No reason would convince me to skip school for days in a row, in the core of the semester to visit people I've never met.

At home, the loneliness protruded through my bones. After the initial excitement of a new place died down, the ambiance became too somber for my taste. No one opened my bedroom door to invite me to dinner or chit-chat tea.

On Thanksgiving, Heather invited me to her house for dinner. I accepted before she finished her sentence. Carl opened the door.

"I already miss this place," I said, strolling in for friendly hugs.

Carl unscrewed the wine bottle I'd slipped on the counter and Heather poured it into glasses. "You can move back in, if you'd like." A new humanoid stood next to Heather.

"Thanks but you guys could use the extra space in your own house and I need to be close to school."

"Alexa, meet Tania, a good friend of mine. She lives in Brenton City too."

We shook hands and I half-smiled, introvert style.

"Nice to meet you," she said.

"You, as well."

By the end of the night, we all hooted at Tania's stories around the dinner table. She reminded me of Maureen in a way. Positive perspective on life. Riveting sense of humour. We trailed each other out of Heather's driveway and down to the highway on our way home. She waved before she dashed off two exits before I did.

When solitude and doubt conquered my insides, I texted Zee from class with a hole in my stomach. "Hey, in class. What's up?" he retorted. "Wanna stay in class?" My turn to ask him to skip. "Yeah, it's a must-attend class." And my turn to be turned down. I fidgeted in my chair with my stare out the window as my brain refused to make sense of the teacher's words.

Later in the day, as I settled at a desk, Zee's shadow dispersed out of the library. "You busy?" I keyed a text his way. I wanted to sit somewhere and talk, connect again like old times. No reply. I pictured him glancing at the phone, shrugging his shoulders and tossing it back in his pocket on his way to class. "If it's so difficult to exchange two words with you, forget it." Nothing again.

By the following week, I staggered through the college hallways in a shredded mood. Zee played his game again, a game that'd worn me inside and out. I dragged myself past the library window stacks when his face glimmered behind a monitor next to the science tutoring hub. We locked eyes and he slipped a pity-smile. Then he resumed his homework and I returned to the front of the library. I dipped into a couch to wait for an available computer. All were taken.

Minutes later, he passed by inches away and exited into the lobby and up to the second floor, letting me squirm in his scent trail. I fought the impulse to chase after him with a text message. "I will never understand you."

Enraged by his silence, I stormed out of the library and up the stairs, cursing under my breath but lost his tracks on the way. I rambled on the hallways from one building to another. I checked the parking lot and ran back through the school doors. He was standing in line at the school's pool bar as I shambled back toward the library with my heart asunder. I stopped in my tracks with dead eyes. He gazed at me with remorse but not enough to talk to me. I carried on down the hall.

I coiled into a ball on a windowsill along the corridor. "Your eyes go straight through my heart," I texted. "Stop," he wrote and the word carved at the ridges of my stomach like a scalpel. I hugged my body and gasped in pain with my gaze out the window. Tears streamed down my face and this time, the heartbreak ripped my soul to shreds. I wailed. I let it all out until I could cry no more.

I retreated to the back of the library — my safe haven — with inflamed eyes and crumpled into an armchair by the fireplace. I tipped my head back and my face at the ceiling with my body numb and arms hanging off the sides. Nothing mattered anymore, not even school. I couldn't comprehend my world without Zee, nothing I could do about it. My whole existence vanished from under me and I couldn't breathe. I didn't want to. I wanted to die.

I slept to freeze the pain and lost myself in homework when awake. My life moving on was like moving mountains but my mom and Maureen lifted my spirits on the phone every day. I still cried myself to sleep at night and hoped I'd cry out my feelings for Zee.

In Social Psychology, Ethan eyeballed me trying to decode the misery on my face. Back from Denver, he'd changed seats to a different desk. On class break, he scurried into the seat next to me.

"Are you okay?"

"Yeah . . . yeah, I'm fine."

"You look tired. Is everything all right?"

"Yes. Homework." I half-smiled. "How was Denver?"

"Okay, I guess."

The class recommenced and he returned to his seat but eyed me until the end. I hadn't forgotten about his sweet nature but I hardly held the emotional strength to deepen the conversation.

Two weeks passed without encountering Zee at school and the pins in my heart subsided and my spirit rose from the dead. Work and school kept me afloat. I took baby steps to revive my senses.

On a late Saturday night, I lay in bed half-asleep after having finished homework with the TV on low volume CP 24. I daydreamed of Zee rolling beside me with his infectious smile until the phone startled me into alert mode. "Hey," texted Zee and I jolted up to the sitting position.

Our telepathy still beamed scolding hot and it happened every time I'd fall in deep thoughts with him. But this time, I'd gained the strength to do what I suspected he'd done most of the times I texted him. I read his message, pushed delete, tossed the phone back on the night table and rolled to sleep with a smile on my face. Not because he'd sent a text but because I had the power to resist his temptation.

CHAPTER
12

When Zee dipped into a library seat across from me on a rainy November day, my pulse soared off the charts. I typed incomprehensible words in my inner delirium. Then he caught my gaze, stretching over the library room before we shifted our eyes back to our desks.

Two days later, I headed down the hall on the third floor, fresh out of Social Psych to descend to my locker on the level below. As I pushed the door to the staircase, a human shadow swayed in the reflection of the glass door. I spun on my heels and cast an investigative eye down the hall.

The masculine frame wore a hoodie and delved through a locker in a slant of light at the opposite end of the corridor. I stepped in his direction with narrowed eyes and my breathing quickened when the unmistakable tip of the nose peeked out of the hood. By the time I closed in his proximity, I could hardly gab a word.

I stopped about ten feet away. "What's up, Zee?" He zipped up his knapsack and slammed the locker door. "Zee." He glanced at my face, then angled away. "What's going on?" I muttered.

"Nothing. On my way to class right now." He spoke with poise and his gaze down the hall as he passed me by. Every muscle in my body was tense. He was aware of the effect he had on me to the point where I could swear he enjoyed it.

"I'm confused," I said with my breath wedged in my throat.

He glided forward but glimpsed back with cold eyes. "Oh, yeah? About what?"

"You act like you don't even know me."

"I know you. I'm talking to you right now." Still two steps ahead.

"But you don't even look at me. Can you stop walking away?"

"I'm late for class. You can walk with me." At the end of the hallway, he pushed the staircase door and descended below.

"You said it wouldn't happen again. The same bullshit as before."

He pulled the door to the second floor. "Alexa, it's not the right time to talk about this now."

"There is never talking to you."

Once in my locker area, he flung the washroom door open. "Have a good day. See you later." Then he escaped inside and the door thumped shut behind him.

I stood in the hallway, frozen like a monument until a volcano of fury erupted through my pores. I barged inside, pinned him against the wall and shouted at the top of my lungs, "No, I will not see you later, motherfucker. And who the fuck do you think you are to play with my emotions like that?" But that only happened in my head.

I pulled my mind back and took a moment to regain my long lost rationale. If someone called security, I could kiss my seat in the Paramedic Program goodbye. I couldn't afford to throw my hard work on sleepless nights with sore eyes away for a moment of rage, courtesy of Zeke.

I hobbled around the corner, rooted my car keys out and charged through the school doors. I drove on the highway in tears. I wailed a cascade of anger that I'd fallen back in his trap.

When my phone rattled on the passenger seat, I jammed the earbuds in my ears, wiped my cheeks and answered, expecting a girl's voice at the other end.

"Do you want to hang out? Because you need some time with Zee." My heart skipped a beat. It was the first time he called himself Zee and I held from speaking. "You're all right?"

"I'm fine."

"It's sad to see you sad, Alexa. I'm sorry. And I'd like to hang out but I don't like being made to feel like I'm a monster."

"But when —"

"You looked good today. Alexa, you should slap me. I'm a bad boy and you should punish me."

"Punish you?" We paused, then burst with laughter.

"I'm glad I can still make you laugh. It seems lately, I only make you sad but I don't mean it." I listened in silence. "Are you free right now?" he asked, his tone sweet.

"I'm driving to work. I promised my friend I'd take over for half a shift, so she could do errands."

"What about tomorrow?"

"I work long hours on off-school days, you know that. By the time I make it home, I'm exhausted."

"You're right. Eager me."

"Eager to do what, see me? Didn't you just run away from me at school?"

"I had class."

"That was the shortest class I've ever heard of."

"All right, I'll let you text me when you have some time. I'm sorry about today. I hate to see you sad."

"Then don't make me sad."

"I'll try."

"Try harder," I said — these words familiar — and hung up.

Sunday evening, when I stepped foot inside my lonely home, I shot a message with his name, in spite of my fatigue. "At a friend's house. Can you pick me up?" he wrote. "Yes." And a flutter tickled my gut. "I'll text you soon."

Soon turned into hours and I climbed into bed in indignation. "Alexa, did you fall asleep on your prisoner of war? I surrender." And as soon as I finished reading his text, he called.

"Hi, gorgeous. You sleeping?"

"You're terrible with timing." Beats of silence. "Where are you?"

"I'll text you the address. Please, come to my rescue." This guy was an infinite conundrum.

I picked him up outside someone's house, somewhere close to school.

"Where to now?" I asked.

"I guess your place would be more comfortable."

I revved into the night as he hovered over me and showered me with kisses. He kissed my cheek, my shoulder, my arm, my hand on the wheel. He pinched my chin and turned my head, so he could kiss me more.

"I need to watch the road."

"Afraid we'll die? At least we'll die together."

"And you called *me* crazy."

He leaned back in his seat. "Tell me, did you think intensely of me for the last four days?"

"Did you?"

"Maybe." Still proud and stubborn, not wanting to give in an inch. "I thought about texting you but you said you were busy, so I thought, 'what's the point?'"

"You can still text if I'm busy. I can always read it later," I said, scolding-like.

"You still want to write that book?" he asked.

"Do you really care or you're just making conversation?"

"You're only saying about the book because I said it first."

"Don't you get tired of being a dick all the time? And I'm not saying it because you said it first. I mean it," I briefed him in a low, weighty tone, "and you're the main character." He chuckled and didn't believe a single word.

I parked in my driveway and pointed to the side entrance door. We sloped down the stairs and roamed inside my apartment. He dropped his windbreaker on the floor and scouted around.

"It's cozy. I like it."

"Make yourself at home." I threw his jacket on a hanger in the wardrobe.

"Is the furniture yours?"

"No, I rented it furnished."

He opened the fridge. "You have wine?"

"My landlord gave it to me as a welcoming gift."

I unscrewed the cork in the kitchen as he dipped into the chenille couch. Then I plastered the open bottle and two glasses on the coffee table.

Zee poured the wine and raised his glass. "Cheers."

As I flung the glass to my lips, I absorbed the sight of him on the couch at my place, hard to believe the reality of it. And as much as I wanted him here, I dreaded the following days when his scent would linger in the air, tearing my insides apart.

But for now, I allowed myself the momentary joy. We drifted into small talk with animated faces and giggles in our hearts. Our conversation flowed like a river, so good to be together again.

"Do you have music?"

"Yes, here."

I put the glass down and led him to the laptop, which happened to rest on a bedroom night table. He leaped on the bed, as if from a trampoline into a water basin and lay on his belly to toy with the laptop. I sat on the edge of the bed. He set it on You Tube reggae and rolled on his back, his eyes burning into mine. Then he jerked his head with an invitation to move closer. I climbed on top of him and sat on his hips.

"Why do you hurt me so much, Zee?"

"I told you, I don't mean to," he said, his tone like butter. "But from now on, I'll be your teddy bear. I promise."

Promises-promises. "You promise? I cannot believe you left me standing outside the washroom."

He sat up and cupped my head. "That's because I wanted you to follow me in."

"I was this close," I said, pinching the air with my thumb and index. "But I didn't want to get in trouble at school. What if someone called security?"

He brushed my lips with his thumb while he whispered in the lotus position. "Well, they don't know passion."

"How could you even expect me to follow you in? You were ice cold."

"You know what you do the next time I'm being an ass? You throw me against the wall and kiss me."

At that moment, I grasped I'd done it all wrong with Zee. He wanted me to take control, be a bitch even, the way I was at the beginning when he chased me around like a puppy dog.

"I ran after you one day when you walked out of the library —"

He fell on the bed. "I was wondering when you would follow me out of the library one of these days."

"And when I did, you stared me away from the pool bar."

"Yeah but I wanted you to do the exact opposite."

"You like playing games. Okay, you're unpredictable, I give you that. But come on, haven't you made me suffer enough?"

"Not even close." He yanked me on his chest.

"You missed me once, you'll miss me again. But one day, I won't be there anymore."

He thrust me to the side and pinned me against the bed, his lungs panting out of his chest. He kissed me violently and when I pushed him off, his turn-on level soared through the roof. He liked it aggressive, I knew that by now. We pushed and pulled on each other between the sheets, like a love-hate relationship. Our clothes flew in a wrath of hunger and anger on my side. I had my fair share of frustrations to let out and I almost punched him in the face. And the harder he pumped, the more I wanted to box him, reset his genius brain on Alexa mode again.

"Wait, I think the condom broke." He peeped down below. "Yes, it did." He huffed and rolled on his back. "I only have one."

"I have none. I didn't know you were coming."

We stared at the ceiling in the nude and in perfect silence, the moment adrift anyway.

"You know what I always wanted to do?" he said.

"What?"

He hugged a pillow. "Sleep next to someone."

His nothing-can-touch-me shield concealed a lonely guy in desperate need for affection. I tried my hardest to fill the vacancy in his soul but despite my determination, I could never break through his invisible wall.

"Do you want to sleep here or do you want me to drive you back? It's your call," I said.

"Let's go." He jumped out of bed and into his clothes, passing the chance to sleep next to someone.

In the car, a text from Zee popped up on my phone between my legs. "You won't say and I can't ask. Is it you or me?"

"What's this message about? I'm right next to you. Can't you verbalize it?"

"Nah, forget it," he muttered, gazing at the road ahead.

"I hate when you do that. I'm not a between-the-lines reader."

"There is this girl . . . who promised to move in with me last year September but moved away with her boyfriend instead. Then she called in March, told me she wanted to move back and give us a chance but then, I didn't hear from her."

My stomach dropped. "That's the reason why you turned your back on me in March."

"Then she moved back to Brenton City in the summer and called me again to try things out. Next thing I knew, she fell in love with some other guy and got herself another boyfriend."

"Are we back to this unfortunate story? Don't tell me this crap. I don't want to hear it. I don't give a shit about this story. And why do we have to do this every time?"

His eyes plunged to the floor. "Because —"

"You'll never have her, okay? Get it through your head. She doesn't love you. She's playing you, don't you get it?" He gazed through the windshield, quiet again as my heart turned to stone. "What are you doing with me? Am I your bandage? Because I'm not interested in being your fucking bandage."

"Alexa, do you want to get married and have kids someday?"

"What?"

"So do I and my kids have to look a certain way but it'll never happen."

"It will happen."

"How do you know?"

"Because I know you better than you think."

"You don't know me half as well as she does. She's my best friend."

"If she's your best friend, why is she doing this to you? I would never hurt you like this."

"Well, if it's that easy for her to turn her back on me after all this time, then who's to say, you won't do the same?"

I punched the steering wheel. "I would never do that to you. I cried myself to sleep for months because of you. I love you as a friend and as everything you are to me." I had to tell him. I had to tell him because the end was here. He didn't flinch, as if he already knew. And he knew, he'd known all along.

"Then pray for me to get who I want," he said and his words sliced through my insides like daggers.

"Why couldn't you leave me alone in September? I was fine before you barged back into my life."

At a red light, I rolled the car to a stop on the bridge at Grant Street as he stared ahead in silence. I tossed a look down below at the highway with my heart shattered, the traffic sporadic and lazy. What if I drove the car off the bridge? After all, he said he wouldn't care if we died together. Except, I couldn't be selfish enough to take his life.

We coasted in excruciating hush, back to where I'd picked him up. I pulled over near the sidewalk and he hurdled out of the car.

"Good luck with your book," he said, then slammed the car door shut.

He drifted away, finally understanding that he couldn't yo-yo his way in and out of my life any longer. We both sensed the end of us, each in our own right and that night, a part of me died.

CHAPTER
13

I buried my head in my studies again amidst the end of the semester, the busiest time in college. A period when assignments, projects and presentations screamed due date and final tests rampaged like cyclones.

A couple of weeks into December, I rounded the corner to my locker. Zee rushed in my direction frantic and preoccupied and he wasn't about to stop. When our sleeves brushed, I swatted my hand on impulse and gripped his arm.

"Let go." He glowered at me and ripped his arm from my hand, then vanished down the hall.

I propped breathless against my locker. I recalled the night he sprawled on my bed, commanding with a smirk to pin him against the wall and kiss him, whenever he played aloof. How quickly I'd forgotten about the silent verdict to slay our bond stone cold.

I'd intended to hit the library for homework but I raced out of school instead. I crept to my safe place, kinked in a ball again and closed my eyes to numb the pain.

One day at school, I holed up at the back of the library and dove into unfinished projects. My gaze bounced in mid-air as Zee's glacial eyes cracked from behind the science tutoring hub in search for an available computer. He stopped dead on his feet and retraced his steps. He never understood the impact of every move he made, slashing my heart into gravel dust. He circled the tutoring hub and settled into a seat, two rows ahead. Moments later, he twirled his head, scowled at me, then shimmied behind the hub out of sight. As if he couldn't even stand to expose his back to me.

When I finished my homework, I dragged my feet down the corridor next to the windows. Zee's profile broke in sight tilted in academic conversation with a female student. He patiently coached her, it seemed, the same way he did it with me in our beginnings. I fled the library with a growing hole in my stomach.

A week later, my peers and I brainstormed a project around a table at the rear of the library. I'd styled my hair and splashed a bit of makeup on to wipe the alien mask I'd harvested lately. My good mood resurrected for no particular reason other than sometimes I decided to push Zee to the back of my mind and enjoy my life for a change. Sometimes.

When Zee made an appearance, he caught a glimpse of my cheek beams out of the laughing crowd. But against all the decisions I've ever made relating to Zee, the closer he ambled in my direction, the faster my heart thudded. He crashed at a desk within hand reach from my group but kept his eyes on his notes. I loped to class with my crowd without so much as a glimpse his way, a rewarding sport I should try more often.

Post-class, I returned to the library and toiled over a presentation for hours on end with crippled brain cells pinned on thumbtacks. I cupped my head in my palms to rest my burning eyes when Zee's hearty tone startled me off the seat. I snapped my head to the right.

Two chairs over, he yapped on the phone about a project. An available chair rested between us, waiting for the next drained body to dip. He corner-eyed me while on the phone to ensure he'd caught my attention. Perhaps, he toyed with the option of speaking louder, if he didn't. The moment he caught my glance, he turned his back. After all, he could only ignore me if I'd been aware of his presence. I shifted my gaze back to my presentation with a pounding heart and scattered thoughts. I'd lost my creative rope. His untypical garish laugh spurred through my brain and fanned my concentration far and away. He hung up the phone and roared about a school-related topic with a female student, a different one from the week before. Then he rose from his seat in preparation to leave and talked some more with his back, ten inches from me. He pushed his chair under the desk, then the chair next to me, brushing his elbow against mine. He departed with the girl but I giggled inside. The formerly shy guy, who couldn't look me in the eyes, had become popular with the female students. He dressed in a bodysuit of self-confidence, one I've boosted to the moon and back.

I wrapped up the final test in Social Psych when Ethan tailed me out of class and gently snagged my elbow.

"I wanted to wish you Happy Holidays."

I slipped him a smile with a strike of sorrow. "Thanks. You too."

I laced my arms around his waist and he tightened his hands around my shoulders. In another life, maybe we'll be together again because what broke us apart were not so much my sentiments for Zee but our traits at polar opposites. I left him standing in the hallway, watching me wander deeper into the school building.

When the last day of the semester poured to an end, I settled on the couch in front of the TV with a glass of red. And for once, I embraced the school break. Three semesters in a row had utterly drained my wits and emotions. Relaxation — a strange notion for a student.

I celebrated Christmas at Heather's with her family and New Year's Eve at Maureen's with hers. And what a charity child I'd become. My girlfriends and I bonded like family but I craved someone who shared my bloodline, except she lived across the cosmic fields. Throughout the winter holidays, I chatted with Mom on the phone for hours on end but the moment I'd hang up the phone, I'd missed her so much, I wanted to spread my wings and fly.

CHAPTER
14

My first day back at school, I showed up with a less than fresh and ready for class January mood. I'd studied myself to death and pushed myself to the limit in the semesters prior. I'd memorized the Chem and Bio textbooks like my own name and feared I'd remember nothing at the same time.

I'd taken Criminology to round up the required Gen-Eds for Paramedic and strike the filler courses out of the way and I loved it already. The syllabus marinated in correlates of criminal behaviour and theories of crime, an assignment on Jeffrey Dahmer, two on crime typology and a presentation on a notorious criminal of choice. I'd do mine on Charles Manson, I decided.

After Crim class, I sparked up for school again but I dreaded a run-in with Zee in the hallways. I preferred not to. I didn't particularly desire to see him strut around like a peacock, pretending not to know me or going out of his way to avoid me, to make a point that he could.

When Advanced Biology, which spread over two semesters, ended for the day, I pranced out of school and paddled through the snow. I stumbled in shock when a smiley face gleamed in the snowy coat of my car. Someone had finger-drawn two eyes on the windshield and a curved mouth on the hood and a lopsided grin arched on my face. I pictured Zee jotting it with his cute finger but it couldn't have been him. That would've been too much to ask.

"Thanks for the smiley face," I texted Ethan from the driver seat before sticking the key in the ignition. "What smiley face? It wasn't me." I shifted my gaze in every direction. How could this be?

The next day, as I scrambled up to the third floor for my second half of the split Crim class, my eyes scanned down the hall for the ghost of Zee by his locker. He stood in the dim light at the end of the corridor again and gazed my way with a tilted head. I veered around the corner to class. By the weekend, he emailed me an invite to join him on Facebook but my account was best left erased. I tossed his request in the virtual trash.

When I browsed on the college website to check what's new and exciting, his name came up on a student achievement list. He'd won an environmental planning award. In my rush to praise him, I ventured up to the third floor in search for his locker, one day after class. I carried my heart through my teeth. I didn't want to find him there. I could hardly remember his locker from the row, all with a three-digit combination dial padlock, like mine and his, but we both had the habit of sticking the rental plastic locket on the right side of the shackle. Yeah, that had to be it.

I stared at the locker, unsure if an inscription on the door would be a good idea but after all, he sent out the signals first. "Congrats on your award. I'm proud of you. I always knew you were a genius. I said it first." I wrote it in pencil and drew a smiley face to re-gift the grin he'd plastered on mine in the parking lot, on the first day of the semester.

The weekend passed and on Monday, I paid a visit to his locker. As I plodded closer, the sight of the missing lock and the smudged letters on the door came into view. I swung it open and an abrupt surge of angst flashed through my body. It'd been emptied out. I bolted down the hall and all the way home with anguish tears bursting out of my eyes. How many times could he break my heart before I had a heart no more?

CHAPTER
15

On a Saturday afternoon — and a day before Valentine's Day — I wrote the Paramedic examination at Brimley. I sashayed to the testing room with a flickering stomach of a pending exam but tons more confident than the previous year. I blocked the nonsense out of my brain and focussed on the correct answers. I flipped through the virtual exam with incredible calm, so untypical of me and stepped out self-assured.

Then I savoured a post-exam leisure session at the coffee shop around the corner from school. Alone and placid with the book Maureen bought me for my birthday. I could finally sink my teeth into it with a fresh latte next to me. I took to a table in a discreet corner.

"Hey, I know you," a voice echoed from across the shop. I whipped up my head as a voluptuous brunette headed for my table. "Remember me?" I tilted my head. "Heather Preiss, Thanksgiving last year?"

"Tania, right?"

"You still remember my name," she said, delighted.

"It's probably because of your sense of humour."

"And you're . . ."

"Alexa."

"Right. I came in to buy a coffee and run but . . ." She glimpsed at my table.

"Please, have a seat."

"That night, Heather told me you work for her but I think someone mentioned that you go to school," she said as she lounged in the next armchair.

"Yes, I came from an exam to clear my head. And I recall there was some talk about you and the world of promotions."

"I organize bashes and special events, if you ever plan on throwing a graduation party. I'm the best person to call."

"It's a long road to graduation but I'll keep that in mind."

"Or if you'd like to attend one of my parties —"

"I'm not the partying kind but thanks."

"What do you mean? Isn't that what college is for?" I creased my forehead. "Joking. I graduated myself three years ago. Business and marketing. I still remember the bustle of studying, which is why you look like you could use a break."

I raised my book in the air. "I'm taking a break right now."

"I'll leave you my business card. Put it in a safe place, you might use it someday. Good luck with school." As she trotted out of the shop, a positive vibe drifted in her trail.

On Monday after class, I fiddled at the library with Criminology textbooks and brainstormed my first assignment with gusto when the entire school computer system crashed. Students herded out of the library grounds in spurts as Zee strolled in and took the far sided corridor to the back. I lurched in my chair on the phone with Maureen when his magnetic aura dazzled my instinct into spinning my head his way. He stood tall, gazing at me from three rows behind, then shifted his glance to a monitor and descended into a seat, even though he knew the computers were dead.

I giggled on the phone with my bestie when his shadow appeared at a desk closer, as if waiting for me to finish my conversation but I wouldn't. I asked Maureen to stay on the phone. Minutes later, he pranced out of the library with a deflated gait.

I hung up with Maureen and toyed with my phone. Maybe he did try to talk to me. "Did you draw a smiley face on my car on the first day of the semester?" I figured the worst case scenario would be Zee ignoring my text, which would tell me that he wasn't, in fact, trying to talk to me. "Who is this? And no, definitely not." I guess I haven't thought about the worst possibility because I sensed the blood drain off my face as I read his text. I gathered my notes with trembling hands and rushed out of school with that hole in my gut again, by now a canyon in the pit of my stomach.

In the driver seat, I dipped my head in my hands. I never understood why he used himself as bait, then turned a cold shoulder when I bit the hook. I raised my gaze through the windshield, unsure what to do. I didn't want to go home, modern and comfy as it was, the solitude would kill me right now. I didn't want to drive to work on my day off again but I had to get away from campus. I rooted in my tote for Tania's business card and flipped it in my hand as I calculated my decision. I couldn't go wrong with a funny girl for company, even for an introvert like me.

She answered on the first ring and I suggested a cup of coffee at the shop where we last met.

"It's freezing outside and I just put on a fresh pot. Why don't you come over?" she said and it sounded like music to my ears.

Tania lived in a semi-detached townhouse, in a discreet neighbourhood, not far from my school. She opened the door with a warm smile and before I stepped foot inside, the pressure in my heart diminished to half.

"Come in. I'll bring the coffee. Then you can tell me what's wrong."

She'd briefly met me but she was good at sensing and I liked people who sensed hidden emotions and answered on the first ring.

The townhouse interior was designed in bright and neutral shades with yellow and white walls and earthy hues upholstery. The place stemmed a cozy ambiance and a flavour of tranquil. No wonder she exuded yummy vibes far and wide. I wilted on the couch to absorb the soothing solace.

She placed the cups on the glass top of the coffee table, next to a vase of white lilies and I inhaled their perfume as aromatherapy for the soul. Then she leaned back on the love seat. "All right. I'm all ears." I took a deep breath and unloaded my story with Zee.

PART TWO

SPELLBOUND IN U

CHAPTER

16

O n my first visit to Tania's, we bonded so well, the stopovers became an after-school ritual. By March, I waved my lonesome apartment goodbye and moved into her place.

"You should come with me on a trip," she said one morning.

She traveled for work as an event planner and organizer. At twenty six, she knew everyone who was anyone in the world of entertainment promotions within a five-hundred mile radius.

"It's not that simple with school and work."

"Come along on a weekend. It'd be good for you."

I booked the Saturday before reading week off from The Beauty Bar. Tania had planned an event to promote a new beverage for a major client in a modernized locale north of Brenton City.

The morning of the drive, I woke up fresh and upbeat and ready for a road trip with my brand spanking new roommate.

"Morning coffee?" she asked as she poured it in the cups.

"What could be better right now?"

"I could name a few things."

We dunked into the couch and I bounced my feet in the air.

"When are we leaving?" I asked.

"Relax, it's no big deal."

"Speak for yourself. I stressed about what to wear all week."

Late afternoon, we jetted out the door sprinkled and decked out. On the way, we grooved to the music and shared life stories. Two hours later, we arrived in Cape Kay, a dreamy town anchored by the lake with tiny shops and animated parks. We parked in front of The Tavern, a rustic bar emanating countryside comfort and ease.

"I never knew northern towns were so idyllic," I said, scanning the surroundings.

Tania shut the car door. "It's a nice break from the city, not that Brenton City's much bigger but it's closer down south. It picked up the urban vibe from Toronto."

We made our way inside where dim music and lilac incense gushed in the air. A serving bar, a dance floor and tall, narrow tables along its edges made up the interior. Kiwi coloured paper lanterns with matching wicker chairs and tables decorated the wooden deck facing the lake.

"Well, if it isn't the legendary Tania Malone. Welcome back." Two women about our age with long onyx hair and identical height scooped from behind the serving bar in our direction.

"Alexa, meet Nikki and Kara Holloway, the two sisters who own this place."

"Nice to meet you both. I love the décor."

"Your new business partner?" Kara asked Tania, scanning my frame.

"No, she's my friend and roommate. She came along for the fun."

Nikki turned to me with a smile. "First time in Cape Kay?"

"Yes."

"Drinks?" Nikki asked, trudging behind the serving bar.

"I'm fine, unless she wants something." Tania pointed at me.

"I'll take an iced tea for now."

Tania drew near my ear. "The best part about attending an event in a new town is that everyone wants to know who you are. Enjoy it while it lasts."

I preferred to relish the atmosphere from the sidelines with a tasty cocktail in hand but that would come later. For now, the break away from the school pressure pacified my sentiments.

"Lemon mint green iced tea specially made for our new guest. Enjoy," Nikki said and I smiled back.

"I have work to do. Go socialize. You need it," Tania said.

"I'm fine over here."

She jerked her head. "Three o'clock."

A slender male figure with hazelnut hair and a wide smile slightly bowed his head from the crowd.

I snapped my head back. "No way in hell."

"He's your type," Tania said.

"I don't have a type."

"I can describe yours in five words right now."

"T, I'm here to relax and clear my head. I'm not in the mood to meet a new guy."

"I thought you wanted to meet new people."

"I never said that. And in any case, it'd be people you casually meet at an event, not a guy who's eyeing me from across the room and you know how the rest of the story goes. No, thanks."

"Then casually talk to him. What's the difference?" she said, before strolling away.

The impending threat approached in the corner of my eye with bouncy steps and curved lips.

"Hello. Having fun?" His deep set cognac eyes glimmered.

I glimpsed at him, "Hi and yes," then away.

"I'm Vinson." He held his smile.

"Alexa. Excuse me." I rushed to Tania's group. "Thanks for leaving me alone."

"He didn't kill you, did he?"

"Who? Vinson Donohue? Not yet," Kara said.

I raised my glass at Tania to back my point. "See? That's why I'd rather not."

"My sister's joking," Nikki said. "Vinson's a nice guy."

"A bit immature for a twenty-seven-year-old," Kara said, glancing in his direction, "but he does run a home foundation contracting business with his father."

"I don't pick them according to their financial worth," I said. "And I don't even know why we're talking about this right now."

"She means he's worth a try," Nikki said, "in a sense that he's a hard working man."

"But I don't even like him."

"You don't want to like him," Tania said. She leaned close to whisper. "But talking to him as friends may help you recover from school boy."

She had a point but I wanted to breathe easy for a while, free from butterflies and emotional earthquakes.

"I'm here to relax and have fun. Not interested in meeting anyone in that way," I said and ventured onto The Tavern's deck for a breath of fresh air.

Tania trailed behind. "All I'm saying is that he may turn out to be a nice guy and you need a nice guy."

"Can I buy you ladies a drink?" Vinson asked from the door step.

"I'll get my own," Tania said on her way inside.

"Where are you from?" Vinson asked, stepping closer.

I moved next to the patio heater. "Brenton City. Well, Toronto but I moved to Brenton City for school."

"Beautiful and smart."

"That's not going to fly with me."

"What?"

"Beautiful and smart."

"I'm speaking the truth. You don't believe me?"

"I don't care to believe you."

He sighed. "I'm even more intrigued now."

"Don't be."

"Intrigue level raised through the roof." A lopsided smirk slipped on my face. "So she smiles." He pointed to the bar. "Care to step inside? You're probably frozen by now."

We shuffled through the crowd to the serving bar.

"Do you want to know anything about me?" he asked.

"No . . . uhm, what's your zodiac? It doesn't matter, I'm only asking for conversation."

"Hold that thought." He angled away and placed an order, then a minute later, he handed me a carbon copy of my first drink. "I believe I owed you this drink half an hour ago."

"Ah, observant."

"To be fair, I asked Nikki what you had last. Gemini."

I snapped my eyes wide open. "Goodbye."

"What did I do?"

I wandered through the bar in search for Tania and nudged her elbow as she mingled with patrons.

"Are we almost done here?" I asked.

"No, the night's not over yet." I slouched in dismay and she pulled me close. "Come over here and lighten up."

For the rest of the night, Vinson smiled every time our eyes met in the crowd. When we waved the sisters goodbye, Vinson floated my way.

"Here's my phone number. I'm open if you'd like to talk sometimes." He handed me a folded napkin.

"I'm closed. Goodnight."

Tania scooped the napkin and followed me outside.

"What happened?" she asked as we climbed in her car. "He looked like he had no clue what he did wrong."

"He's a Gemini."

"That is what happened?"

"It's a curse for me. I went through hell and back with Zee."

"Vinson is not Zee. And he's older by a few good years."

"But I don't even know if I'm ever coming back here. You know how busy I am with school and work."

"You're done school next month and the summer is on its way after that. I bet you will."

"I'll sleep on it. We'll see what happens."

Tania glanced at me, then at the murky highway. "That's the spirit."

I worked the entire reading week at the beauty salon, kicking the boys subject out of mind. When Tania and I gathered at home, we watched movies, shared wine and turned dizzy from laughter. I welcomed the restored normalcy in my life with open arms.

Friday night, I twisted under the covers until two fifteen in the morning when the red flicker on my phone twinkled in the dark. I reached over blindly and read the display with squinting eyes. "Hi, Alexa. Can you call me?" read an email from Zee. I soared to the sitting position in a transient vertigo. Every time my soul drifted in tranquility, he'd stir my senses into a frenzy but only for a heart-beat now. I let myself fall on the bed with the phone beside me and the word *ignore* clouded my mind. The spine tingles faded as I dipped my head in the pillow.

Monday morning, I meandered to school ahead of class time and bounced to the library with coffee in hand to print the lecture out-lines of the day. Minutes later, Zee scanned the library before he paddled to a seat at the back. I shifted my glance to my notes after I caught his stare at the corner of my eye. Ignore, ignore, ignore.

When he dropped into the chair next to me and dissected my face, I held my gaze on the monitor.

"Alexa, how are you?"

"I'm good," I said, unmoving my eyes.

"How was your break?"

I glimpsed at him, then back at the screen. "Great."

"Going to class soon?"

"Yes." I paused. "You?"

"I'm working on a project. I only slept for an hour. Wanna see?"

Before I could reject the offer, he rushed to his desk and back with the project sheets clenched through his fingers. He sprinkled them on the desk and described them with thirst.

"Zee, you emailed me, remember? Have something to tell me?"

"I think so."

"You think so? And how many times will you erase my number only to email me again and again to ask me to call you?"

"We need to talk but what we need to talk about will take more than five minutes."

"Did you ask me if I wanted to talk?"

His lips parted, his eyes widened. "Don't you?" He inched forward as I gaped away. "We need time and right now, I have to work on my project. It's due in a few hours."

"Good luck then. See you later." He eyed my moves as I pushed the chair behind me, chucked my notes in my tote and decamped.

At the crib, I flopped on the couch with my legs up and a fixed gawk up at the ceiling.

"Hey," Tania said, shutting the door behind her, "I have something for you." She waved a large envelope with the Brimley logo on it.

"It's the Paramedic exam result," I said, sitting up.

She put it in front of me. "What are you waiting for? Open it."

I cradled my forehead with my palm, then threw the envelope back on the coffee table. "I'm scared. You open it."

"A fat envelope means good news. Just open it."

I unglued the packet covering with shaky fingers, pulled out the paper binder and unfolded it in slow motion. "Congratulations. We are thrilled to inform you . . ."

We exploded off the couch, jumping and screaming at the top of our lungs, papers flying in mid-air.

"I'm in. I can't believe I made it. I'm going to be a Paramedic."

"You deserve it. You worked hard for this."

When we regained our composure, Tania put on a fresh pot of coffee to celebrate — not that we needed an energy booster — while I made phone calls to the important people in my life to deliver the news, starting with Mom. I couldn't hold my mind from dashing out to Zee. Even in a time when there wasn't much left of us, he was still my lucky charm.

Over the weekend, Tania was bound to travel to Cape Kay and estimated three days in town. I booked them off work in advance and hopped in her car. After all, I'd earned a getaway up north with my roommate, a gift to myself for my Paramedic acceptance.

"Should I text Vinson?" I asked Tania on the way. "I'm in the mood to refresh my life."

"If anyone deserves it at this point, it's you. Drop him a line. Talk, laugh, be friends."

"Easy on the *friend* word. It creates a world of trouble for me."

"Yes but you know better now."

"Here we go." I tapped him a text and my phone rumbled within minutes. "He texted back."

"Did you tell him we were coming?"

"Yes."

"And?"

I gave a coy glance. "He asked me out. Dinner and a movie."

"Perfect. You killed yourself over your studies. You need to go out and live a little."

When we rolled into town, Tania angled into an apartment complex visitor parking.

"We'll stay at a friend's place for the weekend," she said and I huffed at the dread of meeting new people.

"I figured we'd stay at a hotel or something."

"No worries. She's a cool girl. I've known her for some time. And she has a fascinating view of the lake."

I stumbled out of the car and lagged in my roommate's footsteps with pouty lips. When the elevator halted on the fifth floor, we took the right corridor to the end.

An upbeat woman with sour cherry, curly hair, chocolate eyes and caramel skin tone wrenched the door wide open.

"Hi guys. Welcome."

Tania glided in and hugged her friend. "It's been a while."

"Yes, too long," the girl said, shifting her gaze my way.

"Serena, meet my roommate, Alexa. Alexa, meet Serena."

"Nice to meet you."

Serena jerked me in a hug. "Likewise." Then she held me at arm's length. "I heard the big news."

"Big news?" I asked.

"Someone's going to be a lifesaver. Congrats."

"Thanks," I said and darted a glance at Tania.

We slid down the parquet hallway to the living room, passing bedroom doors on the way. A bright apartment unfolded with tall windows facing the marina and baby blue upholstery. A bottle of red wine and three stemmed glasses sparkled on the crystal coffee table. I bobbed my head at Tania.

"I may be working but that doesn't mean we can't celebrate."

"I have a date tonight, remember?" I said.

"A sip for cheers won't kill you. Besides, Serena and I haven't seen each other in a long time."

"A date? I thought you're new in town," Serena said, uncorking the bottle.

"We came to town a couple of weeks ago and I met this guy at The Tavern. It's a superficial thing to clear my head and loosen my emotions, that's all."

Serena poured the wine and raised her glass. "Cheers."

"To friendships," Tania said. "Did you call Vinson?"

"I texted him the zip code posted in the lobby. He's picking me up at eight."

"Then let's get you dressed up," Serena said.

"I didn't bring much. I might as well go with what I'm wearing."

"Nonsense. You need to wear high heels."

"To the movies? No and besides, I left mine at home."

"I have plenty I don't even wear. Let's go play dress up."

We toyed with outfits and makeup while dance music blasted in the air. At eight sharp, I sprinted downstairs with a beaming face. Vinson awaited my arrival in a dusty blue pickup truck. Never mind the pickup, he could've at least stopped at a car wash on the way.

I hoisted myself in the passenger seat.

"Hi," he said, sporting the widest grin I'd ever seen. "Glad you made it back."

He revved the engine on the road and drove to a pizza restaurant. When we stepped in, I peeked at my fancy boots, courtesy of Serena, then at the conventional eatery. My high heels didn't suit the restaurant or the other way around but Tania would've said, "Who cares about the dusty pickup or the pizza joint? Tonight, it's all about the enjoyment of the spirits."

We settled at a table and stewed in first date discomfort. I had no idea what to say, I've never been much of a talker on a date with someone new. I've always dreaded first dates.

When the waitress arrived at the table, Vinson gaped at me. "Lemon mint green iced tea?"

"Steady memory."

"Only when I care to know." He ordered the drinks and then, "What do you think about this town?"

"I haven't seen much of it but so far the scenery is remarkable and the people are friendly. I guess it comes with the territory in smaller towns."

"Did you just call me a small town boy?"

"Northern towns . . . I meant to say Northern towns."

"Teasing, no worries . . . city girl."

"I like the urban lifestyle but I also like landscapes and everything rural. People are more relaxed in towns," I said, sipping on my newly arrived refreshment.

"Should we grab movie tickets when we finish these?"

"Sure."

We decided on a later movie on my phone and made a run to the movie theatre. He jetted inside for the tickets while I waited in the truck to escape the cold.

"Hungry?" he asked as he mounted into the driver seat shivering from the cold.

"Yes."

"All right. Let's catch a bite before the movie."

We cruised to the next parking lot with a fancier restaurant, one with exterior stone walls. After we hopped out, he held his hand for mine and I glared at it through my breathing vapour. But as soon as I gripped his digits, he sped through the parking lot, hauling me behind while I drowned in laughing hysteria.

"What's so funny?" he asked as we rumbled inside the restaurant lobby.

"You, pulling me like a rag doll."

"It's freezing out there." He held the second door. "But I'm glad you find me funny."

As we nibbled on dinner, the tension faded away and our small talk flowed into a giggling fever. Then we roamed inside the movie theatre with chortling faces. In line for popcorn, I propped my face into his shoulder to fight back the bursting laughter.

By the time the movie started, my stomach muscles hurt from amusement. The film turned out a bore but I hoped to be the longest one I'd ever seen. He winched my legs over his knees and held on for dear life. I corner-eyed him from time to time in disbelief. Up to a month ago, I couldn't see myself with anyone else and yet, I'd unknowingly gone on a date with the funniest man alive. I freed my legs and loomed close to him. He pulled me into the slope of his shoulder.

I couldn't recognize myself into my grins, an out of character notion on my ordinary days. I cringed every time the word *smile* echoed in my trail and immediately sensed the urge to fly my fist through the summoner's face. But Vinson triggered an uncontrollable glee inside my body and he didn't even have to try. He came as a natural joker with the charm of a paramour.

"You know what I like about this . . . date or whatever it is?" I said as we stepped out of the theatre hall.

"What?"

"That you're not trying to pull info out of my mouth like people usually do on first dates."

"I'm also a believer in letting personal information come natural and in due time," he said and I smiled.

We stumbled out of the cinema in a chuckling hoopla and made a run for his truck through the bone chilling wind. I shook off the cold in the passenger seat as the ghost of Zee flashed through my mind.

"You okay?"

"Yeah, cold."

"You'll warm up in no time," he said, cranking the ignition.

At the apartment complex, he idled in the driveway. Our eyes locked and he inched closer until our lips grazed in a gentle kiss.

"Goodnight," I whispered.

"You too."

I leaped out and turned to wave goodbye. He stared at my trail, frozen in the driver seat.

"How did it go?" Serena asked upstairs.

"I don't know what to make of it yet but unexpectedly good. Is Tania still working at The Tavern?"

"Yeap. She should be back soon."

"I'm hitting the bed to make sense of what happened tonight."

"Goodnight."

The next day, Vinson called in the afternoon as I chit-chatted with the girls over coffee.

"Would you like to watch a movie with me tonight?" he asked.

"The movies again?"

"No, I mean somewhere quiet."

"Where?" I asked, my tone wary.

"I have this place where we can go and talk, be with each other, if that's okay with you."

I paused for a rapid reflection. "Pick me up at seven and we'll see."

He texted from downstairs ten minutes before seven p.m. I padded down to the same beaming face waiting in the same grubby pickup truck. He roared the beast on the road to Thunder Hill, a

Cape Kay neighbourhood and pulled into the carport next to a pearly-white house with olive shutters. He turned the engine off and gaped at me with bright eyes.

"I'm house sitting for a friend and feeding the cat while he's on vacation with the family."

"Does this crappy line work on every girl you bring here?"

"It's not like that at all. We connected so well yesterday, I wanted us to get to know each other, away from the noise. We could sit in the car, if you'd like."

I wrenched the truck door open and jumped out. "Are you coming?"

"Right behind you."

A fluffy grey hairball greeted us at the door. I picked him up for a cuddle.

"That's Eagle," Vinson said.

"Eagle?" I said, petting him. "He doesn't look like an eagle."

"It's because he's fast and strong."

"It's so nice of you to feed your friend's family cat."

There was something about a man taking care of a cat that melted my heart as fast as a Popsicle forgotten under the sun by the poolside in July. My heart turned to liquid in one, two, three.

We dipped into the living room couch with random talk while Eagle settled in his favourite armchair and our words blended into a surreal vibe. There was a shifting energy between us that raised my blood to sweltering levels and my cheeks flushed with heat into a headache. A good headache, if such thing even exists.

"Where did you come from? Everything is so —"

"Weird? You seem kind of unreal too. You make me laugh and that says a lot about you already," I said.

"Why? You don't like to laugh?"

"I do but I'm not the laughy-laughy type of girl and yet, I get so bubbly with you."

"I'm glad I can do that for you," he said as he deepened his gaze into my eyes.

"It's strange but when I'm with you, I turn into someone I never met before."

He gently pinched my chin. "Yeah?"

"Yeah," I murmured, lost in his eyes.

He raked his fingers through my hair. "I hope you never stop looking at me like this." The words sounded premature for a second date and yet, they fell into the right place.

Something incredibly attractive lied inside this trim and lean Northerner, who trotted around town in steel-toe boots all day. He shared Zee's deep piercing gaze along with the zodiac and I was scared to death. But after months of Zee's icebergs, Vinson's warmth and affection buttered the chambers of my heart.

He glimpsed at my lips and shivers raced down my spine. Then he drew his mouth into a sensual curve and tested my lips.

"If we ever get to a point where we're bored of each other, let's remember this moment right here, right now," he whispered an inch away from my face.

"Vinson, we don't even live in the same town. I mean, what are we talking about here?"

"You can't deny our chemistry."

"No, I can't," I muttered, terrified.

We took turns to elaborate on what we liked about one another or what we liked in general. We discovered infinite similarities in mutual shock and to the point of fright.

"The energy between us is so intense, it's difficult to process what's happening," he said.

"What's happening is unreal."

We lay flat on the couch and he wrapped one arm around me. "The compatibilities between us keep on piling up. I think you'll be stuck with me for a while."

"You decided?"

"No, but I have a feeling you're going to have me wrapped around your finger like a puppy." He smacked his forehead. "And I probably shouldn't even tell you this."

No, you shouldn't. "We should go," I whispered.

"Something I said?"

"No, it's late."

He rose off the couch and held his hand for mine again. We stepped out of the house and parted as we climbed in the truck with our eyes fixed on each other.

"G'night," he said in the driveway, whispering against my lips.

"You too," I murmured as my ears caught on fire. I opened the truck door in slow motion and departed with startled eyes.

Tania and I shared the spare bedroom but she hadn't returned from The Tavern yet, so we could talk. Serena was holed up in her bedroom and I wouldn't impose a man-conversation on her. Not yet, anyway. I tried to digest the events on my own under the duvet. Whatever I had or didn't have with Zee became a faded contingency compared to the intense moments I'd shared with Vinson over two nights. Two nights and my heart was pumping on steel again.

I flipped my eyes open with inner ecstasy budding on my face. Over morning coffee, I bored my friends with my Vinson deliria. He'd set the shine back on my face and the vigor back in my heart. He'd brought me back to life.

In the afternoon, I joined Tania for company's sake at a daytime restaurant for a pre-scheduled business meeting. She introduced me to people whose names I'd forgotten the instant they spoke them to me. I slipped a couple of polite smiles and nods from time to time. I was mentally somewhere else.

Hours later, I raced downstairs and hopped in Vinson's truck with a case of the giggles for another date. We drove to the same house in Thunder Hill and after feeding Eagle, we parked it on the couch in a bundle.

"Do you feel like watching a movie?" he asked, his tone sensual.

"We might as well since we didn't do it yesterday."

He flipped through the channels. "*Blade Runner* okay? There's nothing else on."

"I love *Blade Runner*." I guess that was going to put a damp on the *Blade Runner* memory with Ethan.

"Come here," Vinson said and drew me closer. He fell against the back of the couch with me in his arms. "Did you think about me today?"

"Mmm, a little."

"Only a little?" he asked, his voice delicate. "That's okay. I thought about you on double time."

"Of course I thought about you silly. How could I not?"

His face brightened into a smile and his eyes dropped on the edges of my lips. His mouth neared close until it caressed my lips into a spark.

"I love your lips. They're so soft," he said.

"Pretty sure all girls have soft lips."

"But yours are different."

"Oh, yeah? Cause yours have a magic wand," I said, glancing at his lips every time they pulled away and back.

"You're a perfect fit for my lips, for my arms. We're a perfect fit." Another rash statement brought my face into a frown. "You never told me what you're taking in school," he continued.

"I'm going for Paramedic."

He bowed his head in admiration. "Like I said, beautiful and smart."

"I'm not there yet. I finished a preparatory program last summer, then took individual courses to help ease the load when I do start the Paramedic Program in September."

He jerked his head back. "Wow, you have it all figured out."

"You do too. You work with your dad at the family company, you'll take over someday."

"You've been informed." He paused. "When are you coming back to Cape Kay?"

"I'm not sure. I thought I'd come here once and that would be it."

"But you came back and I hope you will again, even if you'll be busy with school."

"I'm done with the semester in April."

His eyes lit up. "And you're off in the summer?"

"Off from school but I do work at my friend's beauty salon. I'm an aesthetician too."

"My point proven how many times now? You must love school."

"I do." I lay on his chest, one leg bent across his knees.

"Oh, baby. I'm so comfortable, I don't have a care in the world."

Did he just call me *baby*? "I could fall asleep in your arms," I said, snuggling deeper.

He stroked my hair. "So do I . . ."

As dawn spread on the horizon and warmed our cheeks, we flicked our eyes open, still glued to each other.

"Morning, doll," he said, glancing down.

"Morning?"

"You fell asleep. I didn't want to wake you. You must be exhausted from school and these long trips."

"Crap. Tania's going to flip. We're supposed to leave town early."

"It is early."

"It's never too early for Tania."

"Do you ever stop and breathe?"

"No," I said on the way to the bathroom. I speed-freshened up and when I ambled out, Vinson waited by the door.

"I fed Eagle. Now let's get coffees."

I followed him to the truck, giggling to his jovial morning observations about whatever he set his eyes on. I imagined that life with Vinson must be like watching a theatre play every single day. Even as we waited in drive-thru, he had me laughing with my head tilted back. He had a way of turning something random to utter parody and I couldn't keep a straight face. Not with him beside me.

When he dropped me off, he pecked my lips and said, "Keep in touch." Keep in touch? Wasn't *keep in touch* another version of *I'll call you later*, which meant *never*?

I headed upstairs, unsure they'd be the best words to hear the morning after I'd spent the night in the arms of a guy who'd touched my heart in three strikes and by strikes, I mean days. But in a case of contagious positivity, I accepted keep in touch for its literal meaning.

Tania lurched by the door with the car keys dangling off her index finger.

"You two are up already?" I asked as I glided to the living room.

"Up and waiting for you." Tania's tone dropped across the five words from snappy to slightly sour to sugary sweet when the scent of fresh coffee drifted in my trail and I figured as much.

"But it's not even eight o'clock."

"You know I'm a busy woman." Back to bossy sour.

"It's Sunday, chill. Have a coffee, Vinson's treat."

"Vinson's rubbing on you already," Serena said.

"You know him?" I asked as I sat on the couch.

She took a cup from the tray. "Vaguely. In this town, everyone knows each other, more or less."

"You're beaming. You said you'd keep it superficial," Tania said.

"And what should I do? Wait for Zeke forever? He doesn't even care and we were more like friends anyway. Vinson's the real deal. He's sensitive and he wants to get to know me."

"Yeah but take it easy."

"I am taking it easy. We talked all night and I fell asleep in his arms because I'm so damn tired from all the commotion in my life. And who encouraged me to talk to him in the first place?"

"All I'm saying is keep your emotions in check," Tania said.

I thumped the cup on the coffee table. "I'm ready when you are."

"I'm taking my coffee with me."

"Thanks for having us over again," I said to Serena at the door.

"Anytime. Let me know when you guys are coming again."

Tania winked at Serena. "I don't know. It's debatable."

"I caught that," I said as we shuffled out the door.

"I meant for you to catch it."

"Are you coming back to Cape Kay with me?" Tania asked as I arrived from school. I crashed my tote on the kitchen counter along with a smile. "So, you're coming. Can you give me a hand with some of this stuff?" she asked, facing her laptop.

"*You* need my help?"

"I'm trying to fit everything in my schedule." She huffed. "If I only had four hands. I keep saying I should hire an assistant but do I have the time to go through the hiring process? No."

I climbed on a bar stool by the counter. "What can I do?"

"See this?" She pointed to an extensive business email list. "Each email needs a reply but a professional one. I spend enough time on the phone with potential and recurrent clients. I don't have the time to write emails too."

"Why don't you send out automated replies?"

"Because they won't come back. Every email must be tailored according to the business relationship I have with each one. Some, I've worked with for a couple of years while with others, I'm establishing a connection now."

"Okay, I get it. But I don't have experience with business talk."

"Didn't you take Business Communications at Brimley? I saw the textbook here somewhere."

"We composed memos, resumes, proposals, that kind of stuff."

"I'll coach you at first and then you can do it on your own. There's also designing the leaflets for each event and sending them off for printing, managing social media."

I pretended to faint off the chair. "Like I'm not tired enough from school and work and the trips."

"Let's start with the emails and take it from there."

I rubbed my forehead. "I'll give it a try but no promises to step into your assistant's shoes. I already have a job."

"Wouldn't it be easier to work with me? Aren't you tired of the long drives to work every weekend?"

"I am but I can't drop Heather. She let me stay with her when I needed a place and she's a good friend."

"She's my good friend too. But I thought she'd return to work full time by now. Don't leave her hanging but run it by her, see what she says."

"After I give business emails a try first."

"Do you want to give it a try now?"

I nodded and absorbed her instructions, despite a creeping headache and by bedtime, I grasped the idea. I could handle business emails for now and working with Tania meant time to travel with Tania. And I liked the sound of that thought.

On Wednesday — my classes ran on Mondays and Tuesdays this semester — I hurdled to work with Tania's words lingering in my head. The truth was I'd grown tired of the drives to a different area code every weekend. I reflected upon the manner in how to approach the subject the entire way to The Beauty Bar. I texted Heather if she could drop by the spa, so we could talk but she anticipated a new recipe to occupy her day in the kitchen. She invited me to her house instead.

At closing time, I locked the salon and zipped up the street, an elongated one but soon enough, I rounded into the driveway.

"Glad you could stop by your old home," she said and made it even harder for me to drop the question.

"What are you making?"

"Spinach pastries. I hope they'll come out good."

"I forgot that I inherited the taste for spinach from you."

"Where is Little Carl?"

"Big Carl took him to my in-laws."

"Uhm —"

"What's on your mind?" She lifted her head from peeping inside the oven.

"I'm going to ask you something but only if it accommodates your lifestyle too."

"What is it?"

"Are you thinking of going back to work full time?"

"Why?"

"Tania asked me to work with her but I won't do it if you're not ready. The spa is your other baby and if you'd have to hire someone new, I'll stay but if you think —"

"I've been ready to go back to work full time for a while but I didn't want to leave you without a job. Especially because you're in school."

"Really? You don't mind if I —"

"No. If it's convenient for you to do something else, by all means do it."

"Because of the long drives."

"I figured this day would come sooner or later."

"How did I get so lucky to have such good friends? Do I even deserve you?"

"You deserve to do what's good for you."

"See? That's exactly what I mean."

Heather inched closer into a hug. "Do your thing. Just don't forget to come over once in a while."

"I won't, I promise. And if you ever need me to work the odd shift because you need to do errands or whatever, please call me."

"I will."

I handed over the spare spa keys, as if I'd given up a portion of my arm. But once on the highway, I unrolled the window and welcomed the March sunrays. I let the wind breeze through my hair and my newfound freedom.

I sprinted inside the townhouse and splashed the news to Tania. "It's done."

"That was fast."

"Heather was planning to go back to work anyway but she didn't because she wanted me to have a job."

"Beautiful," Tania said, planting three different colour binders on the kitchen counter. "Now let's get to work. Here's the email list for tonight. Then see if you can come up with a design for the flyers for my next event. It's another beverage. They're putting quite a bit of money into the campaign and it has to come out in mint condition."

"No pressure or anything."

"We'll work on the flyers together. The extra pair of eyes is of extreme value to me."

"I'm glad to be valuable to you." And just like that, I'd become my roommate's assistant.

In the morning, Tania opened my bedroom door a crack and called out my name.

"What time it is?" I asked, rubbing my eyes.

"It's wake up time."

I reached over to my phone. "Seven o'clock. Do you ever sleep? This is worse than school."

"Get up. We're heading up to Cape Kay."

"Right now? Today's Thursday, isn't it?"

"A prospective client moved our meeting today. I have to be in Cape Kay by the afternoon. Let's go. We'll get coffees on the way."

"Working with you was supposed to be easier."

"It is," she yelled from the kitchen. "Think of the long drives you don't have to do anymore."

"You kidding me? I gave up the long drives, so I could go on longer ones," I said, rolling out of bed.

"Yeah but these ones are fun filled. And correct me if I'm wrong but there's someone waiting for you at the other end. Someone, I'm pretty sure you're eager to see too."

When I texted with Vinson earlier in the week, he said he'd be busy with visiting relatives. My senses weren't overflowing with joy in relation to this week's trip up north.

"All right. I'm up," I said, on my way to freshen up.

When we pulled into Serena's visitor parking lot in Cape Kay, she waved from the balcony sporting a wide grin on her face.

"You can't love us that much," I said, strutting in the apartment.

"I sure love the company. My boyfriend works way too much."

We gathered on the couch for a girly chit-chat over a glass of red wine and chill-out music, each with a story to tell. Serena, who shared Tania's age, worked as a paralegal and found herself in a two-year relationship with a workaholic attorney, who couldn't commit to moving in with her. Tania dated some dude for a year, whom I have yet to meet and who wanted to marry her but she had trouble fitting him into her schedule. And I had no idea where I stood anymore but I was willing to sail along and find out.

When a knock at the door interrupted our damsel giggles, we gaped at each other with questioning eyes. Serena vamoosed down the corridor and returned within seconds winking at me.

"It's for you."

I rose off the couch and glided to the front door.

"Hi," Vinson said, leaning against the door with his signature smile. "I called your phone. I heard you're in town."

"Sorry, I started yapping with the girls and forgot it in my tote. You heard I was in town?"

"Someone saw Tania's car at a red light. I assumed you came with her."

"Seriously?"

He shrugged his shoulders. "You can't breathe in this town without someone knowing." His eyes bore into mine as he took a step forward. "I wanted to see you. I hope you don't think it's too much."

"No but you said you'd be busy with family."

"Yes but I missed you."

"Come in," Serena's voice echoed from the living room. I pointed my arm down the hall and he obeyed with flushed cheeks.

"Hello ladies." He eased into the couch and talked about his encounters with Serena's attorney boyfriend, who happened to represent his father's company, then asked Tania about upcoming events at The Tavern.

"Speaking of which," she said, "duty calls. You two have fun."

"I'm heading to my boyfriend's for a surprise visit," Serena said.

Left alone in the living room, Vinson's jokes unraveled in his quest to turn my life into a merry-go-round. He was a bilingual, born into a French Canadian family. I pestered him to speak French for the enjoyment of the tone. And the French gust on his lips speckled a sexier vibe on his character, not that he needed the help to boost the portrait I'd already constructed in my mind.

"Keep talking, I like it," I said.

"But you don't even understand."

"A bit here and there but who cares? You sound sexy."

"If you say so . . . but I'll stick with English for now," he said, then pressed on my lips, pulled away and tested my lips again. "How come you never close your eyes when I kiss you?"

"Habit, I guess. But that doesn't mean I enjoy it any less."

"Are you sure?" He pinched my chin and caressed my lips again, sealing our kiss deeper and deeper. "What time are your roommates coming back?"

"Serena will probably sleep at her boyfriend's, it's the only time she sees him and Tania will be back sometime after two. Why?" His eyes gleamed with desire. "No, I can't. It's not my place and I don't feel right about it."

He exhaled into a slouch. "You're right, I'm sorry. I let the mood carry my mind away. Find a movie on TV?"

I handed him the remote. "Movie it is."

We set the TV on a movie we didn't care about and wasted the evening kissing and cuddling on the couch. By the end of the film, I had no clue about the content, the characters or the plot. Vinson's lips and tender touch fired up a sweet arrow inside me, one that I'd never experienced before.

"I should go," he said, gently pulling away. "Where are you on Saturday? I'm visiting friends in Toronto this weekend."

"We might be heading home around the same time. We drove a day earlier for Tania's business meeting."

"Perfect. I'm driving down south on Saturday afternoonish and maybe I could pay you a visit in Brenton City on my way back."

"I'd like that."

The corner of his mouth quirked up. "Let me know."

As I followed him to the front door, he spun and leaped in a theatrical manner to steal an ephemeral kiss.

"Goodnight, doll," he said after slipping into his navy Gazelles. No more steel-toe boots and Adidas never shone so bright on anyone else before.

I flipped through the TV channels until Tania's return, then asked about our Saturday plans with a level of eager I couldn't control.

"Yes. We'll be home by Saturday evening and he's welcome to come over," she said and I hugged her so tight, she could barely breathe.

I couldn't put my finger on whether my friends' will to accommodate my get-togethers with Vinson was out of pity for my pre-Vin deplorable love life or genuine devotion. But it was more than I could ask for.

The next day, Vinson asked early in the day for a get-together later on. "Yes and we'll be in Brenton City on Saturday. You're welcome to come by," I typed. "Great news. I'll call you soon."

But he didn't and I crept in bed dejected. I beat my head against impractical analysis before Serena coiled at the end of the bed to reveal the story of how she met her boyfriend, Kyan.

The phone trill startled me in the sitting position. I scouted the room and blew out my cheeks. I'd fallen asleep during Serena's life story. I craned the phone to my ear.

"Hi, doll," Vinson said, his tone upbeat. Music and multiple voices echoed in the background.

"What time is it?" I asked, groggy.

"Shortly after midnight. Can I come over?"

"Right now? No, I'm sleeping."

"Oh, sorry . . . but if you change your mind, let me know."

"Goodnight," I said, unimpressed and hung up the phone.

Saturday morning, we cruised back to Brenton City and by the evening, we scattered snacks on the coffee table in anticipation of Vinson's visit. Tania opened a bottle of Merlot while I dialed his number to clear the confusion floating around his silence. His voicemail kicked in and I tossed my phone aside.

"I guess it's us, the snacks and the bottle of red."

"Why?" Tania asked while pouring the wine in the glasses.

"His phone is off."

"I'm sorry."

"Don't be. It's his loss," I said, gloomier than I liked to admit.

The first two days of the week passed miserably at school, mostly me shambling from one class to another absent minded. At home, I wrote business emails, brainstormed the design for the flyers for the upcoming event, squeezed in homework and studied before bed. The next day, repeat.

On Thursday, we coasted up north. Vinson shot a couple of casual texts, as if nothing happened. I broadcast my arrival in Cape Kay without mentioning his late call or the forgotten visit.

As soon as we landed in Serena's apartment, my phone rumbled.

"Hi, doll," Vinson said. "You in town yet?"

"We just drove in."

"Can you squeeze me in for a date?"

"I'll get back to you on that. Let me check my schedule," I said, my voice sharp. He paused but his deep breath resonated through the phone line. "I'm kidding, of course I can."

"All right, gorgeous. I'll pick you up at seven."

Suddenly, *gorgeous* shot me back to Zee but only for a second. I shook off the flashback and toyed with clothes to wear.

At seven sharp, I pressed the elevator button but before it caught the chance to ascend, I took the stairs down two steps at a time. In the lobby, I caught my breath and shifted my pace to a stroll.

The eternal dusty dark blue pickup truck waited patiently down-stairs. Vinson's glimmering face welcomed me in the passenger seat. All smiles as usual, pleasant and affectionate.

"Nice to see you, doll."

"Can I ask something of you?"

"Yes, gorgeous."

"Stop calling me gorgeous."

"Someone's in a bad mood."

"I just don't like that word." I did but it belonged to Zee. "Can you keep your word when you make a promise from now on?"

He scratched his head. "Okay?"

"When you say you'll call at a certain time and then call hours later? Or not at all? It doesn't feel good."

"Got it. Keep my word. Where do you want to go?"

"I don't know. It's your town, you pick."

He cranked the key in the ignition while the confusion lingered on his face. He had no idea why I said what I just said.

We rounded into a parking lot and wandered inside a hollow bar. One person chatted with the bartender at the serving bar. The wooden walls, dim lights and giant bellied, bald bartender remin-ded me of the saloons in the classic Westerns where they crashed chairs and tables on each other's heads until the bartender would shoot a bullet up at the ceiling to break the collective fight.

"What would you like to drink? I doubt they have lemon mint green iced tea here."

"Surprise me," I said, taking to a table in the corner.

He returned with two large tomato-red glasses in hands. "Do you like playing pool?"

"I'm not good at it. I'd rather not."

"I'll teach you."

"The game bores me to death, to be honest."

I took a sip of cocktail and contorted my face. "This is the worst Caesar I've had in my life."

My voice echoed a bit too loud for comfort because the bartender and the only other customer in the pool bar turned their heads and gave me the death stare.

"I shouldn't have said that."

Vinson rested his glass on the corner table. "That's not why they're staring."

"But why?"

"They can tell you're not from around here. And I agree with you about the drinks." The stares at the serving bar remained unmoved. "Tell me what you want to do. I'm at your command," he said.

"Let's get out of here."

"Good idea."

In the truck, Vinson's gaze scorched the side of my face.

"Now you're gawking too?"

"Yeah but for different reasons. You're beautiful."

"You're only trying to flatter me, so I could overlook your broken promise on Saturday."

"No, it's true about your beauty. And by the time I made it down south, my phone died. Sorry."

"If you had called earlier in the day, I could've given you directions." I jerked my head. "Never mind. Let's go to Serena's. We have the place to ourselves again."

We picked up snacks and soft drinks on the way and parked it on the couch again. Vinson couldn't shake his gape, even in the living room.

"Why are you with me?"

"Am I with you?" I asked, turning the TV on.

He tipped my body to a horizontal line and kissed me playfully. Then, "You want to be?'

"We should have gone to see a movie," I said, pressing on his chest to sit myself up. "We haven't done that since our first date."

"Why don't we do it tomorrow?"

"Should we do it like a group thing? I'll see if my roommates want to tag along. You can pick us up. Your truck is big enough."

"No problem." He slipped half a smile and I questioned if hitting the movies with three girls in tow was too much for truck boy.

We played a movie again while our tongues danced in our mouths and our laughter leveled out of proportions. He kissed me goodnight and sauntered out of the apartment as Tania stepped out of the elevator.

The next day, I beamed with excitement. The girls happily agreed to join Vinson and me to the movies but Tania wanted to tie loose ends at The Tavern before heading to the theatre.

"Why don't we all go to The Tavern and Vinson can meet us there?" Serena asked.

"I haven't been there in a while. I'll text him," I said.

"Neither have I and I could use a drink," Serena muttered.

"You'll have to tell me about it over one then."

When the three of us strolled inside The Tavern, the sisters welcomed us with hugs, Nikki's warm and tight, Kara's, superficial like ice in the spring.

"I missed you guys," Nikki said to Serena and me. "I love Tania too but I see her all the time."

Kara rolled her eyes. "You love everybody."

"And what's wrong with that?" Nikki said.

"Loverboy is here," Kara said, eyeing the door, then me before retreating behind the serving bar with her sister.

I arched my mouth into a smile with my gaze through the crowd until Vinson stepped closer with a friend in tow. A man we haven't met, a stranger to us. My tight expression must have read like an open book because he approached with knitted brows.

"Hello, ladies. I brought a friend with me. He'll come with us to the movies," he glanced at me, "if that's okay." I hoped the friend joined him for the ride to The Tavern and stayed here for the night. He introduced his friend to us, then loomed close to my ear but shouted through the blaring music anyway. "You don't mind, do you?"

"We made the plans for us four," I snapped and he widened his eyes in pure shock.

"What she's trying to say," Tania said, "is that we don't know your friend and it might be awkward."

"But I just introduced him to you guys."

"Yeah but we don't know-know him," I sneered. "You should've come alone."

Vinson held a disconsolate stare for a moment longer, then dissipated into the crowd, friend tailing behind.

"Don't you think you were too harsh?" Tania said.

"No, not at all."

"I see your point but think about it, he would be the only guy in a group of three girls."

"And what's the problem? I'd go to the movies with my guy and his two friends."

"Yeah but he's a guy. Guys don't function like that."

"Are you done with your loose ends?"

"Yes."

I stepped off the bar stool. "Let's go home. I lost my mood."

"Aren't you telling Vinson we're leaving?" Serena asked.

"No."

We waved a cab outside The Tavern and swarmed inside, Tania in the front, Serena and me in the back.

"Well, that was short lived," Serena said. I glared sideways. "I mean, the night," she redirected, "not you and Vinson."

Once at the apartment, I couldn't stand still. "Do you guys think I overreacted?"

"I'm staying out of it," Serena said. I shifted my eyes to Tania.

"A little bit. I could understand his point of view too."

"Should I call him? Maybe the night is not shot to hell?"

"Give it a try."

His phone rang and rang and rang. I tried again before bed but to no avail. As much as I half-recognized I'd been in the wrong, the way he turned his back on me and my friends shook me.

The next day, Tania and I drove back to Brenton City. Neither of us — Vinson and I — called in the upcoming days. At school, I shuffled down the hallways lost in space again. I drowned in a world of reminiscence about my connection with Vinson and my truncated concentration screwed up my final Advanced Biology test. But I still wrapped up the course in the nineties.

At the library, Zee whipped up his head when I strolled by but I wore my indifference as a crown. Even school, my sanctuary at one point had become too heavy to carry. I craved for the semester to end already. I longed for a break. After four semesters back-to-back, a four-month vacation from school sounded liberating. And I couldn't wait for the summer.

CHAPTER
17

"A re you still coming to Cape Kay with me?" Tania asked, juddering my mind out of daydreaming.

"I guess. What am I going to do here alone over the weekend?"

Thursday night in Cape Kay, I followed Tania inside The Tavern in a pretend-cheerful mood. I painted a superficially unaffected psyche but a premonition of an encounter with Vinson made my heart bounce in somersaults.

The Tavern theme party for the night was April Fools' Day. By midnight, the place jammed up and good time vibes poised the atmosphere. Tania mingled around, carrying the triumph of the event turnout as an invisible halo. The sisters couldn't keep up with the orders and glowed with content behind the serving bar.

I removed my jovial mask and kept to myself in a corner, holding on to a lemon mint green iced tea for dear life. I couldn't even indulge. I was the designated driver for the night.

"What the hell are you doing here by yourself? Come over and socialize," Tania said. "The sisters are asking about you."

"So, according to the theme, should I play jokes on people?"

"Yeah but with your mood, don't tell them you found out their grandmother died."

"This is beyond stupid."

"Are you calling my idea, stupid?"

"No, I'm sorry." I stirred the ice cubes in my glass. "You're brilliant at what you do. It's my mood. I'm just going to sit here."

"Don't worry, Vinson will show up. Everyone in town is here."

"Everyone but him."

"He'll show up. Where else would he go? He's not the stay-at-home type, especially on a night like this."

Serena pushed her way through the crowd with welled up eyes.

"What happened?" Tania asked. "Didn't you go to your boy-friend's house?"

"We got into a fight."

"Join the brooding club," Tania said, jerking her head my way. "I'll be back."

I drew Serena into a hug. She leaned back and wiped her eyes.

"What are you drinking?" she asked, lifting my hand up. "Iced tea? Let's have a real drink. I could sure use one."

"I can't. I'm driving."

"We'll cab it home and come back tomorrow for your car," she yelled through the ear-splitting music.

"I don't want to leave it overnight. What if a drunk will kick it or something? Besides, it's almost one a.m. If I haven't had one by now —"

"I'll get one for myself." I tailed Serena to the serving bar.

"How's your night going?" Nikki asked.

"Good." I half-smiled. "Great turnout tonight for you guys," I said, shifting my eyes between the sisters. Kara darted glances my way as she poured cocktails for patrons.

I scaled on a bar stool next to Serena, who chatted with a man who knew her boyfriend while Tania roamed around to wrap up the night. My heart sunk lower in the grasp that I wouldn't be granted the sweet sight of Vinson after all. Our ethereal beginning ended before it blossomed. My imprudent temper ruined my own chance at happiness and I grew madder at myself by the minute.

Tania raced in breathless from the front door. "Vinson's outside. He's here. He's here."

I leaped off the chair, screaming in glee and jumped up and down in a near-hyperventilating state. Tania hopped with me, holding my hand.

"Calm down. He'll come inside at any moment now." She spun her head to the shrinking crowd at the front door. "And there he is," she said and waded away.

An anxious Vinson rushed to my side and stood still an inch away from my face. "Are you still mad at me?"

"No. Never."

"I apologize for not taking your calls that day but I didn't know what to do," he said with troubled eyes. "I didn't want to let the argument escalate."

"And I'm sorry for yelling at you. I shouldn't have done that."

"OK. Can we move on now?"

"I'd like that."

"Come here." He pulled me into his arms and tightened his grip around me. Then he held me at arm's length. "Let's go somewhere private. I want to hold you in my arms."

I grinned. "I was just your arms."

"I want to lose myself in your eyes, cuddle you and there's too much commotion here."

"You came in with your friends and I don't want to steal you away. We'll get together another time. I'm glad we cleared the air." I promised myself that if we made up, I'd be a good sport when it came to his friends.

"Come on, let me introduce you."

He hauled my hand toward a group of men and introduced them one by one. I couldn't make a word of their names through the music and my exhilaration. They bowed their heads with smiles of approval. And Vinson beamed as bright as the midsummer sun.

"The girls and I will leave shortly. Tania's almost done," I said, scouting around for her. "We'll talk tomorrow." I angled toward his friends. "Nice meeting you all."

"I'll call you shortly."

I nodded and strutted away. I doubted he'd ditch his friends to meet with me. We waved our goodbyes to the sisters and other people the girls knew and retreated to the apartment.

"Ah, silence," Serena said, exhaling through the apartment door.

"My sentiments exactly," I said, falling on the couch.

"I'll make a pot of tea for a chat before sleep," Tania said.

After our bedtime chick-chatter came to an end, I scooted under the covers when my phone buzzed.

"Vinson?"

"I told you I'd call. I promised to keep my word."

"And I appreciate it but have your night with your friends. I don't want to disturb —"

"No, I —"

"I don't want to come between you and your friends again. We could always get together next time."

"No, I don't care if I have to wait for you in your parking lot all night. We're getting together tonight. And I don't care where we are going to be, as long as you'll be next to me."

"I'm in my pajamas."

"Get dressed or come down in your pajamas, however you please. But I'm picking you up in a cab. I'm on my way."

He taxied his way over and waited downstairs.

I clambered in the back seat next to him. "Where are we going?"

"The house in Thunder Hill?"

"Why don't we take my car? I haven't had a drink all night."

"Let's go then."

We spilled out of the taxi as Vinson apologized to the cab driver and slipped him a fat tip.

"Why are we always going to your friend's house?" I asked, scooting into my car.

"Well, I'm living in my parents' house at the moment and I dread taking you there. Not because of my parents but because it's an improvised bedroom in the basement. I don't want to turn you off." I tilted my head while sliding my seatbelt on. "Six months ago, I moved out of a five-year relationship and into my parents' basement. The house we shared . . . my house is empty right now until the post-split paperwork is settled in court."

Had I known he'd spill the beans on his past love life, I would have kept my head straight.

"I didn't mean to pry."

"It's all right. What about your last relationship?"

"I don't like to talk about the past," I said, hitting the road.

"You'll have to tell me eventually."

"No, I don't."

On the drive to Thunder Hill, we'd become oh-so-conversational and playfully fought over who should speak first. We acted like two kids at play, animated and overly enthusiastic to be together.

"I need directions," I said, trying to hold my emotions in place. "I don't remember the way since you drove there before."

"First left, then keep straight." He angled his body toward me. "Alexa, do you know how much I respect you?"

"What? I mean, thanks but where is this coming from?"

"It's coming from here." He tapped over his heart. "Usually, I'm an independent, stubborn motherfucker but you . . . I don't know how you did it but you've got me. You've got me big time."

My own heart skipped a beat but I wanted to play demure. "I want us to take it easy and not rush a thing, like, be friends first, you know?"

"Ohhh, we'll be more than friends." He shifted his eyes on the road. "The house across the street from the convenience store."

When I rolled into the carport, he took my hand and bore his eyes into mine.

"Being with you feels so natural . . . but please, please don't ever play me. I'm begging you. Don't ever hurt me."

"I'll never do that to you. Come on."

Once inside the house, he catered to my comfort like a butler, then he fed Eagle and inspected the cupboards. "There's nothing here. I'll make a run to the convenience store for snacks."

"Wait, maybe I should come with you," I said from the kitchen entryway, cuddling Eagle in my arms.

"Why? You think it's going to be one of those freak moments when a car will run me over, just because everything is perfect?"

"That's exactly what I'm thinking."

"I'll be fine."

He sprinted to the store as I waited by the window and it seemed like forever since he left my side. He returned empty handed.

"The store is closed. The light inside is deceiving. Would you come with me to the gas station a couple of streets over? I don't want to spend another minute without you."

"I wouldn't let you go alone anyway." I eased Eagle into his favourite armchair and followed Vinson out of the house.

"Give me your hand," he said, before we crossed the street.

"Why? There are no cars driving by."

"Just in case. You never know."

"You're funny," I said, giggling. But deep down inside, I understood what he meant.

I heard countless times that when you meet *the one*, you just know. I never believed it. "How would you know?" I always said. But the moment we barreled across the hollow street holding hands in the core of the night, I knew.

We navigated through the peaceful neighbourhood of Thunder Hill, the only two humans on the sidewalk. He decelerated his pace and waved his hand back and forth.

"The connection between us is unbelievable. I never thought something like this existed."

"We're perfect for each other. I already came to that conclusion."

"You don't think I'm crazy?"

"No, not in the least."

We chased each other up the street in a euphoric state and barged into the gas station with bursting laughter.

He opened his arms wide open. "Pick anything you want, baby. The world is yours." The clerk chuckled.

We picked up refreshments and sauntered down the street, hand in hand again. I don't know why we bothered to charge across the street back without a single car in sight. But Vinson came to a stop in the middle of the road.

"What are you doing?"

He cupped my head. "Could you do this with me forever?"

"Yes. Yes, I could."

"I don't care if I live in a one bedroom apartment and eat Kraft Dinner for the rest of my life. I want to do this with you forever."

"What makes you think we'd live in a one bedroom apartment and eat Kraft Dinner for the rest of our lives?"

"It's my way of saying that I'm prepared to face whatever life throws at us, as long as I'm with you."

The intensity of his words raced my pulse through my veins and rushed my blood to my cheeks. The two of us standing on a deserted road in a neighbourhood of Cape Kay at three in the morning, declaring our undying devotion to one another was surreal. Like a scene out of a movie. And I wished it'd last forever.

He kissed my hand. "But of course, I want to give you so much more. I want to give you a palace."

"I just want you. I don't care about the rest. Now can we cross the street?"

We made a run for it in chortles. Then he stopped on the house doorstep to add to the collection of declarations.

"Alexa, if I have to make you laugh until the day I die, that's fine by me. And I want to take you to meet all my friends and family."

"What? We only met a month ago."

"Yes but what's happening here is insane." He stared into my eyes with excitement and fear at the same time. "Do you realize what I'm saying here? I'm saying I have feelings for you."

"And I have feelings for you."

"I usually don't have feelings for someone until much later but I don't know what you did to me. I thought about you every day. No, I thought about you every minute. I even read your horoscope every single day. I was scared you wrote me off."

"Seriously?"

"I wanted to call you on Monday. I had to find a way to get back to you but I wanted to do it in person. I'm crazy about you, Alexa." I held my breath for a moment to let the words sink into my brain. Then he added, "I had a terrible week. I know how it feels to be without you and I don't want to ever go through that again. Please, let's not fight again. And let's not play games. I hate games. Let's not hold back from talking again because of pride."

I tried to douse the burning intensity of the verses pouring out of his mouth before my wits spiraled into insanity. But the truth was, I loved everything about him too.

We wandered into the house and folded on the couch.

"For once in my life, I feel like I'm on the same page with a girl. You know those situations where a guy likes a girl more than she likes him or vice versa?" he said and I nodded. Did I ever. "That's not us, we like each other the same way."

"It's fate."

"Alexa, do you know you're beautiful? I mean, do you really know you're beautiful?"

"What?"

He threaded a hand through my hair. "Have you looked in the mirror lately? Because I can't even believe you like me."

"*Like you* is an understatement," I said, testing his lips.

He pulled away. "Let's make this work then."

His affection astounded me. Tears of joy trickled down my face as words made of sangria kept pouring through his lips like tennis balls out of a tennis ball machine.

"Don't cry, baby. I don't ever want to make you cry. I want to make you happy." His eyes charred into mine as he kissed my tears.

We fell on the bed, kissing to death while we ripped each other's clothes. We couldn't get enough of one another. His lips nibbled on mine and a sensation of heat traced my body. He cradled my frame under his smooth skin while his fingers browsed along my thighs. His sensual touch electrified my flesh and spread frissons on my back.

"You fit in my arms perfectly," he whispered.

I played with his hair. "I agree."

His tongue tasted the sweetest, like the crude acacia honey I mixed in my tea before bed. And his body moved like a snake, up and down my arches, shooting my senses into a pleasure vault.

"You feel so good. I could do this for twenty four hours. Want to try?" he murmured against my ear.

"Stop. You're making me laugh."

Our lips molded into a scorching bliss while his hair patted my cheekbones. Our bodies swayed in unison succumbing to the relish of deliria. He glided his hands down my arms and threaded his fingers with mine as we reached the apogee of desire. We'd become one body, one soul.

We laced our arms against our naked figures and cuddled under the covers for slumber. An indulgent glow trekked from my legs to my stomach and my insides turned into feathers. I might as well have slept on a cloud. Could nine. Because I must have been living a dream.

"Morning, doll," he said as I pressed my legs across his.

"Hey."

"How did you sleep?"

"Do you even have to ask?"

"Yeah, me too."

I rolled out of bed, picked my clothes off the floor and tiptoed to the bathroom to freshen up. He waited for my return dressed up and ready to jet.

"Eagle's fed and in his chair. Can you give me a ride to a friend's house?"

"Sure," I said, petting the putty tat as he licked his chops with content.

We climbed into my car and before I swerved the steering wheel on the road, I glimpsed at the house with affinity. I had no clue who owned that house and I didn't care. I loved that house. It had become our hideaway, a place for devout spills, love and affection.

On the way, Vinson kept up his cheery character, making me throw my head back with laughter.

"Have a good day. Talk later," he said after he kissed me.

He strutted away with his sexy tresses sprawled down the nape of his neck. I adored his hair. I adored him.

Back at Serena's, the scent of brewed coffee awoke my senses from the hypnotic clout of Vinson.

"Grab a cup. I made a fresh pot," Serena yelled from the living room as I made an appearance in the hallway.

"You're here. I'm ready to go," Tania said, coming out of the bedroom. "I packed you too. You're welcome."

"What would I do without my girlfriends? One cup and we'll go."

"Make it fast," Tania said.

"Are you ever not in a rush?"

"No. So, what's the story?"

I sipped on sizzling coffee as I shared my elation with my friends. The girls cheered on my delight but as soon as our empty cups touched the coffee table, we made our way out the door and back to Brenton City.

On Tuesday when I came home after school, a note waited for me on the kitchen counter. "Out doing errands. Pack up. We're heading up to Cape Kay today. In case you wanted to come along."

By the looks of it, she'd finished packing hers. I gathered my belongings and folded them into my mini-suitcase. As I organized my clothes, Vinson texted, "Hi, baby. How are you?"

My skin tingled every time he called me *baby*. He made it sound so good and unique, like no one has ever said it before. "I'm leaving soon," I replied. "Today? I can't wait to see you."

Once in Cape Kay, I texted him from the apartment. He called eagerly, asking to see me.

"No, sorry. I'm too busy for you," I said, my tone stern and he paused. "I'm joking, of course I want to see you." He exhaled. "I have the apartment to myself tonight. We can hang out here."

"I'll come over after work."

Serena's boyfriend, Kyan had whisked her to the Caribbean for her birthday after they made up and Tania hosted an event at The Tavern. The modern dungeon with a view of the marina was our playground for the night. Vinson showed up early evening, waving a couple of DVDs in hand.

"Do people still watch movies on DVD?" I asked with a whiff of arrogance I sensed after I'd already spoken.

"The night is young and I don't want to rely on the TV channels," he said, gliding down the hallway.

"We have Netflix."

"I didn't know," he said, lifting me in his arms when he stepped into the living room. He planted a kiss on my lips. "I missed you."

"I missed you too."

"The days I don't see you are terrible. Nothing seems to work. But we're together now, so that's all that matters." He nudged me closer. "I counted the minutes until I could see you again. I hope I'm not suffocating you."

"Don't worry. The feeling is mutual."

"Yeah?" he asked as we sank into the couch. "It doesn't seem to be the same way for you."

I toyed with his smooth hazelnut hair. "It is."

His eyes dropped to my lips, then he matrixed his mouth onto mine. So much zeal in such a short time touted with the unreal but nonetheless, a blazing heat of passion struck both of us with equal damage to the brain.

He gently leaned back from our kiss and burned his eyes into mine, driving me to mental fuzziness. Shivers darted down my spine as he parted his lips with desire. We dashed to the bedroom, dove on the bed and within seconds, we embarked on a fantasy trip to the love island of Vinson and Alexa. He caressed me as if I was a porcelain doll and I couldn't love his sensuality any more than I already did.

When he snuck in the shower behind me, I could hardly explain to myself the level of comfort between the two of us but it was there, as if we'd known each other for years.

"Is this happening for real?" he said. "I keep thinking I'll eventually wake up from a dream and it will all be over."

"No, it's real."

We showered between kisses, then I hopped out.

"Choose the movie you want to watch first," he said from behind the shower curtain.

Vinson pressed play and joined me on the couch with his arms around me. We chattered about trivial-not-so-trivial topics but the more we attempted to dig up symmetries in our traits, the more differences surfaced.

"I thought you wanted to watch movies," I said, my tone snappy.

He peeked down at my head, resting on his chest. "That's just for background noise. Please, continue."

"So, I like odd numbers. Like, the volume on TV has to be on an odd number, never an even one."

"I like even numbers," he said, gliding his fingertips on my arm. I frowned into my goosebumps. "I was born on May 24th. I'm bound to like even numbers."

"I'm on the 24th too but I still like the odds."

"There's a similarity right there. Our birthdays are on the 24th of the month, even if they're different months."

"Ketchup or mustard?" I asked, hopeful.

"Ketchup."

"Yikes, mustard. See, it's happening again."

Since our first date, our compatibilities kept *piling up* as Vinson said it but not tonight. No matter what one of us said, the other had a different perspective, down to the small and insignificant matters.

"I don't like it Vinson, I really don't. It's a bad omen."

He tightened his grip around me. "That's inevitable, baby."

"No, not to us."

"We're still two people, it's normal to be a little different. Not much but a little."

When I turned my head away from the TV, I met Vinson's gaze. He pinched my chin to face him.

"Baby . . . baby." His whispers melted my insides as my chest rose with rapid breaths. "What is it, baby?"

"It's nothing," I murmured.

He turned me on simply by talking. The sensual tone in his voice echoed with such erotic vibrations, I could have died in his arms.

"Baby, I forgot my contact lens case in my truck." He scooted from under my body and off the couch. "I have to bring it from downstairs, that way I don't have to worry about it later."

I shifted in the sitting position, then up on my legs. "You wear contacts? I'll come with you to hold the entrance door."

"No need. I'll take a bottle of water and put it in the doorway."

I fell back on the couch with narrowed eyes and buckling knees. These words came from the guy who refused to go to the gas station store without me a week before. I aimed my gaze at his phone and as the thought — if he takes his cell — crossed my mind, he touched it and a burning arrow lanced through my heart.

After he pranced out the door, I turned the lights off in the living room and retreated to the bedroom. A considering amount of phone conversation time later, he returned upstairs. I lay under the covers with a textbook on my lap.

"What's wrong, baby?" he asked, crawling in beside me.

"Nothing."

"We both know that's bullshit," he said, seducing me with his gaze in the meantime. He hovered over me and kissed me tender. "Tell me." He tasted my mouth. "Tell me." He cupped my jaw and deepened his eyes in my soul, transfixing my brain to desire. He swayed his body like a serpent, glided his fingers along the edges of my physique and left kiss-imprints all over my body. And despite the scenario, perhaps concocted in my mind, I craved him inside me like bees crave for spring bud pollen.

By the time we arose from our sexual rumble — three of them back-to-back — I'd changed my mind about the trip downstairs. Maybe I did overreact. Maybe it was nothing.

Wide awake and back on the living room couch, we curled in each other's arms for the second movie. Halfway through the film, his turn-down for my company to the truck scuffed at my wits in suspicion. Maybe it was something.

"Are you single?" I blurted out before I could stop it.

"What are you talking about, baby? You know I am, you know my story."

"Can you answer my question?"

"Yes, I'm single. Are you?"

"You know I'm single. And don't turn this around."

"Well, you're not from this town. I don't know if you have a boyfriend in Brenton City too."

"You don't know if I have a boyfriend in Brenton City, too?"

"No, I don't know."

"You don't know if I have a *boyfriend* in Brenton City, *too*?"

He paused for a momentary reflection. "Yeah-yeah, I am. I'm your boyfriend," he said, hugging me coy.

I shifted the topic to a positive note. Too soon for doubts and it'd only cause our affection to lose its purity. I sought to keep it innocent, untainted. I refused to spoil the night any more than I already had. Maybe it was nothing after all.

We stopped the movie before the ending and rushed under the covers. Another smooch session revivified the nocturnal ambience. We kissed ourselves to sleep.

The morning alarm stirred our sleepy eyes into consciousness. He still lay wrapped around me minutes after the galling buzz.

"Mmm, it's so hard to let you go," he said, winding his body against mine.

I kissed the top of his head. "It is." He shot a one eye glimpse at me. "I meant, it's hard for me to let you go too."

"I don't want to go," he yelled, like a child repudiating school.

"Don't go."

"I wish work was that simple." He shimmied out of bed and fifteen minutes later, he granted me one more kiss before tearing out the front door. I rolled over and left it unlatched.

"Good morning. Breakfast is ready," Tania said.

"What?"

"Wakey-wakey. We have work to do."

"Where did you sleep last night?" I asked, groggy and savouring the first sip of coffee at the kitchen counter. I've never been a morning person.

"I took Serena's bedroom. I saw man shoes by the door."

I funnelled a piece of toast to my mouth. "Sorry about unintentionally kicking you out of the bedroom."

"Don't be. Her bed is softer anyway. Now here's what we have to do today," Tania said, pointing to her laptop.

I blew out my cheeks and braced myself for work I was in no mood to do. I hovered over promotional materials for upcoming events with a whinging face while Tania yapped business on the phone. In all truth, I wanted to spend the day in bed doing zilch but daydream about Vinson.

"What did he do to you last night?" she asked.

I raised my head from the laptop. "We watched movies."

"How many movies did you watch?"

"Ha-ha funny. I'm having one of those days. Nothing to do with Vinson."

Tania's nose crinkled before dialing out another call. I wedged my ear buds in my auditory canals and let the ambient music drift into my brain while I worked on promos. Later in the day, I texted bedtime wishes with Vinson.

A good night's sleep was what I needed to restore my energy and the next day, I woke up fresh and upbeat. I even offered to ease Tania's load of business calls, much to her delight.

"Are you coming to the wine tasting event? Tania asked. "You worked hard on the promo flyers. You might as well join me."

"No, I'd rather stay in bed and study. My school is not over yet."

"You know, I like Vinson, he's a good guy but ever since you met him, you stopped coming to events."

"I'm not much of an event goer and you know it."

Tania groaned under her breath and glided to the bedroom to dress up. I scattered my school notes on the bed. Attention to my studies came in order. I'd shoved them on the back burner lately.

"Have fun," I said to elegant Tania as she sauntered out the door.

I hadn't heard from Vinson all day. So, I tapped out a casual text. He retorted, "Getting out of the shower and ready for bed." A dozen flirtatious messages later, we wished one another goodnight. But not before we planned a movie night the next day, his idea. A snuggle on the couch with him sounded like the perfect plan for a midweek get-together and I couldn't wait.

He called in the afternoon to announce later working hours than expected in a drained but affectionate tone.

"I'll make it to your place around ten but at least we'll have a couple of hours to cuddle together. Are you still up for it?"

"Yes. I'll wait up for you."

I waited until midnight with Vinson a no-show. I crept into bed disheartened, especially since I'd made it clear that I loathed being made to wait in confusion and left to draw my own conclusions.

"Hi, baby. I'm sorry for last night, I fell asleep. I'll give you a call later," a text signed by Vinson flickered on my phone display in the morning. "No problem. Call me when you can."

I kept busy working along Tania throughout the day but by the evening, my phone remained silent. And when he left my call un-answered, my stomach swivelled like a blender.

"Relax, he'll call. You know how he is," Tania said.

"Something feels off."

"You're overreacting. The man is tired. He works too hard."

"I'm serious. I don't feel good about this."

Not a word from Vinson came through the next day or the day after. Not a word the entire weekend.

By Monday school, my desolation deepened tenfold. On my way to the library, Zee bowed his head at me from a distant hallway while chatting with a peer. He waved the student goodbye and marched my way. I was in no mood for his antics. I rushed down the stairs and into the library. When I spun my head around, I'd lost him in my tracks. I breathed easy. I dreaded social contact with anyone. Even Zee. I raced out of school halfway through my last class of the day.

Tuesday passed in a daze. After class, I worked on an upcoming presentation with a classmate, then I fled home. I couldn't grasp the reason for Vinson's deadly silence. Didn't he miss me? Didn't he want to see me? Be with me?

"Maybe he's just going through a phase," Tania said.

I shot her an ironic look. "A phase?"

I had to give it to Tania for her effort to generate reasonable doubt and keep me from jumping to irrational conclusions. But I knew better. And so did she.

"We're not going to Cape Kay this week. I'm busy here in Brenton City," she said on Wednesday.

"You're not going but I am."

"To do what?"

"I don't know. I'll figure it out when I get there."

"Maybe you should give Cape Kay a rest."

"I should but I won't."

I asked Serena, who'd returned from her trip, if I could come to her place alone. "Of course, you don't even have to ask. Take the spare keys from Tania, in case I'm still at work when you get here."

Tania handed me the keys. "Be careful."

"I'm not going to war."

"Call me if you need to talk."

The solitude of the apartment in Cape Kay weighed heavy on my shoulders, it dug deep at the roots of my sanity. Minutes after I announced my arrival in a text, Serena called from work.

"I'm sleeping at my boyfriend's tonight and heading to his place straight from work. Are you going to be okay alone? Maybe call Vinson over?"

"There's a problem with Vinson but I'll tell you later. Happy belated birthday."

"Thanks. I could cancel my night with Kyan and come over if you need the company."

"I'll be fine. Enjoy your night."

I delved through the kitchen cupboard and pulled out a bottle of red in triumph, as if I'd discovered Vinson apologizing on bended knee. I dipped into the couch, poured myself a glass and recalled my last encounter with him. I disseminated every word, every glance and every move.

When the wine untied my senses, I picked up the phone and grazed my reluctant fingertips over the keys. "I want to know why. Tell me what happened and I will understand." No response and I drowned my sorrow in wine until I fell asleep on the couch.

The next morning, my phone played dead in my hands with an empty display. Pressed against my poor judgment, I insisted with a text. "That's it? It ends here? Just like that?" Nothing again. How could someone disappear without a trace after declaring his undying devotion?

I dialed his number despite the obvious. I had to know I tried until the end. When he ignored my call, the epiphany cleared in my head that he wouldn't answer anymore. The revelation hit like a blazing truck, shaking my body to the core. I pressed my hand to my chest to annihilate my quivering breaths. My eyes flooded with tears and I let it out. I screamed the emotional pain out of my body but it still hurt like a thousand machetes. Who says, "let's make this work," only to vanish a week later?

Serena opened my bedroom door with a creased forehead when she found me in bed by early evening.

"Is there anything I can do?" she asked after I relayed the story.

"No, it's okay. How was your Caribbean trip?"

"Amazing. It brought us closer. Why don't I put a pot of tea on and I'll tell you about it?" I nodded but instead of leaping out of bed, I slid under the duvet. Only until the tea infused.

I woke up in the morning drenched in my own clammy morose with a cold tea cup on the night table. I levered out of bed and texted Serena at work. "I'm sorry I fell asleep on you. I'm heading home today. Thank you for your hospitality." "No worries. Anytime. Come back soon."

I drove to Brenton City with my heart asunder and disconsolate for failing to solve the Vinson enigma. Tania was right, I should've given Cape Kay a break.

On Monday, I handed in my last Advanced Biology test with relief. I could hardly concentrate on school anymore. I'd grown tired of homework and studying. After a year and a half straight, my academic fuel was running on empty.

After class, I strolled to the library to review my Criminology presentation due the next day. I slouched at a desk and flipped my notes in a daze. I instinctively whipped up my head when Zee's voice traveled to my ears. He stood no more than twenty feet away, conversing with a student, once again pretending to be unaware of my existence.

On Tuesday, I exercised my last resource of enthusiasm to exhibit my presentation on Charles Manson in Crim class. At the lockers, I removed my lock off the encrypted door and tossed the rest of my textbooks, notes and whatever else into my tote. I glanced at Zee's former locker, zipped up my tote and navigated down the hall. I meandered out the college doors and welcomed my summer freedom with arms high up in the air.

CHAPTER
18

At the beginning of May, I was faced with a dilemma. I'd received early acceptance for Bachelor of Science in Nursing and tossed the letter aside in my relentless wait for the Paramedic result. But lately, I've pondered over my slender ability to carry a patient on a stretcher, a requirement of a two-hundred-and-ten-pound lift with a partner in the first year of school. A safe technique existed in place but in the face of self-honesty, my body lacked the muscle mass and strength that paramedics possess. It was a thought I'd shoved in the back of my mind until now.

I stirred in bed night after night. I dreamed of the moment I'd squeeze into the paramedic student uniform since the day I stepped foot at Brimley. Only I could breathe my way into the Paramedic Program, spend days on end and sleepless nights killing myself studying to pass the entry exam and when I finally did, I considered other options. Only I could be that senseless.

In the end, I made a gut wrenching phone call to the college, one that shattered me to pieces.

I jaunted to The Big Smoke to lunch with Maureen, the epitome of a modern woman who juggled a promising real estate career, a solid marriage and motherhood to perfection. She came as a walking encyclopedia in four languages. We could chat about hair products, ancient history and pending political issues at the same sitting. And I couldn't wait to see her.

I parked my car in a spot and my behind on a stone décor by La Rocca's front door. Never a minute late, she stepped out of the car with her mahogany hair, lustrous and bouncy, flowing in the air.

We hugged tight and pranced inside with beaming faces. Then we dissected my emotive troubles over lunch.

"You should have gone for a shrink career," I said and she smirked. No need to search for a top therapist. Just call Maureen, the cemented ballast in my life.

Our lips still rambled as we strode through the eatery doors. We'd need months to spill all we had to say to each other.

"Text me when you get home to let me know you made it safe, okay?" she said in the parking lot as rain drops dribbled on our cheekbones.

"I will. Give me a hug. I don't see you often enough."

She pulled me tight in her arms and all of a sudden the sun shone brighter, even on a rainy day.

"Love you," I said, watching her glide toward her car.

"Love you too," she said, before shutting the car door.

I waved wishing I still lived in Toronto. But one day, I will again.

Three weeks had gone by since Vinson and I made contact last. I tried to forget his sensual portrait but my stubborn mind had other plans. Some days, I swung through lighter moods where I'd conclude that he lost a chance at true love. Other times, the urge to call tickled my fingers to the point where I could hardly fight my own hands off the phone keys. I passed Tania my phone and begged her to hide it in a secret place. Then I demanded it back and fumed with anger when she refused to hand it over.

By mid-May, Tania and I kept busy with local events in Brenton City. I'd mastered the paperwork and business emails and learned to create posts for Tania's new blog. I also honoured Heather's appeals to stand in for a handful of shifts at The Beauty Bar whenever time off came in handy for her.

On her birthday, I treated Tania to dinner at a newly opened upscale pizzeria downtown Brenton City. We settled on the patio overlooking the bay as the music from the clubbing area resonated from two streets over. To our left, the parking lot where I once strolled through with Zee on our way to the apartment-turned-recording-studio was now crowded with sleeping cars.

"What happened to that guy you were dating? I never had the chance to meet him," I said, to break the silence.

"He's long gone. I couldn't find the time."

"Gone? You didn't tell me."

"You had school and Zee and Vinson. Too much on your plate. It wasn't important."

"Speaking of plates," I said as the waitress planted a jumbo veggie pizza on the table, "forget about my crap. Today we're celebrating you."

"Can't argue with that."

After dinner, we sauntered along the boardwalk taking in the late spring scent in the air.

"Let's go home and spark up our own party," I said.

"Good idea. There's a fine red waiting to be opened on the kitchen counter."

I scattered snacks on the coffee table while Tania let the red wine flavour mix with the Freesias' perfume into a sublime aroma. She always set a vase of fresh flowers in the living room. We turned the music up and laughed our way through the night until the booze dunked our bodies into inertia.

On Victoria Day weekend — a time when festivities sprint in a chain reaction in every club, bar and establishment of the kind under the Canadian sky — Tania and I dashed to a club and let loose on the dance floor.

On Monday, Vinson celebrated his twenty eight birthday. At least, I assumed he did. I debated the entire morning, if sending him a birthday greeting fell in the appropriate check box. By mid-afternoon, I shot him a "happy birthday" text with no reply. I'd waited for him to come back to me for weeks on end but on his birthday, I finally accepted the bare reality that he wouldn't. But it didn't mean I'd given up my reminiscing jiffies in bed, late at night with my eyes closed.

CHAPTER
19

One June evening in particular, I reached my lowest point in solitaire. I'd cried myself to sleep the night before, still unable to wrap my head around Vinson's disappearance. His face and his words imprinted in my head loud and clear. I longed to spend one night together to talk it out, to grant me an explanation for closure. Even if he told me an excruciating reason for his vanishing, at least I'd know the truth.

Meanwhile, Ethan's attempts to rekindle our brief relationship fizzled faster than the flickering light of a ninety-nine-cent lighter. He tapped out a few texts to claim he missed me — they all do in the end — and suggested a get-together. "I'm sorry Ethan but our train had left the station long ago," I texted. "What train?" That's exactly why I ended it in the first place.

We talked about school and I bragged about my Paramedic acceptance, skipping the program switch details and hoped he'd rub it in his mother's judgmental face. Then he updated me on his one year Brimley suspension for failing three courses. "What the hell, Ethan? You were so close to graduation." Only a handful of courses, less than he could count on one hand kept him from receiving his college diploma. He worked at a fast food restaurant now. Damn it, Ethan. I hope your momma's proud.

"I'm heading up to Cape Kay," Tania said.

I lifted my head from the laptop. "What?" I heard what she said but I wanted to hear it again.

"Did you finish the design for the promo flyers for next month?"

"I'm working on it but that's not what you said."

"I'll be in Cape Kay this weekend. Are you on board?"

I couldn't decide if Tania dropped good news or bad news. Somehow, I'd found a way to hold my emotions on a string by shifting focus. But the temptation snarled its teeth at me with an invitation I couldn't resist. The event took place at The Tavern, upping the chances of a Vinson encounter. My heart bled in the town of Cape Kay but I could bulldoze my closure out of Vinson's mouth. And that alone was worth the ride. "Yes."

On Friday, we took to the highway and coasted up. The northern we drove, the faster the butterflies batted their wings against the pit of my stomach. When we passed the *Welcome to Cape Kay* sign on the highway, Tania and I eyeballed each other. I took a deep breath as we landed on the off-ramp.

A bottle of Chardonnay on the coffee table awaited our arrival, courtesy of Serena. We nestled on the couch in our ritualistic wine group therapy with plenty of chatter to catch up on.

The next day, I swirled around the house breaking in sweats and nervous laughter. But in the evening, I pranced inside The Tavern flanked by Tania and Serena and cool as a snail.

"You're irrationally calm. Have an energy drink," Tania said, digging a rainbow coloured can in my hand.

"I don't drink energizers. I'll get my lemon mint —"

"I'm promoting this drink tonight. Just hold it in your hand while you mingle for a bit."

"Who said I was going to mingle?"

"I don't suppose you'll be staring at the walls," Tania said, before she strutted away.

"How is it going with Vinson?" Nikki asked as I climbed on a bar stool. "I'm guessing by now the two of you have moved on to more . . . serious things, shall I say."

"Actually, we haven't spoken in a while."

She knocked a cocktail bottle into submission on the serving bar.

"What happened? You looked like lovebirds-united months ago."

"Believe me, I don't even know."

"He hasn't been around here either. I wonder what he's up to. I might know where to find him. Want to come for a drive?"

"Aren't you busy here with the event and all? And no, I'm not going to look for him, it screams desperate."

"My sister will be here soon. Do you want to see him or not?"

"I . . . can't." I feared I'd faint if I looked into his eyes but I still considered Nikki's proposal. I scanned the crowd for my friends.

"They stepped out on the patio."

"OK, I'll go," I said as Kara sashayed behind the bar.

"Go where?" Kara asked with inspecting eyes.

"Wait for me outside. I'll be there in a minute," Nikki said.

"I'll tell the girls first."

I swam my way through the packing mass and by the time I reached the patio, Nikki caught up with me.

"Your car or mine?" she asked. "No, I should drive. I know my way around."

Tania inched closer. "Where are you going? Just stay here, you don't know this town."

"I have to know. I have to know why."

"I can't come with, I'm stuck here."

"I'll go with her," Serena said. "The more support, the better," she redirected when Nikki twisted her mouth, as if to say, what am I, chopped liver?

We ambled out of The Tavern under Tania's scrutinizing gaze and climbed into Nikki's red pickup truck.

"What's with all the pickups? Everyone drives them here."

"You ain't a true Northerner if you ain't got a pickup," she said, swerving out of the parking lot. Serena rolled her eyes. She drove a sedan.

Once on the main road, our route kicked into my comprehension and my heart pumped infinite beats per hour. Nikki drove to Thunder Hill.

"There is a place he sometimes goes to on Saturday nights. I'm thinking he might be there," she said.

Serena gave me the fretful eyes from the back seat. I turned my head to the road ahead, the same one Vinson and I took two months ago. I swallowed hard to fight back my tears.

"Here we are," Nikki said, angling into a parking lot.

I hopped out of the truck with tingling legs and a stomach drowning in anxiety. I hastened my pace toward inner Thunder Hill, then turned it into a gallop in my desperate search for the house where we made love for the first time. It couldn't have been far and every step would bring me closer to my memories, to Vinson.

Serena caught her breath behind me after she hooked on my arm to stop me. "This is why I came along. Can you get a hold of yourself?"

I pointed ahead. "It's that way. The house is that way."

"Okay, it's that way but calm down and let's see what Nikki has in mind. That was the idea in the first place." She jerked her head toward the truck and a pair of hesitant moments later, we traced our steps back to a wide-eyed Nikki.

She stepped toward a building that resembled a dive. "I'm going in." She waved her hand in a circling motion to Serena. "Try to calm her down."

"I'm all right," I said.

A minute later, a crestfallen Nikki stepped out. "He's not here today. Sorry, I was kind of hoping he was."

"Is that a bar?" I asked.

"It looks better on the inside."

"You didn't say I was looking for him, did you?" I asked, opening the truck door. I scrambled into the back seat.

"No, I told them I was." Nikki shifted her focus to Serena in the passenger seat. "Is she always like this?"

"Most of the time."

"I am not," I riposted from the back.

"Only when you're in love," Serena said.

"Only when I'm in love with a guy who vanishes after feeding me tons of bullshit stories about how he doesn't want to spend another moment of his life without me. That's when."

Back on the road, I sank in my tears with my gaze out the window. And when the convenient store unfolded under the sky, a hole burned in my chest.

"Stop the car."

"Where? Here?" Nikki asked.

"Yes. Pull in, on the left."

"At the convenience store?"

"Yes."

Nikki gawked at Serena with eyebrows raised halfway across her forehead. Serena knew about the convenience store, the gas station, the house and the fact that they had become like artifacts at a museum to me.

"Don't ask," Serena said to Nikki.

I hurdled out of the truck and eyeballed the store, as if it was a monument with flashbacks to the night Vinson zipped across the street. The gas station sign shimmered up in the sky two streets back. My tears must have been in the way when we passed it by. I pictured the house behind me and drew in a long breath. I closed my eyes and spun around, then flicked them open and gasped in pain. There it lay across the street, the house with alabaster siding and olive shutters, just like I remembered it.

An army green SUV rested in the carport — clearly the owner of the house had an affinity for shades of green — and the lights shone bright in the house. I raced across the hectic road and slalomed among the honking cars. The world had turned into a blur, except for the wonder house.

My foot touched the sidewalk at the same time Serena clenched her fist into the back of my denim jacket and a few design jewels scattered on the pavement.

Her face flashed fiery red. "Are you fucking crazy? Are you trying to kill us both?"

"This is the house . . . where it all happened."

She stood strong in front of me with her back at the house. "I get it but fuck, what are you doing?" I angled to the right and so did she. "You're not going to the door."

"I have to talk to these people. I miss their couch. I miss their cat. I have to ask about Vinson."

"Can you listen to yourself? These people don't know who you are. They're going to think you're crazy. They might even call the cops. Do you still want a career in the medical field?" My eyes swam in tears. "You have to get a grip here." I threw myself in her arms and wailed. "Cry as much as you want. That you can do," she said, tapping my back. "Let it all out and then we'll go."

I bawled in a hysteric wave, right there on the sidewalk, in front of the memory house in Serena's arms as Nikki looked on from across the street with her eyes the size of onions and her jaw flat on the ground.

When my tear-well dried up, I shambled across with Serena. I flung Nikki's truck door open and crept in the back seat as she tried to control her stunned expression.

"I'll drive you guys home. She's in no shape to go back to The Tavern," Nikki said to Serena.

"Good idea," Serena said.

"Stop talking like I'm not here. I want to go home anyway."

Nikki steered back on the road. On the drive, we kept to ourselves to digest what happened while I chased my demons back into their cave.

In the driveway, I stumbled out of the truck with Serena.

"Get better," Nikki said. "Take care of her," she said to Serena.

"I'm not sick, just a bit overwhelmed," I said.

"A bit overwhelmed?"

"Thanks for today," I said by the driver window.

"No problem. Sorry I couldn't find him for you. We might have better luck next time." She winked and the right corner of her mouth prodded into her cheek.

Upstairs, I faced the windows on the edge of the couch to enjoy the nocturnal view of the serene lake. Tiny boats navigated in the distant water, sparkling into minuscule laser lights.

Serena served two cups on a stainless steel tray.

"I made tea for us, chamomile, to relax us. I called Tania to tell her we're home. She was frantic."

I peered at my drawn face in the tea sheen. "I have to give it to her. She keeps her emotions in check but deep inside, she cares. She's a good friend." I shifted my eyes to a nodding Serena. "And so are you. Thank you for tonight and everything else. You welcomed me into your home when you didn't even know me."

"I knew Tania and that was enough for me."

"I'm sorry for dumping my drama on you." I fetched the tea cup to my lips.

"Hey, what are friends for?" She scooted closer. "Come here." We drew into a hug, then downed our teas in silentio.

Serena dropped the empty cup on the coffee table. "Get a good night's sleep. You need it," she said on her way to the bedroom.

"Goodnight."

I sat in bed, holding the tea cup under my chin and my gaze into the room to reminisce some more until I parched the reminiscing cellar and fell asleep.

The morning coffee aroma revived me from the dead. As I roamed to the kitchen, my friends stopped mid-conversation.

"Look who decided to wake up. What the hell happened last night?" Tania asked.

I poured myself a cup of coffee, sashayed into the living room and as I strained my mouth open, she cut me off.

"Rhetorical question. Serena filled me in on the details."

"Great. Then I don't have to recall them."

"Good to see you're feeling better," Tania said, savouring the last drop of coffee. "Is there any more left?"

"Yes."

An hour later, we voyaged southbound on the highway.

In the following days, I wondered if Vinson heard about my Cape Kay disaster. The sisters and Vinson belonged to the same entourage. They grew up in the same neighbourhood, attended the same school and hung out at the same diners. Someone must have relayed the drama to him. Perhaps, the story reached his ears through the grapevine and he probably concluded that I was a bona fide psychopath.

Tania dreaded to announce a trip to Cape Kay and I wouldn't have blamed her if she secretly planned to forget me behind.

"I'll be fine, no worries," I said.

"Promise?" she asked as we picked our clothes for the next trip.

"You have my word."

Serena welcomed us with wine glasses on the kitchen counter.

"I'll sip on water tonight. You guys enjoy the wine," I said.

"I'd make your favourite — what is it, lemon mint green iced tea? — but I'm missing the ingredients," Serena said.

"Water is fine."

The three of us chatted the evening away as usual. Well, the two of them did, mostly. I nodded with my eyes on the phone. I still hoped Vinson would call after hearing about my Thunder Hill house visit attempt and ask about my well-being but no such luck.

The next day, Tania and I ambled inside The Tavern while Serena retreated to her boyfriend's place for the night. The place jammed with bar goers and music, the atmosphere upbeat.

Tania eyeballed me sideways. "You promised. You know how much I hate drama."

"I hate it too but for some reason, it always finds me."

"It finds you because you let it find you."

"I won't. Besides, there are no more houses to visit. Now let's have a good night, shall we?"

"You look a lot better," Nikki said as Tania wandered into the crowd. I gave her a smile and she pulled on my wrist. "Come on, let's mingle. You need to meet people. I'll introduce you."

I roamed with Nikki around the bar, stepped on the deck and back inside in a continuous social laughter. I nudged Tania's elbow from time to time to show off my good disposition.

I admired Tania for her ability to blend business and pleasure with precision. She never strayed from a business-like mind, even at a party. She was detached. Her work meant fun, the reason why she'd become so good at it. At The Tavern, the busiest place in town, she saw a business opportunity at every corner. She tirelessly charmed the sisters with new marketing ideas, ideas that generated prosperity for both parties. She was the best promoter and event organizer money could buy.

Tania approached with Kara in tow as I climbed on a bar stool at a side table.

"Cheer up."

"I am cheered up, just quiet," I said, peeking sideways at Nikki's sister. "You know these places tire me up."

"These places?" Kara said with a contorted face as Tania trotted away. I gaped at my friend dissipating into the crowd like a six-year-old ganders at his mommy after dropping him off at grade school for the first time.

"No, I like your bar. It's the place to be on Friday night. I meant parties in general, the loud music, the crowded places."

Kara stared at me with a tilted head, as if to study my motions and gestures. She probably giggled inside about my last week's escapade, tried to envision my pity performance and regretted missing the chance to witness my making a fool of myself.

"Hello, ladies," a man's voice said, polite and husky.

I gyrated to a robust man with dark chocolate hair and goatee. Whoever you are, I owe you a drink for saving me.

Nikki perked up beside him. "Alexa, you know Sloan, don't you?"

"Hi, Sloan," Kara said and headed toward the serving bar.

I tapped my chin with my index. "Hi." We shook hands as he bowed his head.

"Can I buy you ladies a drink?" he asked.

I raised my glass. "I'm good. I'm still working on my iced tea."

"I'm okay, too. I still have to run this place," Nikki said.

"Your sister is here," he said.

"She is but on a night like this, it takes two of us. So, have you talked to Vinson lately? I haven't seen him around."

I stirred my head. "You know Vinson?"

Tania made a brief stop by our table, yelped, "oh-boy," and wandered off. Nikki swallowed with concern that she might have opened a can of worms.

"They work together every day," Nikki said to me, then broke away from the table.

"Really?" I asked Sloan.

"I know who you are."

"You do?"

"I met you when you guys first started dating. Plus, he talked to me about you. He's my best buddy."

"We met before?"

"We met here," he pointed his index downward," on April Fools' Day. You two made up after a misunderstanding or something like that. He introduced us but you might not remember."

"Now that you mentioned it, I do. There was a group."

"A bunch of us. It's hard to remember everyone."

I took in a deep breath. "How is he?"

"He's okay," he said, unsure about what to say next.

I almost asked him on impulse to say hello from me but changed my mind on the spot.

"I'm glad he's all right." I fought creeping tears.

Sloan knew the depth of the story about Vinson and me and why he vanished. It was written all over his face in golden letters but I wouldn't put the burden on him to spit out the details.

"Vinson is," I said, swallowing my tears, "the coolest guy I've ever met." I couldn't hold the next wave.

"Oh, I feel bad," Sloan said as he rubbed my arm.

"Don't. It's not your fault."

"No, it's nice that someone feels this way about my best friend."

"Okay, I'm taking over," Nikki said, fresh on her feet. She patted my back. "Do you want to go freshen up?" she asked, then nodded and answered for me. "Yes, you do."

I took her command to the ladies room. I bet Tania snapped at her for reviving the topic of Vinson. But there wouldn't be any drama tonight. Sure, my emotions spiked but the volcano hummed in its mantle and returned to the dormant state.

By the time I returned to the table, I'd waved the burst of tears out of my system. I joined Nikki and Sloan in conversation about life, human existence and reincarnation. I didn't mention Vinson's name. But Sloan did, as soon as Nikki ripped away from the table.

"The thing is . . . he freaked out at the way you felt about him because he had just come out of a relationship."

"He felt the same way, Sloan. He said he had feelings for me. He said he wanted me to meet his family and friends. And what do you mean by 'just'? He told me his relationship ended six months before he met me." Sloan tapered his eyes, either in skepticism or to compare mental notes. "It happened six months ago, right?"

"Yeah but sometimes the end of a relationship can drag on for months," he said and rocks tumbled in the depth of my stomach.

The night Vinson declined my company in his quest to bring his contact lens case from the truck, the trip downstairs could have been tied to a phone call after all.

"But his ex . . . she has nothing on you," he said.

"Oh, yeah?" He nodded like a bobbing toy-dog's head on a dash-board. "But I don't care about that, Sloan. Looks have nothing to do with it."

"I'm just saying. You," he glimpsed down, then back up, "you are exceptional. You can get any man you want."

I chortled inside at the irony. My love life transpired as a disaster and I couldn't have any man I wanted. I couldn't have Vinson.

I put on a brave face for the rest of the evening. Sloan kept mentioning Vinson while Nikki stirred the chat in a different direction. I stayed on neutral grounds and didn't say much.

Before I left The Tavern, Nikki nudged my arm. "I hope you'll show up tomorrow. I expect Sloan to fill Vinson in on his encounter with you." She inched closer. "And he will. Goodnight."

"Goodnight, girls," Tania waved to the sisters. "Who was that guy and why the commotion?" she asked on our way out.

"Nikki didn't tell you?" I asked as I climbed in the driver seat.

"Briefly."

"I'll fill you in on the way home."

I returned with Tania to The Tavern the next evening to wrap up a two-day event. After a night of ear-splitting music in a sweaty crowd, I'd typically devote the next to studying or reading a book in bed. But my eternal hope for a solid conclusion had given me the extra push for a double party-cipation.

"You look like you need a cocktail shot," Nikki's voice echoed from behind. She never bothered with formal greetings and boring small talk. She aimed straight to the point.

"Why is that?"

"I'm sure Sloan relayed the message. Prince Charming might make an appearance tonight."

"Why do you care?"

"Because ever since I've known him, he's been in unhappy relationships. I want my friend to be happy and you're the one who can make it happen."

"I can't do it alone."

"Speaking of the devil," Nikki said, peeking sideways in triumph. My spine stiffened as I pinned my eyes on her face and my heart pounced faster. "You can look. He's at the opposite end."

I rotated my head in slow motion to the sight of Vinson and Sloan across the bar. His grown locks peered out of his cap at the nape of his neck and his energized physique swayed with a cheerful demeanor through random conversation.

I turned my head back to Nikki, who inspected my reaction like a science project.

"He's looking this way," she said.

"Of course he is, now that I turned my head."

"Someone probably told him you were looking."

My heart pumped more blood to my face than it should and I needed to pull myself together. Fast. I spun my head in his direction again and we locked eyes. He waved with a smile and another flush crept up my face. Then he gestured two legs walking my way with his index and middle finger on his palm.

I scouted for an escape, a place where I could come to my senses and regain the ability to talk without jitters. I dashed toward the washroom right before he zipped through the crowd. He jumped in my tracks before I could squeeze through the door.

I gasped as he held my gaze in silence. Up close, his body was scant, unhealthy, as if he'd recently battled challenging times. I fought my tears back at his tarnished physical semblance alone, never mind the tête-à-tête I'd yearn for so long coming true.

"I want you to know that . . . I'm not mad at you," he stuttered.

Strange but his equally high strung nerves put me at ease. His transient lack of self-control spoke louder than words. I'd made a bigger impact on his state of mind than I'd thought.

"Why would I think that?" I asked, calmer than I expected to be.

"You know, because of the way I took off."

I stood still and lost my eyes in his vision. I'd long planned to let him have it, give him the words he deserved for vanishing on me, then give him the cold shoulder. But it all winged out the window at the sight of the shadow of his former self. I raised my eyebrows instead, in my wait for an explanation.

"I had some personal problems . . . and some other kind of problems. I couldn't deal with everything. I wanted to go into hiding for a while." And leave me heartbroken?

I held my thoughts as I still processed the notion of Vinson standing in front of my eyes, flesh and bones.

"How have you been?"

"Take a wild guess."

"I'd like to take you out to dinner," he said, his voice shaky, "if you want." I dug deeper into his eyes, unsure his request bore any weight. I searched beyond the surface of his skin to discover concrete sentiments. "Do you still have the same phone number?" he asked and called it out, area code included.

"You know my number by heart? Yes, it's the same one."

In 2010, the era of high technology, where numbers rested programmed into our phones, I could hardly remember my own. Many times over, I'd blank out and double check my phone info when asked to confirm it along with the address over the phone by some bank or cable company.

"It's good to see you," he said.

"Good to see you, too."

"Come here, give me a hug." He drew my body closer and we froze in the hugging position, immersed in the sensation I wished would last forever. "It's good to feel you again," he whispered, his sensual pant brushing the hair away from my ear.

I couldn't fight my love for him no matter what. It was penetrated in my soul and ran deeper than the seaport of Nanaimo. We leaned back with lingering arms and gazed into each other's eyes some more.

Nikki elbowed my arm. "Tania is looking for you."

"Where is she?" I sauntered behind her and away from Vinson.

"She isn't, really. I wanted to know what's going on."

"We were talking," I said as Vinson joined his friends.

"Don't worry, he'll be here all night. Let him chase you around."

Nikki had a point and a damn good one. I wandered through the crowd in search for Tania who, surprise-surprise, discussed new prospects with some dude wearing a suit.

On his side of the boat, Vinson mingled with friends. We'd glimpse at each other every now and then but soon enough, he made his way by my side. Sloan and Nikki followed.

"Thank you," I mouthed to Sloan. He winked.

Vinson and I giggled as he whispered sweet nothings in my ear. Our faces grazed so close, they could touch but we kept a two-inch distance, just to make it more intense. Then he pretended to whisper and kissed me when I turned my face. His lips were softer than silk. I'd missed every part of his body. I missed him whole.

"What's the plan for tonight? Would you come out with me?"

"We're out already," I said.

"I mean, somewhere we can talk . . . just you and me."

I huffed and rightfully so. "Oh, Vinson."

I should've played hard to get but I'd waited for two excruciating months to see him and I couldn't resist the offer. I figured I'd leave the I'm-so-mad-at-you-for-disappearing-after-all-you-said moral for later.

"I deserve for you to give me shit and I'm here to take it."

"It's not the right place for divulgations," I said.

"Look who decided to come out of the cave and join humanity," said Tania. Vinson saluted her with a lopsided smile, then stepped away to search for his scattered friends. "Don't give in right away. Let him fight his way back to you."

"I'm mature enough to know that."

"Are you sure?"

Vinson rushed back to my side. "Listen, I have to drive a buddy of mine home. I'm the designated driver. But I'll come right back and we'll take it from there together, okay?"

I half-nodded. I held the inner excitement to a low, in case he'd fail to return. But I kept positive, hoping he would.

Half an hour later, my phone rumbled in my back pocket. I picked up but could hardly make sense of what he said against the deafening music.

"Sorry . . . things came up . . ."

"What? I can't hear you very well."

"Call you tomorrow . . ."

"Wait, let me go outside." I held off until I stepped on the deck. "Hello . . .," I said into silence as the voice at the other end had vanished, just like he did two months prior. He'd hung up the phone before he had to explain.

The disappointment, unbearable, numbed my legs into collapse on a patio chair. I winced at my phone. We'd just made up and he already broke our plans. Plans he made himself.

Tania followed outside. "What? What did he say?"

I dropped my eyes to the ground and she sighed away in dismay. I couldn't find the strength to explicate. I didn't need to.

The next day, his call failed to pop on my display and I was unsure if I should be sad or laugh at my own stupidity for believing his lies again. I erased his number from my phone. I dreaded passing his name every time I scrolled through the list for my friends.

A week later on a Friday night, I marinated with Tania on the couch at home in Brenton City. No need to drive to Cape Kay to my relief. Around midnight, I prepared for bed when the red flickering light on my phone advertised a text. "What's up, doll? It's Vinson, at The Golden Casino. Where are you?" Just like that. Like nothing happened.

The Golden Casino spread on the outskirts of Brenton City, about a twenty-minute drive from our place. It was why he texted. He'd driven to the casino on a weekend trip with friends.

I burst into an angry giggle as I read his message over and over. He added *doll* as enticement for temporary forgiveness but I didn't take the bait. I wanted to give him a taste of his own medicine and the taste of his medicine was sour. I dove into bed and pulled on the covers. I stuck my hand out, grabbed my phone and deleted his message along with his number again. Then I rolled back and dozed off to sleep.

CHAPTER
20

Quiet times fanned in July. Except for one weekend, the only one Tania and I drove to Cape Kay.

Serena and friends had been invited to an outdoor birthday party. She'd mentioned it on the phone before our arrival in town but deciding ahead seemed illogical.

On Saturday night, Serena and I dwelled on honouring the invitation. It came through a friend, who'd been invited himself and given the go-ahead to bring other friends.

"I'd love to come but I have other commitments," Tania said, snapping her eyebrows at me.

I shook off the guilt, unapologetically. By now, I dreaded sitting in a corner at The Tavern and watching the door for Vinson to show up. I was dying for a change of scenery and a good time.

"I guess it's you and me then," I said to Serena. Tania shot me the evil eye. "*If* we go. We're not sure yet," I added.

Around nine p.m., Serena received a phone call. We'd been on the decisive edge because the destination called for a half an hour drive to the border of Cape Kay. Not quite enticing when you're bound to have drinks at a party, which meant one of us would have to drink soda.

Serena rested the phone on her shoulder and turned to me. "My friend will drive us there and back."

"In that case, we'll go," I said, scouting the apartment corridor for Tania. The front door slammed shut. "I feel bad but I thought Tania loved her job."

"She does but she got used to us being there too."

"My being there won't change anything. She's always busy anyway," I said, before we scattered to get dressed.

Forty minutes later approx, Serena and I hopped into a car with Todd and Kelsey. Not a romantic couple, just friends. At destination, we leaped out of the car and a bulky man introduced himself as Justin. The birthday boy.

"Hi. Thank you for coming. There's beer in the ice bucket."

"Happy birthday and nice to meet you," I said. Serena echoed my words as we stopped by the bucket and scooped two cans of beer from the ice.

"Come on. Let's head over to the bonfire," said Justin.

"I love bonfires," I said.

"You guys should have been here earlier. I had the party going all day. My yard was jammed packed."

As we approached a group seated around the fire, I feared awkward momentum. I mean, what could be worse for an introvert than attending a party where the only person she knows is her friend? But after the birthday boy introduced us to his relatives, the good times rolled. They treated us with cushy seats next to the fire and more food than we could handle.

Soon enough, Serena and I howled with tears of laughter. There's always an aunt or an uncle or a cousin — this time an aunt — who takes over the party and gurgles jokes the way luggage pops up on the carousel at Pearson. Tales and puns unraveled under the stars with music in the background and plenty of laughter.

Sometime later, a group of people of our generation made their way to the bonfire. Justin's cousin dated the most handsome man Serena and I had ever seen. His name hung in the air as Preston as soon as he darted out of nowhere while Serena and I giggled with the funny aunt. He was well built with dark hair and dazzling brown eyes, a total cliché of the handsome type, the kind you read about in erotica and magazines for chicks. But he was real and shone like a sculpture, right before our eyes. We froze in our seats.

The vibe between model boy and his girlfriend was hostile. She paid no attention to him but me and my friend did. We couldn't take our eyes off, so out of character for us. We both spurned the notion of gawking at another woman's man. But the beer had taken over our brains and this man was immortally gorgeous.

As soon as sculptured boy grasped on our stares, he jumped in the game. At first, Serena and I tried to deter our shameless glances away but when Preston returned the favour, we batted our eyelashes viciously. We hooted our tipsy moods in the patio chairs as stunning dude sat back across the bonfire and shifted his eyes from me to her. By the end of the night, his eyes stationed with me. A palpable attraction drifted in the air, physical and forbidden. But Preston and I pursued the game of the night only to enthrall our senses and brighten the party for ourselves.

His poor girlfriend chatted with her friends without spitting a word at us, not even so much as a dirty look. And if she had, we'd fully deserve it.

Before we decamped, we gathered in a circle for farewell hand-shakes and kisses on the cheek. Justin's relatives started the trend and we happily obliged next to the bonfire. Preston's gaze and firm handshake turned equally mesmeric. The moment his eager lips touched my cheek, I melted like butter inside. We kept it brief like the others and I moved along.

When I headed toward our ride, Preston trailed in my steps. I shook my head and he stopped with regret in his eyes. I waited with Serena next to the car for Todd and Kelsey to make their way from the crowd. Before I leaped in the back seat, I waved at Preston goodbye. He waved back stepping forward. I glanced at his wanting-to-be-oblivious girlfriend to discourage any ideas drifting in his head but I did share his momentary sorrow.

Before Todd sparked the ignition, he spun his torso to me.

"You know what Preston told me before I left? He said 'take care of the blonde'. I think he likes you."

I waved once more as he held my gaze. Then he stepped onto the tire tracks and flapped his hand in the air until we drove out of sight. I smiled the entire way home. I'd never see Preston again but he'd given me the perfect ingredient to spike my disposition.

A harsh cold turned my body to mush the next morning. I'd worn shorts at the birthday party and every time I stepped away from the bonfire, a cool nocturnal breeze turned my bare legs into Popsicles.

I ruled out skipping town before seeing a doctor, so I made a run to a walk-in clinic. Serena advised minimal waiting times at Cape Kay clinics, contrary to a three-hour wait in Breton City. Tania declined to accompany me, said she'd rather pack our bags instead.

I sauntered into the clinic waiting room and breathed a sigh of relief at the half dozen scattered people. After registration with the front desk, I took a seat at the back of the room and picked up an outdoor magazine. A couple of pages flipping through, I tossed it aside and pulled out my phone.

A handful of internet cat videos later, I raised my head when the clinic door busted open and someone hobbled through to the front desk. At first, I thought my cold symptoms played tricks on me but after a quick scan, the reality sank into my weary brain — Vinson.

Now, what were the odds of running into Vinson at a walk-in clinic, on a Sunday morning? When he angled away from the desk, I buried my nose in my phone. In the corner of my eye, he took a seat slantways, facing the front desk. He wore dark sunglasses and a baseball cap, much like a celebrity attempting to hide his identity and I suddenly became conscious of my appearance. I was out of it, groggy and with my hair up in a messy bun, which apparently is sexy if you can to do it right. I never could.

His attempts to hinder his over-the-shoulder subtle peers made his awareness of my presence even more obvious. Luckily for him, my seat at the back gave him the perfect excuse to pretend not to have seen me. I tried to decide if he feared my reaction, had no clue what to say or considered it to be much too early in the day for emotional dealings.

When the front desk called my name, I ambled through a door leading to the consulting rooms with Vinson's gaze tingling at the nape of my neck. Less than ten minutes later, I returned behind the desk with a light prescription in hand.

"Good luck with school," the doctor said. Inevitably, we held a brief conversation about healthcare careers.

Vinson whipped up his head and gawked over the desk at the doctor's regards. I may have not looked my best but at least he caught me smiling.

Back in the waiting room and on my way to the exit, I tapped Vinson's baseball cap visor with my fingers. I didn't know I was going to do it until the moment I did it. He muttered hey but I continued on my path through the exit door.

I hoped for a more notable greeting than a mere hey. I hoped he'd chase me to the parking lot but he didn't. I scrambled into the driver seat and wondered why the inadvertent encounter at the clinic, if nothing came out of it. I pumped the gas pedal back on the road without giving fate much credit but it was a hell of a coincidence.

CHAPTER
21

The first weekend of August, Tania attended an event in a prospect town but I didn't care to follow. Not because I didn't want to join my friend but because I'd grown tired of the new-town-new-people ordeal. I relished the novelty of Cape Kay but I couldn't care less for another destination over the summer break.

I flipped through the TV channels on the couch and mentally prepared for a lazy weekend when Serena called out of the blue.

"Care to join me to the Greek festival tomorrow?"

I joined Maureen at the festival in Toronto many times before but this time, she left for Montreal with hubby and child to visit her parents.

"Sounds good," I said with a whiff of confusion. I figured if Serena would go with anyone, it'd be her boyfriend.

"I usually drive down with Kyan but he has tons of paperwork to go over at the office," she said, unimpressed.

"Why don't you come to my place tonight? Then we'll drive down together in the morning."

"I'll see you soon."

I waited for Serena's arrival with snacks and red wine, the same way she'd waited for Tania and me countless times at her place. We chatted the evening away over glasses of burgundy potion.

"It's weird. Tania's away with work while the two of us are jetting off to have fun," I said.

"It wouldn't be the first time but we'll have to make sure she's included the next time."

I raised my glass. "Definitely ensure of that."

In the morning, we coasted southbound on the highway straight to Danforth Avenue in T.O. Neither of us bore Greek roots but we loved the culture, the music and the food just the same. We strolled around the highly animated streets with joyful people and enchanting music and stuffed ourselves with vegetarian moussaka, squash fritters and spinach pie.

Early evening, we drove back to Brenton City. The two of us fell on the couch to relax with the tube on when my phone vibrated with a phone call. The unsaved number struck a chord of resemblance — no, it can't be him — before I answered with reluctance.

"Hi. May I speak to Alexa?"

"Speaking. Who else would answer my cell phone?"

"It's Vinson."

Serena raised her eyebrows and jerked her head, then my flushed cheeks told her the answer.

"Hi."

"Sorry about that day at the clinic. It was early morning. I wasn't sure it was you," he said. Liar, liar, pants on fire.

"That's okay." It was most definitely not okay.

After his attempt at an excuse for ignoring me at the clinic, he assumed the defense work was done. His voice turned happy and upbeat as usual.

"So, how are you?"

"I'm fine."

"Are you in town?"

"No."

He took in a sharp breath. "Keeping busy?" When his question remained unanswered, he added, "I've been busy myself moving into a new apartment." I'm glad he considered I cared to hear about his news. I didn't. Not in the least. "But I don't want to bore you with the details." Finally. "When are you coming up north?"

"Hard to say."

"Will you let me know?"

I paused for a speedy reflection. "Maybe."

I questioned why he cared to know. He didn't seem to care on our encounter at The Tavern when we reunited two months after he dropped me like the limb of a tree.

"Please. Take care, doll and . . . call me?"

"Bye." I dropped my phone. "Did I just talk to Vinson?"

"Yes, you did," Serena said as the key turned in the front door. Tania surged inside, dragging her suitcase behind. Serena rushed to catch a hug.

"How was the new town?" I asked, coyly.

"Great but exhausting. Please tell me there's something to eat. I'm starving," Tania said, her tone dry.

"There's takeout on the kitchen counter with all kinds of Greek goodies. Feel free to dive in. We're stuffed."

Tania's face brightened as she rummaged through the aromatic cookery bag. "Thanks guys. You're forgiven for having a good time without me."

"Eat up, so we can polish that red begging for attention on the coffee table," I said as Serena waggled her head in approval.

Two days later, sometime in the afternoon, Vinson texted as I stretched on the couch for a minute of relaxation. "Hey, doll. How are you?" I soared to the sitting position with burning cheeks.

"A word of advice from your friend — don't answer right away," Tania said from the loveseat, peeking over the edge of her laptop.

"How do you know it's Vinson?"

"I know the face you make when he texts you."

"I took his call yesterday."

She glided over. "Give me your phone . . . give me . . . give me." She reached for it as I stretched out my arm.

"No, it's my phone."

"I don't want you to look stupid," she said as she returned to her seat empty handed.

"I won't respond now. But I will later." She scowled.

I texted him before bed and he called the minute after.

"I wanted to say goodnight, if you don't mind," he said.

"Are you settled in your apartment?"

"Yes. I still have to put my belongings away but other than that, I'm moved in."

"Sounds like fun."

"Yeah, lots. Goodnight and sweet dreams, doll."

I'd contemplated that when and if he came back, I'd make it difficult for him and let him grind his try at winning me back. But the truth inside me screamed *you're still madly in love with him and you desperately crave his scent on you*.

As I rolled over to sleep, the phone rang again.

"Don't forget to let me know when you're coming to Cape Kay."

"If I'm coming."

"What do you mean?"

"Goodnight."

Two more days later, Vinson called again. This time, we yapped and laughed about silly stories. I'd warmed up on the phone. His consistence impressed me. He repeated the call before bedtime to say goodnight and that meant progress. We'd rebooted our connection and my heart chanted but we kept our conversations light. No dramatic spills, no declarations of love. We carried a natural way of starting over and it suited our moods perfectly.

A week later, I made my way to Cape Kay with Tania. I drifted into my thoughts behind the wheel as we coasted on the highway.

"What are you going to do?" Tania asked.

"What?"

"Are you going to call him?"

"I don't know." I still couldn't escape the uncertainty, the fear of having my heart taken off its hinges again.

"You will. Just be careful. I don't want to see you get hurt again."

"OK," I said as unsure as I was about winning the lottery.

Early evening, we retreated to Serena's and after the usual greetings and hugs, I texted Vinson.

"Do you have plans tonight?" he asked on the phone. His call.

The girls waved their hands, mouthing, "Just go."

"It depends," I said. Answering no, meant eager to see him. Answering yes, meant screwing my chance to see him and kicking myself in the butt, later in bed with my head dipped in the pillow.

"Would you like to come over and see my new apartment?"

"It's kind of a bad idea for us." Against my introvert instinct, I hoped for an outing with friends for an easy restart.

"Come on. We'll sit and talk. Figure things out."

Talk. The magic word for a girl. "Okay."

Close to his place, I decelerated to pay attention to the street numbers. He waited in front of a mahogany house with a beaming face and a summery short haircut. His glinting eyes startled a landslide of emotions inside my stomach. I pressed on the brake pedal in the driveway while his eyes absorbed my visage. He flung the car door open and I stepped out in slow motion to deter my heart from pumping out of my chest. Come on legs, cut the numbness crap out. My love nerves crawled like bugs under my skin.

"Hey, it's so good to see you," he said and tugged me into a hug.

I leaned back. "Likewise."

"It's this way." He led the way along the vinyl siding house wall to a wooden door leading down the stairs. "Hold up," he said and descended the stairs to turn the light on. "Come on down."

He held out his hand for mine on my last step down the staircase. We passed a square lobby designated as the laundry room and he opened a wobbly door in desperate need for repair.

"I'll take care of it this weekend," he said, tapping it lightly.

He'd moved into a bachelor in a house owned by his sister's mother in law. The minuscule apartment emanated coziness, the kind of emotional comfort that brings a couple together in the initial stages of their relationship.

The bed rested against the wall on the left side with the back of the futon at enough distance for one body frame to squeeze through. A russet timber coffee table ran the same width as the futon and a TV had been squashed on a stand in the corner across.

A two-door wooden closet separated the sitting area from a kitchenette posing in modesty to the right side. Despite its unpretentious appearance, I found it perfect and I loved it, just because he called it home.

Vinson opened the fridge as I dropped on the futon. "I apologize, I forgot to buy drinks." He plunked himself beside me.

"It's all right. I should have brought something to drink or even a house warming gift. I'm the guest and I came empty handed."

"Nonsense, I invited you. It should be my treat."

"Debating about it will not magically bring drinks on the table."

"In that case, why don't we order in?"

After he ordered pizza and soft drinks, we chatted to break the first visit fright. Not only did we both tremble with nervous laughter but you could cut the sexual tension with a knife.

Vinson radiated desire and energy. Each time he rested his hand on my knee, my heart skipped a beat. And when he brushed my arm, bolts of electricity spiked through my stomach. Just before the order arrived, he elevated my left leg on his knees and kissed the bare skin on top of my foot. Then he raced to the door while I smelted in my own astonishment.

We reclined against the back of the futon bellies up after we scoffed the pizza. As Vinson lounged in comfort, he raised his bare feet on the edge of the coffee table with toes even cuter than Zee's.

"Why were you at the clinic? I hope nothing major," he said.

"No, just a random cold."

He tilted his head. "A cold in July?"

"It does happen. I wanted to make sure pneumonia was out of the question. It can be sneaky and it can lead to complications."

"All that school is getting to you, making you a bit paranoid."

"You can become a hypochondriac with everything you learn."

"Out of all the clinics in Cape Kay, we both went to the same one, at the same time, on the same day. I can't believe it."

"Why were you there?"

"I injured my back at work and was on medical leave. I went in for a checkup on the recovery progress."

"At a walk-in clinic? That's strange."

"My doctor's office is on the upper floor but she was on vacation and the doctor at the walk-in downstairs substituted for her."

"I see. Are you getting better?" I asked, rubbing his back gently.

"Slowly but surely."

He slouched with his head on my shoulder as his fingers wriggled through mine at the side of my leg. Holding hands in private indoors, a mystical habit I recalled from our last dates. We held hands while we cuddled on the couch and slept in bed.

We sat in comfortable silence propped on one another as our jitters slowly subsided. I withdrew my mind in instant contemplation to process my rekindle with Vinson, the close proximity of our bodies and my hand wrapped into his. I took it all in like a sponge.

When we snapped out of it, the room breezed with laughter just like it used to. In a moment of chatter break, he plunged toward my lips and kissed me and my insides liquefied.

He drew back and shifted his burning gaze from my eyes to my lips. "It's so easy to kiss you. I missed it." Then why wait so long to call? "You're my first guest," he said and his mouth quirked up.

"I thought about that too."

He leaned close and tucked my hair behind the ear as I glanced away, then back at him. "You look beautiful."

I had my fair share of compliments with his name on up my sleeve but I feared my zealous manner would scare him away again. He seemed emotionally braver this time but I refused to take any chances. You're quite sexy yourself, I praised him in my mind.

I hadn't forgotten about the plan to talk about four months ago. I wanted to ask questions, call him out on figuring out, demand reasons for his disappearance. But I was scared to crash the intense vibe between us with solemn words and dreading banter.

"It's really good to have you here." We spoke an inch away from each other.

"And it's really good to be here."

Vinson sprawled on the futon and pulled me close. His sensual face mesmerized me and I drowned in his eyes. He raised his head to taste my lips and I closed my eyes to take it in. Our smooches deepened more and more and my skin tingled under his grip. We wound our bodies against each other while garments flew in the air. His velvet skin against mine shot a ball of heat below the belt and when he slid inside me, he flew me into a world of magic. Our mouths churned one another until we reached the clouds. I rolled off the peak of culmination asking myself — why did I have to miss this heavenly shag for four damn months?

He rested on the futon in delight with my body pasted on top and called me *baby* again. "Yes, baby." "No, baby." I still called him by his name to keep it cool. I gave him a head start on the affection before I'd start on mine because mine would come as heavy duty. We fell asleep naked on the futon, holding hands with our fingers weaved through and our legs tangled up.

A light of dawn slipped through a neglected corner of the shielded window on the upper side wall. When I flicked my eyes open, Vinson's head rested against mine and our hands held still. I raised my head in slow motion and raked my chin against his hair. I tossed two strands off his face and took in the sight of our nude figures, staunched under the covers.

"Morning, doll."

"Hey," I said, my voice soft. "I was on my way to the bathroom."

"Wait. Come here." He swayed his body on top of mine and tickled me into morning giggles. He shimmied off the futon and on the bed with his fingers still twisted through mine. We tittered into kissing and draped our arms around each other, like snakes on prey. Smooching turned to heavy petting and to hell with my plans to freshen up until after the sunrise amorous piece.

Starting the morning with a bang bumped up the day into high gear. Vinson assembled his ATV riding garments for Saturday hangout, testosterone only. We climbed the stairs out of his apartment and stepped on the driveway with laughter. The landlord unfolded cardboard boxes destined for recycling in front of the house and gave us the I-guess-you-two-had-fun-last-night smirk.

"Were we loud last night?" I asked Vinson as I unlocked my car.

"Probably," he said with no sign of regret.

We each drove to the nearest Tim Hortons where I parked to the side while he coasted the drive-thru for morning coffees. Minutes later, he rolled his truck next to my car, hopped out, sprinted to my window and handed me one. Then he slid his head through the opening and kissed me.

"I'll call you later."

"Have fun." I trailed his strut with my eyes until he maneuvered his truck back on the road and dissipated into the traffic.

I smiled behind the wheel, my car static in the Timmies parking lot. It mattered to me that I was his first visitor because from that point on, not only his place would remind him of me but my scent would linger on the futon, the bed and his T-shirt I borrowed to the bathroom to freshen up.

The next day, Tania and I headed back to Brenton City. Vinson didn't call the following day. Or week. I'd have been surprised if he did. I didn't call either. I promised myself I wouldn't until he did. But soon enough, I wondered how soon would *later* be. The anxiety took over my emotions again and insomnia carved at my brain, inch by inch.

Days later, I turned into a ticking bomb and scrapped with everyone in sight, including Tania. She dated a new dude named Hank and to my surprise, she sought my approval. An approval I couldn't give away.

One evening, Tania's new boyfriend took us to dinner. He picked us up in a red Porsche, his cure for battling midlife crisis.

After we climbed into his car, he pointed at my little black Toyota in the driveway and asked if it belonged to me. I answered without modesty. I adored my jewel, fast as the speed of light.

"People only drive what they can afford," said Hank-The-Crank.

I eyeballed Tania from the back but she either pretended not to pay attention or his arrogance didn't faze her.

"I'd drive it anyway. I love the way it sways on the road. I could take it to the races," I said. He pursed his lips with sarcasm and I cringed in the back seat. The guy reeked of conceit.

Over dinner, God's Greatest Gift To Women bragged about every good deed he ever did and I yawned in despair. This condescending arshole spoke to us as if we'd been born yesterday. Tania may have fallen for his false grandeur, only because he had money but I didn't. His pathetic attempts to outsmart anyone in sight, just so he could show off to his new conquest made my stomach turn with disgust.

Tania expected my approval because she emotionally supported me through my rollercoasters with Zee and Vinson. But her new flame's personality hindered even my tiniest will to return the favour. Beside his excruciatingly annoying character, the man was in a relationship with someone else. I kept a polite front and handled his sarcasm in silence but as the days went by, she resented my refusing to socialize with them outdoors.

"You can't expect me to cheer you on dating a double dipper. Why can't you find someone who's single?" I said.

"He is single."

"That's because he left his longtime girlfriend to be with you. Do you think he'll be faithful to you? How can you trust he won't do the same to you?"

"Why can't you be happy for me?" she asked, shooting her usual scrutinizing gaze from the kitchen counter.

"I want to be but under these conditions? How can you sleep at night knowing there's a woman out there crying herself to sleep, just so he could be with you?"

"I can sleep just fine, thank you very much."

"In that case, I have nothing else to say."

I paced up and down the driveway, breathing in the fresh air while I dialed Serena's number. She was familiar with my late divergences with Tania but stayed on a neutral side. I called her for a brightened perspective.

"Listen, why don't you come up to Cape Kay for a few days to clear your head?" she asked. I paused to deliberate. "Still there?"

"I don't want to drop Tania. I still have work to do with her."

"You're not dropping her. You're taking some time away. If you stay, your arguments will escalate and that's even worse. Come over. A break will do you both good."

"I'll be on my way shortly."

I packed up in silence and muttered, "I'll be up north for a while," on my way out. Tania raised her eyebrows but kept quiet as a mouse.

I jetted to Cape Kay and crashed on Serena's couch. After all, her apartment had become my home away from home.

"You two are having a spat. It will pass."

"I'm sure," I said, doting on a fresh cup of coffee.

"I'm flying to B.C. tomorrow to visit my family. I'll be gone for two weeks but you can stay here as long as you'd like."

"Vancouver?"

"Yeap."

"I'm jealous. Vancouver's beautiful. But you should've told me you were going away."

"If I did, you wouldn't have come and you could use some time alone."

"Are you sure?"

"Yes, I'm sure. We've been part time roommates anyway."

When Serena flew away, I remained in solitude. And in solitude, I fell into contemplation. I didn't know when I'd return home but school would follow soon and that required planning.

As I reshuffled the stages of my life on a Friday afternoon, Vinson came in next to settle the eternal confusion about our status. We'd been floating on unsteady waters for months. I called him with full expectations to end whatever didn't exist between us.

"Hi, doll. I'm so glad you called. I had a terrible week," he said, as if our lives could have been more alike.

"Really? Me too."

"I can't wait to see you. When are you coming to Cape Kay?"

"I'm in Cape Kay now," I said, my tone grave, warning-like.

"Great. Can we get together? I have plenty of free time. I'm still on medical leave until Monday. I'll call you in a bit."

"You know where to find me."

He returned the call four hours later to postpone. The reason — having to wake up early morning the next day for work. Then, "I'll call you tomorrow. Sorry about that." I hung up right after *that*. I didn't bother to argue his medical leave. I dumped my phone on the coffee table flustered at my own stupidity. I should have stuck to my guns and give him the heave-ho, even when he answered seemingly happy to hear my voice.

I worked on my laptop on the couch, next to the windows. It was strange to be in Serena's apartment without her but its comfort was soothing. After I finished my work bulk for the day, I emailed it to Tania with business related comments, no personal and she replied with a dry thanks.

I flipped through the TV channels. Five hundred channels and nothing worth watching and I wasn't in the mood for Netflix. Then I scrolled through my contact list. I called Mom, Maureen and Heather. I spoke to my mom and two voicemails. I suck at voice messages. My speech becomes insipid and choppy. And I do enough talking in my head, there's no need to do it out loud in other people's inboxes.

Later on, when the weight of loneliness grew too heavy to bear, I gave Nikki a call. She gave me her number months ago and encouraged me to call on every interaction at The Tavern.

"Hey, girl. It's good to hear from you," she said.

"Really? I thought you might be busy."

"Not overly today. Wanna hook up?"

"Sure. A coffee shop?"

"Screw the coffee shop. Let's go bowling." Her ideas bounced off her head in split seconds. Like now.

"Bowling?"

"Yes, bowling. Let's go."

"I'm terrible at bowling. I can't throw the ball straight down the lane to save my life."

"Who cares? We'll drink cheap beer, wear ugly shoes, throw side balls and talk. You in?"

"I'm in." Her beaming voice lifted my spirits in seconds. I put on clothes in elation and bounced out the door.

We squeezed through the parked cars from opposite sides of the parking lot and united on the steps of the bowling alley. The two of us mingled outside The Tavern once, the day I cried rivers in Thunder Hill. But that day transpired as an emotional blur. So in a sense, I wasn't sure how our get-together would turn out but I was willing to try. It beat staying home alone, straining my brain to death over my life's disarray.

Nikki came as a nonconformist with a petite figure. Her striking dark eyes matched her hair and despite her off the chart spunk, her feminine allure emanated a calm disposition.

On the first game of bowling, we clicked right away. She bore a contagious sense of humour. Our time together passed without a boring moment and before we knew it, we couldn't stop laughing.

"How's Vinson?" she asked, breaking our laughing spell. We sat side by side at a round table with a pitcher of beer and nachos.

"I don't want to know."

She slammed her beer glass on the table. "Again? I thought you two made up."

"We did but that was then and this is now."

"Give it time. It will happen."

"Yeah, sure. I'll wait by the phone," I said, staring at the bowling lane, twitching my mouth. Then when I turned my head and met her gaze, we burst into an explosion of laughter. "It's not funny."

"I didn't say it was," she said and we roared again for a good portion.

"Come on. Let's play."

"I thought you hated bowling."

"I do but it will keep my mind off of how shitty my love life is."

I stuck my fingers through the largest bowling ball in the ball-return and threw it away with anger. It landed in the gutter which prompted another set of laughter.

We played well into the evening and by the time we left the alley, my personal happy score skyrocketed.

I hugged Nikki in the parking lot. "Thanks for today. I needed that."

"I'm happy you called. We'll do it again sometime."

I drove to Serena's place with a smile on my face and for the first time in months, I slept straight through the night.

A week after I bolted out of Tania's place, she called my number. I took a deep breath before I picked up.

"I thought about it long and hard and it's better if we go our separate ways," she said, her tone dry.

"You're destroying our friendship over your new boyfriend?"

"If you can't respect him, you can't respect me," she said, detached. "And he's moving in anyway."

"That's the issue, not my . . . if that's what you want, I hope he'll give you the best."

"It's probably bad timing for you, considering school is starting soon," she said without a remote tendency of sorrow in her voice.

"It is but don't worry about it. I'll survive."

"Okay then," she said, her voice snappy. "I'll drive to Cape Kay tomorrow. I'll bring the rest of your stuff and I'd like the house keys back."

"No problem." Click. Click.

The next day, Tania refused to drive to the apartment. She claimed on the phone, she was in a rush to end business ties in town and I could spare her some time if we met in a public parking lot by the highway. We sure did, like two gangsters engaging in an illegal transaction in a remote location and it gave me a bitter taste that our friendship had been diminished to a farewell on the go.

She stayed in the driver seat with dark oversized sunglasses on while I stepped out of my car and sauntered to hers. She passed me a garbage bag with folded clothes through the window and another with miscellaneous, then pointed to the trunk for my school paraphernalia. After I carried my textbooks and the rest over to my trunk alone, I handed her the house keys and the deal was done. She took off without a word and left me in the dust with my jaw dropped. And she wasn't going to lose any sleep about it.

I scrambled into my car with my stare into the parking lot to let it sink. I wondered if I ever knew the real Tania. My friendship with her would go down in the history of me as the fastest rupture I'd ever gone through.

Back in Serena's apartment, which had suddenly become my only home, my thoughts flew to Vinson. And not in a good way. If it had to be partition day, let it be partition day.

I poured myself a glass of red and gulped it with the same deception in my soul that crawled under my skin for months. I'd reached the point of exasperation in my eternal wait for his phone calls. I decanted a second glass before I picked up my phone and texted away. "I'm not a woman who needs to wait around for a man to call. I'm done playing the waiting game. I'm moving on with my life."

Empowered was the word for the sensation that wildly swam through my veins. I tilted my head back and rolled my shoulders. I lifted a corner of my mouth in a diabolic smile and brought the glass to my nose. I closed my eyes and took in the aroma of ripe grapes harvested in the late fall.

Vinson didn't reply nor would he have had the courage to do so. But my excruciating wait had come to an end and at last, I was pain free.

Cleaning house, a concept my acting teacher taught me during private acting classes in my adolescent years, a time when I filled in as an extra on movie sets on days off from school. American productions, Canadian locations, mixed crews. This astonishing woman, who mentored my steps into my youth for a while, was an American playwright living in Toronto. Her life theory — exclude from personal life people who fail to bring any good to it, or worse, damage it. And that's what I did. I cleaned house of people who didn't give a damn about me and wasted a perfectly good spot in my heart.

A week before school, I registered for Nursing School fall courses at Brimley and coasted to Brenton City to meet with my new landlord. I'd found an off-campus student house online, where I could rent a room across the school period. I dwelled on the notion of sharing a house with strangers at first. But everyone at school did it and seemed to get along just fine. My mind rattled about the way it'd turn out for the introvert in me but at this point, I lacked a basket filled with choices.

When Serena returned from Vancouver, I welcomed her with a bottle of wine on the table. She strolled through the door with a grin on her face for finding me at her place. I updated her on my story with Tania.

"Why don't you move in with me? You won't live at the student house all year 'round," she said.

"That was my idea too. I'd drive to Brenton City on weekdays for courses and return on weekends. I'm used to the long distance drives anyway."

"It's done. You're moved in. I have a roommate now," she said, clapping her hands.

"On a different note, you and Tania had been friends for a while. I don't want to interfere with your friendship."

Serena flapped a hand downward. "She won't hold a grudge for us living together. She can be pretty ruthless sometimes but not to this degree. Listen, why don't you transfer to school here? We have a college and a university in town. Wouldn't it be easier than commuting?"

"It would be but you know how much I love Brimley."

CHAPTER
2 2

Nikki and I pranced to dinner, just the two of us. We bonded ever since The Tavern days and even more after our hangout at the bowling alley. We'd both fallen in love with men allergic to falling in love. Serena had a similar story to a degree but Nikki and I related on so many levels in the men's department, we became confidantes. Our vibe generated good energy and our chat had a natural flow. The topic at dinner zoomed in on the two men who'd taken over our hearts. We irrationally pictured marrying the men of our dreams in a double wedding. Against all odds, two girls can dream, can't they?

On Labour Day, I drove to Brenton City to prepare for Tuesday school. I awaited September school with uncharacteristic dread. A demanding program lay ahead with tremendous work along with sleepless nights and lack of time for a social life and I wasn't mentally prepared. But I told myself I'd take it one step at a time.

I rounded into the double driveway at the student house on Sycamore Drive with jitters. It shone an all-white newly painted exterior and a modern décor inside. The living room opened into a bright space with a minimalist style — a couch with dark grey upholstery, a coffee table and a TV on a stand across. Two students with fuzzies on the mandibula played video games and bowed their heads at me. "Hi."

I passed the kitchen where two steps above the living room level gave way to a narrow hallway that led to the bedrooms. Mine came first on the left side of the corridor, furnished with a bed, a desk and a chair.

I dangled my T-shirts in the closet with a deep loneliness I could hardly bear. I struggled to mentally settle in. The environment was impeccable for student life but all too new for me. I texted Serena, "I don't know if I can do this." "Keep your head up and look forward." But the new setting, hospitable as it was, drained my will to go on. I tried to psych myself that it was something I had to go through. I mean, it was for school, right? On my first night at the student house, I fell asleep curled into a ball.

In the morning, I charged it to the shower across from my room. Silence dominated throughout the house at seven a.m. on Orientation Day, a day that counts as sleeping in, except for first years, if that. I wouldn't have gone either but our presence was required in the Nursing Lab for a signature-nursing-kit swap.

I showed up at Brimley College as a nursing student and with the sense that I hadn't been through the hallways in ages. The four year program would be divided into the first two years at the college and the last two at university. And at the end of the program, I'd turn out a university grad with a freaking degree and the thought gave me an immense sense of pride.

But for now, I strolled through with momentary excitement as much as I could bear but nothing beyond. Butterflies, euphoria, drive, ambition. All gone. I should've beamed with enthusiasm to return to my beloved school, the center of my universe not long ago. But only leftover anguish screamed from the shadow of my soul, engulfing the remnants of my zeal for school. I'd given up my seat in the Paramedic Program, I roomed with students I'd never met, my friendship with Tania had crashed and burned and Vinson and I were history. And I dreaded, just dreaded running into Zee. I lacked the energy to process the emotions required for a conversation with him.

I retrieved my old locker with the notes Zee and I-so-heartily drew almost two years prior still on the two lockers. I slipped a faded smile. Even the locker area, my once ground zero with radioactive heart vibes left me cold in my tracks.

I made a run for the Nursing Lab, waved my student card, signed next to the X and slung the kit over my shoulder on my way out. I tiptoed inside the student house as voices babbled in the kitchen and rushed to my room where I fell on the bed in a pool of agony.

The next day, I wobbled to class hoping the lecture would improve my mood. But I found myself swimming in boredom through the awkward class introductions and syllabus reading.

K building classrooms lined up in the mid-section of two corridors as perpendicular tunnels separated them. As I sauntered to my next class, Zee's shadow appeared through the corridor traffic parallel to mine every time we each stepped at the other end of a tunnel. When the row of classrooms ceased at the corridor crossway, I fled down the stairs to the library.

At the end of the week, I raced to the student house, changed my clothes and coiled my car on the road. On the drive to Cape Kay, Serena's transfer idea mustered in my brain. It would be easier but the downside to transferring was me having to wait a year out and applying for the following academic year. And leave Brimley.

I had grown tired of the commute. I'd lived like a nomad for months, traveling back and forth with Tania and while it was fun and exciting at first, it had worn me out.

Over the weekend, I racked my brain in nocturnal anguish. The idea of college withdrawal, the step back, the easy way stepped on my pride in a way. And the transfer to Cape Kay would drive me farther away from the place I longed to move back to.

Years ago in Queen City, I'd sneak with Maureen on skyscraper rooftops to absorb the beauty of the city scalded in nocturnal lights. Her brother worked atop high-rises and caved in to our rebel urbanites' appeals for the tag along. We stood close to the edge above The Financial District and much to her older sibling's apprehension, fifty-plus storeys high with wide open arms and intoned *The city is mine* at the top of our lungs. Adrenaline rushed through our veins as the metropolis thudded with energy beneath our feet.

My friends in suburbia — the cautious nine-o-fivers — asked the same questions whenever they took a daring Sunday trip to T.O. "How can you live in the city?" "How can you stand the sirens and the heavy traffic?" "How can you sleep at night with all that noise?" On a daintier tone I said, "I'm a city girl at heart. I feed off its vibrant air. I could never live anywhere else." I said it more than a dozen times and yet, here I was moving farther away from my darling city.

After a semi-cold Monday morning shower, I threw random clothes on my back and hobbled to my car, dragging Serena behind for support. She'd called in to work at my request — more like a plea — just this once, because I couldn't do it alone.

I stumbled inside Brimley and headed to the Registrar's Office to fill out the withdrawal's form. I did it in tears. I couldn't fight them back. Despite my detachment the week before, withdrawing from the college that once meant the world to me turned out more difficult than I imagined. Excruciating, in fact.

After I handed over my student card for identification, the receptionist refused to return it to me.

I sobbed in pain. "My card, can I keep my student card?"

"As of now, you're no longer a student at this college. So no."

My precious student card, my pride and joy had been taken away. I lacked the strength to argue that graduating from Pre-Health entitled me to an alumnus status. I'd even received a letter with a sticker for the back of the student card that said *alumnus forever.*

I limped out of the Registrar and across the hallway toward a staircase leading up to a platform in front of one of the theatres. Serena waited for me on a bank, next to a spherical cemented pillar with a tensed expression. I crawled up the stairs, sat next to her, dropped my head in her lap and let it all out. I bawled with chunky tears and violent hiccups. What have I done to myself and my future?

The emotional pain had sent my body in a trembling turmoil, worse than if I'd broken up with the love of my life. My own stupid decision to part ways with Brimley tore my insides apart. The college was the place where I'd grown into an honour student, where I discovered my penchant for science and my appetite for learning, where I loved and suffered, laughed and cried, where I'd designed my future. Letting go came as an agonizing ordeal.

"Let's go to the library," I said when I gained the strength to stand up.

I dipped into a couch next to the bright windows where I spent time without end studying for tests and daydreaming of Zee. As Serena praised the state-of-the-art stacks, I fed my soul with the library ambiance and took a moment to say goodbye. Then I made a solid promise to myself that I was, in fact, going back to school the following year. It just wouldn't be Brimley.

Serena ambled beside me in silence on the way to my locker as I gazed at the corridors, the classrooms and the familiar school spots with a blaze of nausea twirling in my stomach. My heart broke in pieces when I emptied my locker. Just harrowing.

I found it bizarre that up to that moment, I hadn't close encountered Zee. I touched his former locker and mine covered in love notes with my palm in a farewell ritual. These lockers witnessed a bag full of emotions. I closed my eyes for a minute, then opened them and mouthed at his locker, I will never forget you.

We stopped by the bookstore, next to the lobby and after I handed over the plastic locket off my locker — property of Brimley — we herded out the front doors. We drove to the student house where I called the landlord and informed her about my change of plans. Then I packed my belongings and left for Cape Kay.

The strange sentiment of being out of school turned more overwhelming than I'd predicted. Over the summer, I still counted myself as a student but giving up the title altogether came as a disturbing thought. My heart and soul crashed with regrets. After a year and a half of school back-to-back, I had no direction now. I was out of school and out of a job. I'd lost my way again.

Days later, I turned emotionally dead with remorse. I couldn't lever myself out of bed. Serena tried her best to comfort me but I shot the world out and locked myself in the bedroom for days.

As the days passed, Serena uttered outside my door from time to time. "Hey, I'm home." "Stepping out for a bit." "I made you mint tea and leaving it outside your door." "Happy birthday." I snapped my eyes open as she paused her chanting to turn my bedroom door knob and it flung open. "You realize today is your birthday, right?"

I raised my head off the bed. "What time is it?"

"It's after six a.m. I wouldn't wake you up this early if you hadn't slept for a thousand hours already. Plus, I don't want you to sleep your birthday away."

"I'm coming." I forced myself into gaping at the bright side of life. Then I glissaded out of my bedroom with half a smile.

"Happy birthday," Serena said again and drew me into a hug. "I'm glad you're feeling better. I'm off to work now but tonight, it's you and me," she said, holding me at arm's length. I nodded before she left out the door.

I spent the day on the phone with my mom and Maureen, then reading texts and emails from relatives and acquaintances. Even my former boyfriend, the one I'd traded for my trip to Europe tapped, "Happy 25th. Wish we were still together for this," my way. But neither Tania nor Vinson. They played the silent card and I bet Vinson didn't even remember my birth date. Or my name. Or my existence.

"Cheers. To birthdays, friendships and wishes come true," Serena said as she raised her glass.

She took me to dinner at Fusion on the Bounty, her treat for my birthday to the fanciest restaurant in town. I bowed my head and clunk her glass trying to hide the embarrassment of my friend and roommate filling in the spot for the missing boyfriend. But she didn't think it that way.

"My boyfriend's picking us up. He'll drive us wherever we want to go," she said.

"Thanks but you didn't have to bother him for my birthday."

She shrugged my humility off. "Where do you want to go on this fine Friday night? Do you want to go dancing?"

"Hardly. I'm thinking somewhere discreet with soft music."

"Come on. We'll drive around and find something."

After a shared bottle of grape wine from Peru, we scampered in Kyan's car. He turned to the back seat.

"I'm Kyan and happy birthday to you."

Kyan was a man of style with mocha skin tone just like Serena's and Polynesian eyes. I envisioned their future children with his exotic eyes and her kinked hair. They came as the picture perfect couple and I hoped they'd stay together forever.

I shook his hand. "Nice to meet you and thank you for picking us up. I hope it's no bother."

"It's no trouble at all. A friend of Serena's is a friend of mine," he said, glancing at her then back at me, "and I'd rather you two ride comfortable in my car than cabbing it around town." He raised his eyebrows at Serena for directions.

"Let's find a quiet café, something along those lines."

"Actually," I said, prompting both to turn their heads, "let's take the way home but instead of turning left at the intersection, go straight through."

"All right," he said, glimpsing at Serena.

As a given, Vinson popped in my head after two glasses of wine. The coward could have sent me a birthday text, if nothing else.

"Where are we going?" Serena asked and I gave her a lopsided grin until my intention clicked five seconds later. "Are you sure?"

"Yeah."

When Kyan rolled the car to a stop, I leaped out on Vinson's driveway. I kneeled down to his apartment's window. It was pitch black inside and his truck was missing from the driveway but all that didn't say much. He could've left it at a friend's house after a drunken night and he could've been in bed asleep.

I skimmed along the side of the house, then stopped in the night's chilly rain at the wooden door. I'd planned in my head to knock on his door, yell at him for breaking my heart, *thank* him for failing to acknowledge my birthday, slap him even — if the moment called for it — and leave. At least, I'd end my birthday with a bang and give him something to remember me by.

I raised my knuckles close to the door while the rain drenched my hair. I froze my fist in mid-air as the cold drizzle trickled down my cheekbones and shook me back to reality. What was I doing outside Vinson's door chasing broken dreams on my special night? I drop-kicked my sorrow next to his door, then glided back to the idling car.

"Let's go home," I said and climbed in the back seat as Kyan and Serena breathed with relief.

We drove off and into the night, spawning exhaust fumes and dribbling rain in our trail.

The next day, Serena and I sipped on homemade red sangria slumped on the couch and chatting nonsense but I was thinking about Vinson again. He'd become like a bad habit, hard to kick out of my system.

In my most daring thoughts, I contemplated on sending him a text but I hesitated and rightfully so. I feared that ignoring my message would rebound my frustration for the millionth time. But Serena, who'd grown tired of Vinson's unpredictable ways and broken promises, encouraged me to text him this time.

"If he doesn't answer, you're not losing any more than you already have but if he does, you'll get what you want," she said. My mouth snapped open with surprise.

She gave me the impulse I needed. I keyed out a text and nearly dropped my phone when it called back with the big V on the display.

"Hi, doll. Happy birthday," he said, his tone upbeat, as if the last time we spoke was yesterday. But at least, he remembered my birthday.

"Thanks," I said, glancing at Serena, "but it was yesterday."

"In that case, let me make it up to you. I invite you to my place to celebrate it together."

"Only if you promise to make me laugh."

"I come with laughter guaranteed."

I hung up the phone speechless and shifted my eyes to Serena's you-can-thank-me-later chin in the air.

On my way to his place, I still feared he wouldn't be at home as promised less than an hour before. That's how much he'd shaken my trust in his word. But when I curved around the street corner, the truck in his driveway gave me a sense of relief. Rewind to twenty four hours before. My aberrant visit along with the mad speech I'd prepared to spit out before his eyes gave me the shivers and I was so glad I held off my knocks.

I ducked through the rain and made my way to the basement entrance door. He'd left it unlocked and I blew my cheeks out to a greater exhale. I opened the door and descended the stairs in the pitch black hallway. I passed through the lobby with the laundry machines and stopped behind his apartment door. A cocktail of voices echoed from the inside.

I knocked on the door and he flung it open wearing a black T-shirt with jeans and a smile. He introduced me to friends I hadn't met before, then I dropped on the futon next to Vinson. Sure enough, his friends were as amusing as he was. Because apart from breaking my heart — unintentionally, he'd say — his humour lifted me up to the sky.

A dozen socially acceptable laughs later, his friends left and Vinson ordered pizza for a celebration in two. He catered to my needs every minute. The eternal gentleman on every get-together, he made me the center of his world on my birthday weekend.

The energy between us hadn't changed. The time apart hadn't stolen our magic. We embraced on the futon but when he attempted to kiss me, I pressed my palm on his mouth.

"We should talk about what happened six months ago, so we can move on." His expression closed up as he leaned back. "What happened back in March?" My voice dropped to a whisper as I plonked my butt on his lap with my knees enfolding his hips.

"I don't know . . . I just . . ."

He frowned in despair, as if to say, do I have to answer right now? So, I thought I'd pave his way to an answer.

"Our emotions flew to the sky and maybe we should've kept it light but to vanish on me?"

"I freaked out. It was all too much and I couldn't commit."

"Vinson, if I remember correctly, our feelings were mutual. And then you disappeared." His eyes dropped to the floor. "You could have talked to me about it and told me up front what was wrong. And I never mentioned commitment. You were the one who said, 'let's make this work,' remember?"

He plowed a hand through his hair. "I'm sorry." He drowned in discomfort but I figured it didn't compare to the suffering he'd put me through.

"You did to me everything you asked me not to do to you. You begged me not to break your heart," I said, swallowing my tears.

Regret glowed in his eyes as he tucked my hair behind my ear. "I never wanted to break your heart." He brushed his thumbs over my cheekbones. "I'm really sorry. I didn't mean to hurt you. I hate hurting you."

"Don't do it then." He nodded in slow motion. "I have a proposition," I said, optimistic. I wanted to change the tune. Enough sorrow for one day. "Let's be friends for now. We'll get together, order pizza, watch movies and have fun. What do you say?"

His face brightened. "Sounds good." He drew me into a hug as I half-smiled. I gambled with my emotions and sanity but I believed in Vinson's worth.

We slouched on the futon side by side, pretending to watch a movie while our hands found their way to each other's body. He angled toward me and caressed my lips in the most sensual way, sending creeping tingles up my spine.

"The attraction between us is fantastic."

"I agree," he said and kissed me again.

We kissed for hours on end, as if to make up for the lost time. And I could have kissed him forever and a day.

In the morning, I woke up with my legs curled up with his and my head on his chest. I glanced up and met his eyes wide awake.

"What happened?"

"You fell asleep in my arms, like you did when we first met and I didn't want to disturb you," he said, lovingly.

I groaned my way to the bathroom in déjà vu and for having missed a perfectly good night of passion.

"You should have," I said on my way back.

"What?"

"You should have disturbed me."

He picked up his keys off the coffee table with a chuckle. "I guess your birthday weekend, as you call it, wore you out. Besides, you looked so pretty, I couldn't. I played with your hair instead."

"That's what did it. It's been a rough couple of weeks," I said on the way out.

"Tell me later?" he asked as we ascended the stairs. I nodded but when would *later* be?

I'd created a beauty blog. I mean, what was I supposed to do with my knowledge? Toss it in a jar and close the lid? I'd learned from Tania — a money-making machine — the skill to create and monetize a blog. So without expectations, I shaped up my own. I posted articles with tips and tricks to modern manicures and glowing skin and soon enough, I guest-posted on well-established blogs. I even fished a contract to write a bi-weekly article for an online beauty magazine. Temporary gigs, I thought, until graduation. It suited the introvert in me just fine. For now, I didn't have to go anywhere to make a living and I loved it.

On a Tuesday evening, I lounged on the couch for boring TV while Serena made tea when Vinson texted. I didn't expect to hear from him for at least a month. But this time, only two days had passed. I tapped out a short reply and he called ever-so-cheerfully.

"I was wondering if you wanted to come over and watch a movie or if you wanted to go out for a drink."

"I could go either way," I said, trying to sound casual, like his call hadn't disturbed my emotions.

"Let's have a drink first and then we'll go watch a movie at my place. Meet me at The Tavern?"

"See you soon."

I left Serena carrying two cups of tea in mid-living room in my charge to the bedroom to dress up. I rushed out the door and drove through the rain like a mad woman.

Vinson waited for me mounted on a bar stool by the serving bar, chatting with Kara. He was the only customer inside.

"There she is," she said.

"Hi, doll," he said, pulling me into a kiss.

"Your usual iced tea?" Kara asked, her tone unusually warm.

"Yes, thank you." I turned to Vinson and bumped my hip into his chair.

When he invited me for a drink, I thought he was out with friends. To find him waiting for me on his own was a special treat.

"Here you go. Enjoy," Kara said. Then she glanced at Vinson and I questioned if she wished me to enjoy the drink or him.

I climbed on a bar stool and we leaned into each other like two old friends connecting over a couple of drinks.

"You know what I did yesterday? I helped Nikki move in with Brevin," he said.

"Her boyfriend? She moved in with him?"

"Yes. She called me for help to pick up some leftovers while he was at work. I was nearby with my truck. Hers was in the shop."

"I'm so happy for her. She wanted it to happen for a long time. I should give her a call."

"She was . . . ecstatic." His tone changed before *ecstatic* when he clued in to my akin wish. "Ready to go?"

He held my hand on our way out under Kara's sharp gaze. I never knew what to make of this girl. Friend? Enemy? Frenemy?

In the parking lot, he kissed me before we jumped into our cars. We drove alongside and laughed, even raced at times, adrenaline kicking, no different than any other experience with Vinson.

We burst inside his bachelor, kissing and tearing our clothes off. We couldn't keep our hands off each other, we couldn't break away. We dove on the bed and our bodies molded together and our bare skin intensified the head rush. Our tongues boogied inside our mouths as we rolled between the sheets with our fingers woven together. The goosebumps turned to sensual tremors and I wanted to cry tears of joy. I couldn't get enough of him. I could never get enough of him, not in a million years.

Two days later, Vinson blew my mind again with an invite to join him at his place for a movie night. His persistence stunned me to the core. I gunned it to his place, only this time I decided to get creative with our sexcapade. I blindfolded him and made him seek for me around the room while I hid behind the foot of the bed. He found me within five steps and when he did, I drew his blindfolded self into felatio until he could hardly stand on his legs from pleasure.

"Sex with you is amazing," said Vinson in the aftermath, prone on the futon in delight.

CHAPTER
23

I'd gained enough confidence to suggest a rendezvous myself. And when I did, Vinson obliged. Around midnight, I barged into his bachelor pad. He laced his arms around me and fell on the futon, showered me with kisses, hands under my clothes.

"I guess we're not going to waste any time."

"I just want to be inside you," he said. "But I also love foreplay with you, which always leads to incredible sex."

His eyes sparkled like diamonds as he swayed his body underneath me, eager about what would happen next.

"It's both of us, not just me," I said.

He closed his eyes and took in my kiss as he molded his sensual lips around mine. His tongue tasted minty and fresh and I wanted to rip it out of his mouth and keep it with me forever. We stared into each other's eyes in the tranquility of his room, our faces an inch away. For a moment, I had the impression that he fought the words of something important in his throat. A bold statement that I wished upon and feared at the same time. Deep down inside, even good news scared me, which was strange because for the longest time, I'd craved to hear more than anything, I love you.

I'd been back in Cape Kay from lunching with Maureen down south. I was chatting with Serena over a cup of tea to unwind from the drive when Vinson shot a text with an invite to his place.

"I don't know if I should go. I'm quite comfortable here right now," I said, eyeballing the TV.

"You should absolutely not go every time he calls. Show him how it feels."

I reflected for a moment, then bolted for the bedroom to change under Serena's huff. I cabbed it to Vinson's in black track pants, a T-shirt, a jean jacket and running shoes. He waited for me fresh out of the shower and good enough to eat. We lunged at one another and by this time, we'd become comfortably vocal with moans and groans. Halfway through the night, I raised my head to admire his sleeping face.

In the morning, I hoisted myself in the passenger seat while he opened the backseat door, holding his phone to his ear. He was set to pick up a couple of work friends on the way and rushed to clear the abundance of clothes, overflowing the back of his truck.

"Want a hand?"

I turned and swatted my arm toward the clutter. We joined hands in pushing the garments on the floor when a red and white polka dot high heel surfaced to the top. He covered it in haste a minute too late. I twisted back in my seat as an invisible knife sliced my gut into minuscule pieces of squandered flesh. I couldn't mutter a word if I tried. I chocked in silence.

When my mental haze faded away, the shoe had disappeared somewhere in the car and Vinson drove on mute in a mist of uncomfortable silence.

He picked up his coworkers and continued his way to my place. We drove in secret hush while attempts of conversation starters from the back seats scattered in the air. In front of my building, I wished the confused riders at the back and the let-me-pretend-nothing-happened-and-maybe-she-will-believe-nothing-did driver a good day and leaped out of the truck. An inch closer to him would have pushed my nausea to burst into vomit on his face. As far as I was concerned, he could have taken the red shoe and shove it.

I rushed up the stairs with no bother to wait for the elevator and stormed inside the apartment with crumpling knees. I charged past a frozen Serena in the hallway straight to my bedroom, slamming the door behind me.

She sighed from behind the door, "Fucking guy." Then the apartment door banged shut. She'd left for work.

I scuttled in bed and shut my eyes. I wanted to slip away into darkness, the place I'd become so familiar with, it'd grown on me like a second skin. At least, no one could hurt me there.

When I woke up in mid-afternoon, I pushed myself to forget the incident and move on with my day. Piles of work required my attention online, the perfect escape from my heart troubles.

Four days later, Vinson called with his characteristic happy-go-lucky attitude.

"I was wondering if you have plans for later on," he said, sweet as pie.

"Why?"

"I planned a night out with the guys but would love to see you after."

"That's okay. Go with the guys."

"I am but I miss you and would love to see you too."

"Call me when you're done." I should've said no.

My phone stayed silent the entire evening and around midnight, I bounced to bed. His call woke me up an hour later. I let it ring. I understood his social butterfly character and forgetting about everything else in the process but it didn't mean I had to accept it any longer.

And the red shoe mystery still left a bitter taste in my mouth. The image of it was stuck in my head. In the four months I'd waited for him, my instinct told me his disappearance had something to do with his ex. The red shoe must have made its way inside the truck over the summer because it wasn't there when I met him in early spring. Sloan told me she still called him sometimes. He spilled a few pieces of the puzzle at The Tavern. Vinson's ex learned he met someone new and found it difficult to cope with the fact, so she decided to give him a hard time about it.

We never dissected these details. I didn't care to know. Why should I know what happened or didn't happen? I didn't want to poison our sentiments for each other with the past. A past usually has dirt, which is why it becomes the past. I preferred our story, as if nothing else existed before us.

Saturday afternoon, I dropped Vinson a text suddenly missing him. I recalled the positive result on my birthday after I pushed a text into his phone. He called back right away.

"I made plans with my friends but we could get together afterwards." Of course he had plans with his friends.

In the evening, Serena had a proposal of her own after she thumped the fridge door shut.

"There's nothing to eat in the house. Let's go out to dinner."

"I'm seeing Vinson tonight," I said, disappointed. "I wish you'd asked first."

"Is he going to keep his word?"

I curled my lip with a thought. "Hold on." Vinson hadn't called back yet, so I dialed his number to check on the plans. No answer, big surprise. "Get dressed, we're going out."

"Are you sure?" she asked.

"Totally. Let's go."

I'd been stupid so many times when it came to Vinson. But I'd be queen-stupid to turn down dinner with Serena and guaranteed laughs on a Saturday night while Mr Supersocial was out and about.

Serena and I dressed up to the nines and descended downstairs to wait for the cab. No dinner came without a glass of red in our books. As soon as we stepped outside, my phone buzzed with a text. I scooped it out of my tote. "Call me." Call me? Sometimes this dude's audacity bore no limits. Why couldn't he call? Unless he wanted to show off to his friends that I call him, instead of the other way around, which if that, how juvenile! I was done jumping at the chance to be with him whenever he handed me his body on a silver platter. He could sure do a few jumps himself.

"Is that Vinson?"

"Yeah and you know what?" I said, tossing the phone back in my tote. "It's done."

"Proud of you."

En route to dinner, Vinson tapped another text. "Call me back". Strange, because he didn't even call me in the first place. I threw my phone back in.

Only after we settled in our seats, dissected our menus and placed the orders, I gave him a call. Not out of curiosity about his whereabouts but to let him know, I had plans too.

"What are you doing?" he asked, his voice eager.

"Having dinner with Serena," I said, dressed in nonchalance.

"Mmm, what did you guys cook?"

"Oh, no. We're at Fusion."

"Oh . . . I'm still having drinks with friends too. Call me when you get home."

I took my sweet time with Serena chilling in the solid oak high-backed booths while we enjoyed the food, the wine and the pleasant ambiance over storytelling and laughter. I called Vinson from home three hours later.

"I'm still out with friends. I mean, the night's still young, right? Can I get back to you later?"

He still had to be on top, calling the shots. He still had to be the one who made me wait for his call and not the other way around. And I'd grown tired of playing into it.

"Don't bother. I'm going to bed." Click.

Waiting for his phone calls late into the night had consumed my patience. Even friends don't forget to call friends back, if that's what we were.

In a complete paradox, I thought a break would do us good. But Vinson didn't think the same when he called three days later, on an ordinary Tuesday night after I'd curled in bed with a book.

"Hey, doll. Would you like to come over for a movie night?"

"Sounds good and yes, I would."

I galloped out the door. The idea still enticed me. But once in a while, he deserved my cold shoulder to bring him back to step one, the one he'd forgotten about — calling for me.

He left the timber door unlocked and the door to the lobby ajar to help find my way through the dark narrow staircase. I tiptoed through the lobby and inside the apartment. He waited for me freshly showered on the futon with a smile splashed on his face. And as soon as we united, the energy between us sparked like fireworks.

High maintenance, my ex-boyfriend described me as once, not in a financial sense but from an affective perspective. He believed he had to work his butt off to keep me interested and emotionally charged. But to know Vinson was to love him. That's how easy it was for him to hold my rapt attention.

We lay on the futon with our eyes on the TV, our arms wrapped around each other and beaming faces. I never remembered the movies we watched. My mind drifted into fantasy about the two of us living together, our wedding and chasing after our offspring. I wanted to be with this guy for the rest of my life.

"You like the movie?" he asked, rubbing my arm up and down.

I lifted my head off his chest. "Sure."

He pinched my chin and drew it closer. "Yeah?"

"Uh-huh."

Whenever his eyes combed through mine, flurries tickled the seams of my stomach, then batted their way down south, like courteous knights waiting for the king's arrival into the castle.

"Come here."

He hauled me to his level and raised his head off the futon with a sensual vulnerability he hadn't shown before, yearning for my kiss. I shifted my gaze from his eyes to his mouth. His palm caressed the side of my neck while his thumb lost its way across the edges of my lips. The king has awakened and leaped on his horse.

And every time his mouth sailed down my arms, my chest, my stomach, my hips and my thighs, I'd longed for his royal lips back on mine. Our garments slid off and his smooth skin palpated mine. My goosebumps rose to fame until his body's warmth commanded them to retract. He wound his body as if he had no bones, sending off waves of carnal incandescence. We smooched with hunger for each other's flesh. He flipped me under him and when he dipped inside my body, our pulses spiked in a fiery vertigo. His moans urged my synapses into sensual torment high up in the sky until I reached the peak of euphoria and came undone over his kingdom. The king has entered the castle and seized the queen in regal elation.

I flipped my eyes open in the dim morning light. Keys jingled in Vinson's hand, who'd already dressed for work. I raised my torso off the bed with lazy eyes.

"Stay in bed. It's too early for you," he whispered.

"What?"

"Don't worry about getting up now. Go back to sleep. Just make sure you shut the door on your way out."

"Are you sure?"

"Yes, I'm sure. Stay and wake up whenever you want." Was I dreaming?

Before he jetted out the door, he kissed my hair. "Okay, baby. We'll talk later. Have a good day."

"You too." No, it was real. He did go to work and left me at his bachelor alone. I rolled to sleep, smiling under the covers.

Late morning, I freshened up with my mouth coiled into a smile in the bathroom mirror. He called me *baby* more often than not. I loved it but still held back on my part. I strode out of his place and drove home where I dove into my work with an insatiable appetite for creativity.

On Friday, I slipped into my pajamas when he called with a midnight invitation.

"It's late but do you feel like coming out?"

"I'm going to bed and not in the mood for The Tavern," I said.

"I'm at a friend's place. It's low key and I'd like to introduce you."

"Where?"

"You haven't been here before. Meet me in the parking lot at Target. You'll follow my car from there."

It took me ten minutes to get dressed and bolt out the door. We finally parked side by side in a townhouse visitor parking lot and as we united under the October sky, he held out his hand for mine.

"Thanks for coming on such short notice."

I landed my hand in his with a giggle. "You sound like an office manager."

"No, I mean it. It's good to see you."

We strolled to a front door, holding hands. A cheery couple opened the door and I glanced at Vinson with delight. A couple, even better than I thought. I shook their hands in introduction as they welcomed us inside. Lit candles dominated the living room and nostalgic music drifted into the background. We dunked into the couch as Jimmy and Leyla served drinks.

"I'm driving. I'll have a bottle of water," I said to Leyla as she brought a tray of beer bottles.

Leyla, a soft spoken, tall girl with short hair and bangs and Jimmy, a hippish guy with inky-black curly hair and a Zen attitude lived in a place that radiated Feng Shui.

"I didn't know you had friends like this," I whispered to Vinson.

"You mean couples and not the partying kind? I have many kinds of friends. You'll meet them all eventually," he said, cuddling my knee with his palm.

"Do you go to school or work?" Leyla asked.

"I have a beauty blog."

"Ah, the trend of online work."

"It's something to tie me over until I start school again or maybe graduation. I took a year off but going back next year. You?"

She straightened her posture. "Nursing student. Third year."

"Really? That's what I'm going for. How is it?"

"It's hard work and your guy better be understanding," she said, glancing at Vinson, "or otherwise it'll break you apart but it's nonetheless rewarding." She raised her chin with pride. "I'll help you. I'll give you my notes and textbooks."

I yapped with Leyla about academics and everything school related until her boyfriend blurted out a riddle to break the magic bond between us girls. The four of us broke into a good time with jokes, puns and everything in between. When Jimmy joined Leyla in the kitchen to prepare snacks, Vinson swung his hand under my legs and raised them over his knees.

"How come you're so understanding and cool and pretty at the same time?" he asked.

"How many beers have you had so far?"

His gaze shot deep through my eyes. "I'm serious."

"Oh, come on." I swallowed hard. I swallowed my fear of losing him because that's what happened the last time. As soon as the romance weighed heavy on his shoulders, he took off and this time, I wanted to keep it light for a while.

"Ah, you scare me, you, sexy woman, you," he said, threading his fingers through his hair.

"Don't say that. If it's that scary for you, let's hang out and have fun for now, okay?" He nodded and rubbed my thigh with a forced smile but his fearful eyes gave the look of a man falling in love.

I never understood the fear of falling in love. I mean, what's the problem with falling in love? Isn't it amazing to have butterflies in the stomach and know someone else feels the same way? Isn't it incredible to have that warm glow all over your body every time the person you love kisses you and holds you tight? There may be tears, disappointment and heartbreak and nobody wants to experience them but if we didn't, could we ever say we were alive?

"I should take you to meet my dad. You'll love him."

"Okay," I said with my breath caught in my throat. But I couldn't help wondering what title he'd introduce me under. Friend? Girlfriend? Friend with benefits?

Around three a.m., we hugged Jimmy and Leyla goodbye and drove to Vinson's place in my car. The candlelight chat and soothing ambiance had romanticized our night and our moods to the extreme. After we ambled inside his apartment, he stopped in the middle of the room with dilated pupils. He bit his bottom lip before he attacked mine and I gladly let myself fall prey to the hunger of his touch. We undressed each other, panting and moaning. He looked sexy and charming and kissable, like every other time but tonight, he looked his sexiest. We folded on the futon, winding in perfect sync. Our arms traveled in despair up and down our frames, starved for our skin. He ground his pelvis while locked inside me and gasped into my ear.

"Oh, baby. I love to kiss you. And I love your body. I love everything about you."

I ran my fingers through his hair, then pricked my nails into his back, not too deep to hurt but deep enough to heighten the ecstasy. I succumbed under his body's motions, slow but deep and eternally loaded with apocalyptic madness.

We fell asleep on the futon, our bodies naked and glued to each other, our fingers woven together and our legs intertwined. The futon mattress turned soft and plump and I wished time stood still, so I could live this night forever.

On Thanksgiving Sunday, Serena had a dinner invitation to honour at her boyfriend's parents' house.

"Would you like to come to Kyan's parents' for dinner? The invitation is open for both of us."

"That's sweet but I'll stay here and relax. Thank you both."

As much as I appreciated Kyan's intent, it had been less than twenty four hours since my wicked sexcapade with Vinson and I wanted to stay home and daydream about it.

"Happy Thanksgiving," I texted Vinson. "You too. Having dinner with family." Thanksgiving dinner, a family affair indeed but didn't he say the night before that he wanted me to meet his father?

On Tuesday, we found ourselves laughing on his futon over random matters as he swiped his arm under the coffee table. He drew it back with the red polka dot shoe from the back seat of his truck. My giggles came to a stop. I couldn't understand why his smile gleamed as wide as his face.

"Remember this?" The shoe dangled off his index finger and I grounded my jaw. "I'm giving it to you," he said as he forwarded it to me, "to give it to Nikki. You might see her before I do."

"Nikki?" And as soon as I said her name, I clued in with relief.

"Yes. It probably fell in my truck when I helped her move."

"Sure, I'll give it to her." I placed it in my tote with care, as if it suddenly turned into a jewel.

If it only dawned on me when it surfaced in his pickup that it could be Nikki's and was I ever happy I didn't make a big deal about it. I would have looked like such a fool.

"Pizza and a movie?"

"Pizza and a movie," I said as I settled in comfort on the futon.

We breezed through the night the same way we had before. I sprawled on top of him like an octopus, pretending to watch the movie, then later he pulled my chin into a hot and heavy kissing session, which led to delirious sex, which led to falling asleep with our legs laced together.

Three nights later, my phone rumbled next to my pillow while I napped my fantasies away. I flicked one eye open at the second growl and pressed my finger on the display. "You up, doll? Was out with the guys. Just getting in. Would love to see you, doll." I minimized the screen to check the time. Five-o-five a.m. I huffed. I hope you had a good time, I mumbled as I rolled over and drifted back into my sweet morning sleep.

"Sorry if I woke you up last night," he texted in the afternoon as I worked on a post about a coconut oil hair mask recipe. "You didn't," I lied. "Coming over tonight? Much earlier, I promise." Why couldn't he ever ask me out to lunch? "Text me later."

In the evening, he called as I stepped out of the shower and Serena sauntered into the apartment.

"Want a hot tea? I'm thinking mint," she asked, rummaging through the cupboard.

"Make it for one," I said before I answered the phone.

"Hey, doll. I'm at a friend's." Of course he was. Where else would he be, apart from work? "Can I call you back in an hour?"

"I don't know. Try and see if you can," I said and hung up. "Correction. Make that for two."

And from experience, an hour meant three or five or a week or months. But an hour later on the dot, my phone buzzed as I chatted on the couch with my roommate, tea cups empty on the table. "On my way home. Meet me there?" I gave him brownie points for his out-of-character punctuality. "Yes."

He cracked the door open with flaccid eyes and a short smile, then dragged his feet to the futon.

"You okay?" I asked.

"Yeah. Just tired."

"It's Saturday."

"I had to go in to work for a few hours. I didn't sleep much."

We cuddled on the futon with a movie on but he held his eyes on the TV until we fell asleep. No laughs, a few mumbles and most of all, minimal eye contact. I pressed my cheek against the silk of his hair and kissed him before I left him in bed asleep in the morning to rush home to my pile of beauty articles.

On Tuesday, my instinct whispered that he wouldn't call and he didn't. Hard to believe I breathed easy. The nestling nights thrilled my heart but I thought again a break would do us good. I wanted us to miss each other and breathing space would do the trick.

By Friday morning, there had been six days without a sign from Vinson and I'd changed my mind. I didn't want a break after all. I wanted him again, just like before. What was I thinking? As if I didn't know how life without him turned out to be in the first place. As if I didn't know how much I'd longed for him to come back into my life. I'd turned into a nervous wreck again and my heart pounded with fear. The vanishing fear.

Halfway through the day, he finally called and my heart danced.

"Doll? Sorry I haven't called. I've worked long hours all week."

"That's okay. I understand the notion of busy."

"Are you up for a movie night?"

"Yes."

In the evening, he invited me in with a gentle kiss. I flipped through the channels while he took a shower. When he returned, clean and fresh, he kissed me again before he inserted a movie into the PlayStation. Then he dropped beside me and pulled me on top of him while he thumped his back against the cushion. And the thought of having the night ahead to do whatever we pleased buttered my insides with delight.

He shifted his gaze between my eyes, as if he hid a confession at the back of his head. He stroked my hair and kissed me, gently pulling away and then again. He tilted his head sideways and in slow motion against the futon.

"What?"

"I made up my mind. I'm not going anywhere," he said with glinting eyes. A sublime confession on Devil's Night. He tucked my hair behind my ear and my breath quickened. I feared that if I opened my mouth, I'd spoil the moment. "I don't know about you but there's no one else over here and I don't plan on going anywhere," he said, waiting for my reaction.

"No?"

"No. I can't go anywhere. Are you kidding? I'm happy with what we have. But if there's another guy —"

"Another guy?"

"Yeah. If there's someone else —"

"It's never been anyone else. Don't tell me you don't know that," I said and his expression brightened as he drew me to his lips.

My heart burst with fireworks. He'd taken his time to think us through and I believed him. I believed him because this time, we did it right. No rush, no pressure. We shared an easy going mixture between a friendship and a relationship. It was safe to call it a frielationship.

We laughed and cuddled in our chemistry. Our bodies fit in bed as if they had been sculpted for each other, down to the ridges and bumps and the shape of our sexual organs. Impossible not to feel like this was it. I was happy with what we had too, as long as he was consistent.

We rolled through the sheets, bending and tugging our bodies against each other. Our frisky fingers everywhere and our tongues playing *Tag*.

"I want to sneak inside your body and never come out," he whispered.

"And I want to do the same to you." I smiled and ran my lips across his chest.

"You can't do that."

"You can't either."

"But I could try." His eyes gulped me up. "I love everything about you."

"And I love everything about you."

He threw my back against the bed and slipped inside my warmth where he belonged. We grated our hips in unison and devoured each other's lips.

"Oh, baby. You feel so good, I want to be inside you all the time," he panted.

I was drugged by his eroticism and spawned by his charm, his sexual aura and his sensual touch. I was forever doomed to crave for him, forever bound under his spell.

In the morning, I untangled my legs from his and unglued my arms from his body. I kissed the tip of his nose before he crinkled it and trundled over to hug my pillow.

"Bye, baby," he mumbled.

"Bye." I love you, I mouthed as I sauntered out the door.

The next day, Vinson called early in the day to invite me out for Halloween.

"Would you come out with me and my friends? Everyone's going to The Tavern."

"I'd love to but I made plans with Serena."

I ordered with Serena cop outfits online, aviator glasses, handcuffs and all, our first time dressing up for Halloween as adults. We'd been hyped up about this day and planned to flounder our costumes around town.

"Bring her along."

"She doesn't want to go to The Tavern. She wants to go somewhere else, I'm not sure where but it shouldn't be hard to decide considering the options in this town. I'll come over after, if —"

"Yes, of course. I'd love that. But I'll keep an eye out for you at The Tavern, just in case."

Serena and I marched to our bedrooms to jump into the Halloween outfits but left the doors open. Our bedroom doors stayed open at all times, even when we slept at night, as long as neither of us had company made of testosterone.

"Ready?" I yelled from my bedroom, still scanning my attire in the standing mirror, police peaked cap with a badge tipped to the side. Mumbling words drifted out of the next room. I glided to the door as Serena threw her phone on the bed, then herself. "What's wrong?"

"My boyfriend's being an ass. I was supposed to go over later but he wants to go to bed." She mocked his voice. "He has to get up early tomorrow. So do I but you don't hear me complain."

"Why don't you go now? I bet that if you'll wear this outfit, he'll forget about sleep altogether." I'd planned on wearing mine to Vinson's and use the handcuffs on him for the first time.

"I wanted to go out with you first. That's why we ordered these, right?" she said, flipping a see-through bag with cop glasses, fingerless gloves and a glossy belt. "But he completely ruined my mood."

I sat on the bed next to her. "You'll feel much better when we'll go out."

"I don't even like the way this costume looks on me. It's stupid."

"You're only saying that because you're upset. It looks sexy on you and you know it."

"That's okay. You go. I don't feel like partying anymore."

"We've planned this for weeks. I'm not going out without you."

"I'm sure you'll run into Vinson somewhere."

"He asked if we were going to The Tavern."

"No, thanks. You go. I'll just put on a movie."

"And what kind of friend would I be, if I let you do that alone?" She slipped a faded smile. "Movie and popcorn then?"

"You'll prep the movie, I'll bring the popcorn."

I slipped out of the cop suit and tossed it in the closet. I put on pajamas, wiped off my makeup, fixed my hair in a bun and sprinted to the kitchen to scoop a bag of extra-large original popcorn. No flavours. I emptied the bag into a bowl and placed it on the coffee table along with a bottle of red.

"Wine doesn't really go with popcorn but —"

"It does if you want it to," Serena said with a smirk on her face. I dunked into the couch to the fourth installment of Halloween. "I'm sorry for spoiling our night," she said as she poured the wine.

"Stop it. I love this." I pressed the bowl between our thighs, then wrapped my fingers around the glass. "Cheers."

Around one in the morning, after Serena and I devoured the popcorn and polished three quarters of the wine bottle, my phone roared. I picked it up with a lazy hand. "Hey, doll. Still up?" Vinson texted. "Yes." "Too late for a visit at my place?" "We're on a Halloween marathon, chilling in pjs on the couch. Next time, okay?" And just like that, I turned him down for the first time and I wasn't even worried about it. Serena had fallen asleep on the couch but nothing could drag me away from my contented state. I tossed the phone on the cushion, poured the leftover wine and slouched back to finish the seventh installment of Halloween.

*

I kicked off the bed sheets at dawn and took to the highway. Just me, my car, my music and my inner thoughts conquering the wide-wide road southbound to The 6ix.

I lunched with Maureen at La Rocca, bathing in our shared enjoyment over gossip, fresh coffee and all day breakfast. A couple of hours later, I climbed behind the wheel hyped up on Maureen's portion of happy hormones, exuded contagious and raw that boosted my brain cells into motion. No one could understand the point of taking a trip to another city for the sole purpose of dining with my best friend but she was worth every mile on the odometer.

En route northbound, I swerved on the off-ramp and stopped in Brenton City for gas. As my car sucked up the juice, I took in the sight of the peak of my beloved college in the far distance. I held the pump nozzle in the filler neck and slipped a grin when the idea of a visit sparked in my head. I missed it big time.

I veered into Brimley campus, swallowing my tears. My heart ached from the moment I stepped foot inside. I strolled down the hall and lingered by my old locker and Zee's to reminisce, however troubled then, I realized now, they were some of the most memorable moments of my life. But this zone of explosive emotions had chilled without my touch.

Someone else had taken over my locker and left Zee's old scribbles on it. I half-smiled. My love notes were visible on his too but new engraving gleamed near one of mine. "Have a good day, handsome," read one of my old cursives in pencil and underneath, someone wrote, "You too, beautiful". I frowned in my thought — Zee. He must have written it after my withdrawal because I'd have noted it otherwise. It read like his cocktail lingo. Oh, Zeke. How late. So late. Too late. When my absence from school finally sunk in, he took a step forward.

I rounded the corner and continued my wander on the corridors with a hole in my heart. I fretted my way to the library and did a walk around. I didn't sit. I couldn't. It hurt too much. I stood near the exit and scanned the library searching for Zee, unconsciously maybe, while I absorbed the atmosphere. Students worked on assignments and socialized as usual but no sight of Zee.

I ambled out of the library with my heart on a stick and my mind on rewind and sauntered through the locker area on my way out. I'll visit again soon, I promise, I mouthed with eyes transfixed on the Brimley architecture before I leaped inside the car.

On my way to Cape Kay, the analytical me turned the you-too-beautiful note sideways and over in my head. After all, Zee played his part in my college experience and his new message deserved deep thought. He was bound to miss me in the end.

When Tuesday rolled through, I hoped Vinson would call. He texted after midnight when I'd already snuck in bed, ready to fall asleep. "Doll, you awake?" Jesus Christ, why always at this hour? I hesitated but a moment later, the phone buzzed with a call.

"Yeah?"

"May I speak to Miss Alexa, please?" he asked, his tone upbeat.

"She's not in right now. Can I take a message?"

"Ha-ha, you think you're funny?"

"Maybe not but you're way too lively for this hour. I'm hanging up." I hoped he'd call but not after midnight.

"Wait, don't hang up. I'm at a friend's house close to your place. Why don't you come by?"

"Right now? I'm in bed and would like to go to sleep, that's why."

"I miss you," he said and we both paused. Then, "It'll take you less than a minute to get dressed."

"That's what you think. It'll take me two."

"I'll text you the address and wait for you outside the front door."

He did wait for me on the doorsteps and when I stepped out of my car, our longing eyes locked, as if we hadn't seen each other in years.

"Come in," he said, slinging his arm around my shoulder.

Inside the house, two friends shook my hand after Vinson intro-duced me. We sat on the couch close together and he lifted my legs across his knees, the same way he did at Jimmy and Leyla's. The host offered me a beer but I shook my head.

"That's okay. I'll just sit here and watch you guys talk."

Vinson swirled his head at me with a smile lit on his face. He rubbed and gripped my legs while he yapped with his friends about sports and other boys' topics. I snuggled into the slope of his shoulder without registering the details of their conversation. Funny how leg rubs annoyed me when Ethan did it but my body melted under Vinson's touch. I guess, it's a matter of who and how.

"Do you want to go?" Vinson asked about an hour into my visit. I'd nearly landed in dreamland next to him. I nodded and we rose off the couch. "Sorry about keeping you up late," he said as we strolled out of the house.

"As long as I'm with you, I don't care," I said, peeking above the top of my car before I unlocked the door. He climbed into the passenger seat with a frown on his face. What? Too strong of a statement? Damn.

At his place, I sat on the futon with something on my mind.

"Vinson . . ."

His gaze zeroed in on my pupils as he lay belly up on the futon with me planted on top, like an octopus again. "Yeah."

"You know it's always been you since the beginning, right? And I mean, just you. I don't see two guys at the same time, it's not who I am." His speculation that I might have seen someone else dis-turbed me. To even doubt my devotion was insulting.

"No, I meant to say, if there was someone before that I would understand and couldn't blame you for it." I gaped at him with strange eyes and more confused than ever. To me, it was under-stood that he'd been the only man in my life since we first ex-changed saliva. "You know . . . because we're not dating," he added, nonchalant as ever.

I let out a gasp of pain as my stomach clenched and my heart bled, even more than it did at Brimley yesterday. Lately, his words drenched my soul like Scottish showers. Hot, cold. Hot, cold. Good thing I used the word *see,* instead of *date,* and spared myself the embarrassment. We'd spoken about taking it easy and having fun a month before but to point it out so bluntly proved more than I could take. Besides, only four days ago he shoved the notion of fidelity straight into our status. So, how the hell were we not dating?

CHAPTER
24

The first weekend of November, I keyed Vinson a text after days of silence. The wait for his call chiseled my heart out of shape and I couldn't wait any longer. His mixed messages bound me in a state of permanent confusion, a state I longed to escape.

He replied half an hour later, during which time a layer of malaise took over my body. "I'm at my sister's for my dad's birthday. I'll be free around nine."

Close to eleven p.m., he texted that he was at a friend's house and preparing to head home. By this time, I'd been sitting on the couch, killing time watching TV, dressed to go and eyeballing my phone over and over. A friend's house? I tried to keep my nerves under control but I wasn't doing a good job. "Try harder." Zee's words will forever be imprinted in my brain.

The dreadful state of uncertainty had returned. With Vinson, matters could change from one minute to another or better yet, from one second to another. By the time he texted back, I'd turned into a dragon spattering fumes out of the nostrils. He offered to pick me up. And the moment I put my jacket and boots on, my fury subsided, as if he never made me wait at all.

I gunned it downstairs and the sight of his dirty pickup idling in the driveway tossed me back in time. The same décor eight months prior, only clueless about how much he'd mean to me now.

"It's like our first date all over again," I said as I heaved in the passenger seat.

He leaned close and cupped my chin. "It is, isn't it?"

He planted a kiss on my lips with eyes closed. Always his eyes closed. He had his way about him to make it impossible for me to stay mad at him. His smile was infectious for one. And riding in the truck next to him gave me the sense that nothing else in the world mattered.

We rolled into a convenience store parking lot for munchies. I waited in the truck while he wandered through the store with his mouth mimicking a self-debate on what to buy. This modern Peter Pan rocked my world and flipped it to the point of no return.

"You okay?" he asked when we arrived at his place.

My mind spun like a wheel. I couldn't erase *not dating* off my ego. "Yeah."

He bobbed his head. "Are you sure?"

"I said yes."

He shimmied on the couch next to me and took my hand. "Is it because we don't talk every day?" No, dummy, it's the wait. It's the fucking wait I hate so much and also not dating. "Because I feel bad when we don't talk every day and sometimes I wonder if you are mad when I don't call for a couple of days."

I tore my hand away. "We don't have to talk every day. If you don't call for three days, I'm not mad. If you don't call for a week, I'm not mad. I like the way things are now too, okay?" And as soon as my mouth spilled the words, I swallowed them with regret.

He glanced at my freed hand and back to my eyes, then bowed his head. "OK."

Stupid me, instead of clearing the not-dating crap and bringing Vinson to recognize our feelings, so we could evolve to relationship status, I'd taken us ten steps back. What the hell was I thinking?

This is what I was thinking. I wanted to make him comfortable with the notion of us and keep him from disappearing again.

"I'm a pretty hard catch too, you know," I said.

"Oh, I'm sure." He patted my legs up and down, giving me the same seductive gaze he always did, right before we were about to fornicate.

"So, don't think I want more from you than what you want from me, because I don't." What a straight out lie but I wanted my pride back or at least a slice of it.

"Got it." He pulled me into his embrace until his tongue snaked inside my mouth.

The sexual vibe swallowed us whole. Our lips glided down to our necks and rib cages while our fingers swarmed in pleasuring habits. He whispered doting words in my ear as his pant tickled my lobe. I pulled him into me where I could have him all to myself, forever and ever if I could. We devoured our bodies in every way, kissing and nipping at our skin while pumping and grinding in tandem.

Vinson hit the shower after I did. I dug out one of his T-shirts from the closet and slipped it on. I pressed it against my chest with a lopsided grin. Inches away, a red one from nights before lay in the laundry basket crumpled and sad. When he made his way back, I cracked a joke.

"I guess you threw the red T-shirt in the laundry. I only wore it once but you thought 'ew, she wore this last night and I'm not wearing it after her, so it's going straight to the laundry', right?"

"I wore it to work the next day. That's why it's there," he said while he rummaged through the closet for something to wear.

"You wore it to work?"

"I wear all the T-shirts you sleep in the next day."

"And do they smell like me?" I asked, astounded.

He scored his head through a fresh T-shirt. "Yes, they do."

I smiled into the room. Like I said, Scottish showers morphed into statements. I considered ditching my pointless fears. No man wears a T-shirt the next day after a girl had worn it to bed the night before without nurturing affection for her. Otherwise that piece of garment would make a straight beeline for the laundry.

In the morning, my eyes snapped open while my nose dug into his hair ends at the nape of his neck and my arms cradled his rib cage. I raised my head off the pillow and threaded my fingers through his locks.

"Hi, baby," he said with a sleepy smile.

"Did you sleep well?"

He rolled on his back and slung an arm around me. "I always do when you're here." He caressed my hair with his gentle hands until my eyes sealed in comfort.

Late morning, after we finally pulled ourselves out of bed, we hopped in his truck and drove around town. It'd be the first time he took me along for Sunday errands and the joy beamed on my face. Never mind dating, this smelled like a relationship that had yet to be recognized out loud.

On Tuesday evening, exhausted from overworking my brain over beauty posts, I wrapped up my day chatting with Serena in the living room. We savoured a glass of wine when Vinson called.

"Hey, doll. I'm out playing pool but would you like to get together after?"

"I'd love to."

"All right, doll. Call you later." But he didn't. I drifted to sleep with the phone next to my head.

In the morning, I checked it for messages, hoping for an apology but the stubborn display refused to impress. I fell backwards on the bed with a pout. Just when I thought about ditching my fears, the frustration kicked in again.

By Friday, I tapped him a text. I anticipated his response in distress and as the minutes dragged on, I checked my phone with a burning gut. Before panic could melt my insides, I called his cell. I had to know he was all right.

"Hey . . . doll . . . can you hear me?" An indistinguishable noise in the background spiraled through the phone straight to my ear.

"Hardly."

"I'm . . . hockey game. I'll buzz . . . home." I exhaled with relief.

I drove to his place in a torn mood. Pleased to see him but disheartened about broken promises. At his place, our connection was off and detachment lingered in the air like a cold draft on a winter night. I questioned the point of my visit.

I jolted off the futon. "I'm going for a walk. I need fresh air."

"Now?"

"Yes. I need to refresh my thoughts."

I sprinted up the stairs and out on the street where I inhaled the air. It'd stopped raining and the petrichor had dispersed into the atmosphere. In the misty nightfall, I paced up the road to reflect upon questions I feared to ask myself from the beginning.

I wondered if his *now* question served as the purpose of elucidating if I'd return to his place tonight, so he could decide if he should hit the bed. I asked myself in the lonely night, if I vanished right now, would he search for me? Wait for me? Call for me? Would he even care or would he move on, as if nothing happened? I traced my steps back to the driveway, buckled up behind the wheel and revved the engine on the road. No point in my being at his place. None whatsoever.

At the crib, Serena's bedroom door stood ajar as TV chatter echoed from inside. I squeezed my head through. She was fast asleep as the screen rays reflected on her curls. I craved the girl-roommate-friend chat about love blues over tea. But I tiptoed in, turned the TV off and retreated to my bedroom.

I lay in bed in the dark with my eyes up at the ceiling. Vinson hadn't called about my whereabouts. I pictured him checking the time, shrugging his shoulders and crawling into bed. I deserved someone who loved me as much as I loved him. And for the longest time, I hoped Vinson would be *him* someday soon. But I wasn't so sure that day would come anymore. I'd done my part. Eight months of love and devotion was all I could give without much in return. Having to eternally suppress my feelings out of fear of driving him away was pure torture. Having him in my arms and wondering when I'd see him next, proved much more difficult than not having him at all. After months of holding on to our memories, the time had come to let him go. At least in time, the pain would go away.

Wednesday evening, I lay in bed with a glass of Cabernet on the night table and zoned out to my iPod with my eyes closed. Serena was gone to her boyfriend's. I immersed my psyche in the *Blade Runner* soundtrack and reminisced my time at Brimley as I fought a tide of tears. I insanely missed my college and school altogether.

When my phone vibrated next to me, I flicked one eye open. A text from Vinson gleamed on the display but I didn't bother to read it. I closed my eyes again and moments later, the phone rattled with a call.

"Doll, is everything okay?"

"Yes. Why?"

"The way you left on Friday, I was worried something happened."

So worried that it took you five days to call? "Nothing happened, I just —"

"I'm on my way home. You up for a visit?"

"I'll be there soon." I slouched on the edge of the bed with tears running down my face.

I cabbed it to his place and once I passed the timber door, I descended the stairs in slow motion. I wasn't eager to confess the end of our frielationship but it had to be done.

He greeted me with a smile painted on his face. Great. Make it hard on me, why don't you? Sloan had dropped him off in the work van and gave me a hug on his way out. Vinson took my hand, sat me on the futon and kissed me tender.

"I missed you," he said. My eyes bore into him as I kept seconds away from spoiling the mood. "Did you miss me?" he asked. I glanced away and he leaned back. "So, how was your day?"

"I worked on my blog, the usual."

"I had a funny day at work." He yapped about his day and I didn't stop him. I wouldn't. ". . . Which made me think of you . . ." His voice trailed away again. I loved listening to him, no matter how random the speech but this time, my brain registered intermittent verses. ". . . And when you answered the phone, I thought 'that's my sweet Alexa' and I rushed home."

"If that's how you feel, why not call sooner?"

"Oh, Alexa," he said, cupping my chin. "Just because we don't talk every day, it doesn't mean you're not on my mind. Because you are, more than you know."

"I don't get it. I really don't get it," I murmured under my breath as he stepped to the TV stand and inserted a disc.

This guy possessed an emotional radar inside his body. Whenever I planned a drastic move closer or away from him, he counteracted, ripping my intentions to shreds.

He retreated next to me and drew me into a gentle kiss. The instant his delicate lips touched mine, I forgot my farewell speech. His kisses conquered my convictions and weakened my emotions.

"Wait, I forgot to press play." He lunged toward the PlayStation and the Pink Floyd sound filled the room with magic. "This is my favourite tune," he said as he plonked his back on the futon with me on top of him.

"What's the name of the song?"

"*On the turning away.*"

"I love Pink Floyd too but why is this song special?"

"I love the words. I already wrote it in my will that I want this song to be played at my funeral," he said, his tone solemn.

"What do you mean at your funeral? We're still young. Why are you thinking about this now?"

"I buried too many of my friends, so I had to think about it."

I jerked my head back into a frown. "What happened to your friends?"

"Car accidents, crazy stuff."

"Define crazy stuff."

"Don't worry about it." He dropped his eyes to my lips, then pressed my head into a kiss, one that melted my insides.

Indeed, he lived on the edge, maybe too much partying at times and to no surprise, his friends led similar lifestyles. And damn it, why did I have to fall in love with such a man?

I wedged my tears in my throat and slid my lips down his neck, then his chest in a bid to hide my eyes. He let me be. He always let me be. I glided back up an inch away from his face.

"Don't you dare die on me, do you understand me?"

"Don't worry. It won't happen for a long time."

"I'm serious."

"Come here." He slung his arms around me, then jerked his head away to inspect my expression. "You're too much," he said with a chuckle.

Now I wanted to confess the opposite of what I'd planned. I silently decided to keep him in my life along with the tortured, sleepless nights, the tears and the anxiety. After all, I couldn't bear my existence without him.

He set *On the turning away* on repeat as we kissed between the sheets. The dreamy ballad amplified our thirst for our flesh and bones. He kissed my tears and I played with his hair. His body bladed into mine, starved for carnal ardor. I wrapped myself around his frame and arched into him to satiate my appetite for his raw touch. He panted on my lips, his breath honeysuckle and mint as euphoria numbed my legs and thrust my mind into vertigo.

Vinson followed me to the bathroom this time. He brushed his teeth while I enjoyed the sweltering drops slither down my body.

"Peekaboo," he said, jerking the shower curtain open at one end.

I jumped with giggles. "Seriously?"

He opened it at the opposite end. "Peekaboo."

"Stop it," I said, howling. I didn't want him to stop.

He clowned around several times, probably for the sake of making me laugh. And these priceless moments, I'd cherish forever.

He chased me back to the room where we leaped on the bed, roaring with laughter. We embraced into smoldering kisses and we couldn't get any closer.

"Wait." He dove out of bed to press play for more action.

When we cuddled under the covers, exhausted from a night of lust, he gazed at me with erotic eyes.

"Baby, how are you getting home in the morning?"

"Cab."

"You can take my truck. Sloan's picking me up in the work van."

"No, that's okay. I'll cab it." His offer thrilled me but I couldn't bring myself to say yes. And I didn't know why.

"I'll leave you the keys on the coffee table and you can decide in the morning."

At dawn, Vinson kissed me and raced out the door. I rolled back to sleep until the alarm woke me at nine. I freshened up, called a cab and dragged my feet upstairs. I leaned against his pickup in my wait. I should've taken his truck. I didn't even check on the coffee table for the keys.

Two days later, Vinson called to invite me out. "I'm at The Tavern with friends. Would you like to join me?"

"I could use some socializing time, why not?"

I'd been cocooned in my apartment, busy with work collaborating with Heather to promote the cosmetic products sold at her spa through my blog and after hard work, came the harvest. My income soared on commission, always a fruitful alliance with Heather. I also spread my wings to affiliate marketing with more promising revenue and I wanted to celebrate.

I sprinted inside The Tavern with delight. Sloan waved from a table where he sat with a friend, so I headed in their direction with a smile on my face. After Sloan gave me a hug, he turned his head in Vinson's direction. He chatted with a girl at the serving bar under Kara's evil eye. No sign of Nikki. Vinson's and the girl's body language showed familiarity with one another. They must have known each other for some time.

"I don't want to interrupt. I'll wait here with you," I said.

"Should I call him over for you?" Sloan asked.

"No, I'm cool. She's probably a longtime friend. No big deal." Except for Kara's stare. I doubted it was in my favour. What was her problem? Or did she know something I didn't?

I caught up on random matters with Sloan until I shot a glimpse in Vinson's direction, only to see the girl hanging off his body and Vinson whispering in her ear. The music interfered with speech at times but Sloan and I didn't whisper in each other's ear. We spoke up a notch or two and understood one another just fine.

I ripped my eyes away from the serving bar.

"They're just friends," Sloan said.

"We're friends but I'm not all over you." He glanced at his feet.

When I turned my head sideways again, anger inched up my throat. This jerk invited me out, just so I could watch him flirt with someone else.

Sloan touched my shoulder. "Are you okay?"

"It's not about jealousy, Sloan. It's about respect."

"I agree with you."

I understood the notion of hugging a female friend once, at first sight, like Sloan and I did but over and over? And she burst out with laughter every time he spoke close to her ear.

It came close to half an hour before he made his way to our table, even though he'd been aware of my presence the minute I arrived. But by the looks of it, the degree of my importance oscillated, depending upon whose company took over his undivided attention.

"Lemon mint green iced tea for my baby," Vinson said as he placed the glass on the table. I glanced away with disgust. "I used to be good friends with her ex-boyfriend when I lived in Montreal, so we had a lot of catching up to do."

"I bet you did."

"No, really —"

"I don't care. You don't have to explain yourself to me," I said as Sloan and the friend wandered into the crowd.

"I want to."

"But I don't. Besides, why would you? We're just friends, remember?"

"We're more than friends and you know it," he said, caressing my hand.

I snapped my hand back. "And what exactly are we? Because I'd like to know." He gazed at me baffled. "That's what I thought."

I deserted the table, my untouched drink and a puzzled Vinson. I bolted toward the exit. But before I had the chance to bang through the lobby doors, he leaped in front of me.

"Come on, she's just a friend. I don't like her in any other way. You have nothing to worry about."

"Oh, yeah? Have you always hugged your friends' ex-girlfriends to death? Because I don't hug my girlfriends' boyfriends. And I'm not worried about it. I don't even care."

The front doors opened and shattered my speech. Bimbo made her way into the lobby reeking of cigarettes. She smiled at me and lifted her index finger across her lips. Then she tiptoed behind Vinson and covered his eyes.

"Guess who?" she asked, proud of herself. She uncovered his eyes, burst out in a squeaky laugh and jogged around to hug him from the front.

He froze like a statue while his face turned pale with fear. But I bet mine turned red with anger. He didn't make a move to stop her and my blood boiled through my veins. I reeled on my heels and charged out the door. I couldn't allow to be ridiculed any longer.

CHAPTER
2 5

O n the first Friday of December, Serena and I relaxed on the couch with two cups of mint tea steaming away on the coffee table. We'd engaged in a light banter over the choice of movies on Netflix for the evening. I loved horror and sci-fi, she preferred comedy and romance. We argued about the pros and cons of our favourite movie genres when our phones rumbled in unison. She took her call in the bedroom. I ignored mine.

"My boyfriend asked me to go over but I don't want to leave you alone," she said, back to the living room.

"Go over, if you want. We can do this anytime."

"Was that Vinson?"

"Yes."

"Are you going to answer?"

"Regardless of what I do, you should still go."

"You don't mind? We planned a movie night," she said, two steps closer to the bedroom.

"Don't be silly. Go."

Minutes after Serena stepped out the door, my phone rang again.

"Hey, doll. Still mad at me?"

"I haven't decided yet."

"Come on, it was a stupid argument." He broke his speech and I let him stew in silence. "I'm out and about but will be home soon. Would you like to come over?"

"Call me when you get there."

Ten minutes later, he texted me from home and I jetted to his place but strolled in calmer than ever. His welcoming smile filled the room. I didn't mention the argument anymore and neither did he. We left it where it was — in a dead place. It wasn't important. If nothing else, our mind blowing sex had to be worth saving whatever we had between us. And also his sense of humour. No one I'd ever met made me laugh the way he did.

Early morning, Vinson hopped out of bed and into his clothes for a short day at work. As he waited for Sloan to pick him up, he crawled back in bed and spooned me. When his phone buzzed, he sighed and kissed my hair before he shut the door behind him.

We did it again on Tuesday, our undeclared rendezvous day. We snuggled on the futon while compliments surged through his teeth in every direction.

"You know what it is about you?"

I raised my head off his chest. "What?"

"Your attitude," he said with sparkling eyes.

"What about it?"

"I love it."

"I thought you said I scared you, you freak."

"No, I mean it. You're patient and understanding and cool."

"You already said that once before."

"Because it's true. Except for two weeks ago."

I slammed my fist on his chest and his body shuddered. "Oh, yeah? I might not be that way for much longer."

"I hope you never change."

He slid my body up to his lips and we turned the room into another erotic chamber, drugged on each other's natural high.

Three days later, after I scored another juicy commission through my blog, Vinson called again. Every time I swam through a good day, he popped up at the end, as if he kicked the good luck my way prior to his arrival.

"My parents invited me over but I'd love to see you after."

"I have the apartment to myself. Serena is at her boyfriend's for the night. Why don't you come over?"

"We could use a change of setting. I'll call you after dinner."

I jumped in the shower and lingered under the hot spray of water expecting to hear from him no sooner than three hours later. But when I leaped out, I shot a peek in my phone's direction and the red light flickered on. I dashed to the phone, towel-turban on my head and another towel wrapped around my body. A missed call and a text from Vinson and my eyebrows almost busted into my hairline. I skipped the text and returned the call.

"I've been buzzing you from the intercom. I'm downstairs."

"Downstairs?"

"Yes. Can I come up now?"

I buzzed him into the building, shook off the towels, ruffled my damp hair and slipped into a fuchsia house dress.

"I thought you were having dinner with your parents first," I said after I wrenched the door open.

"Postponed until Monday."

"Why? I hope nothing happened."

"Nothing happened. I couldn't wait to see you." I wiped the gloat off my face on our way to the living room. He skimmed the apartment. "I haven't been here in a while. It looks huge compared to mine."

"Get comfy," I said. He collapsed on the couch with a glad-it's-the-weekend huff and unloaded his phone and keys on the coffee table. "I'm going to dry my hair for a minute."

"Pizza?" he shouted.

"Pizza," I said and pressed on the hair dryer.

We munched on pizza, drank Dr Pepper and laughed ourselves to death over chatter. Then his expression grew sensual and his eyes spun me over inside. He pressed his tender lips on mine.

"Wait," I said as I rose off the couch. "I'll be back." His intrigued stare followed me to the bedroom door.

Moments later, I sashayed to the living room and a prone Vinson soared in the sitting position, his lips parted. I donned a lace bra and shorts, knee-high stockings — his favourite — and skyscraper heels. All black. As I loomed closer, he bit his bottom lip while his eyes raked down my body. I took his hand and tugged him to the bedroom where I shoved him on the bed.

"Wow, that's a part of Alexa I haven't seen," he said, sitting up, bulging eyes and all. "But I like it."

I ripped his clothes off and pressed on his chest until he fell flat on the bed. I leaned to the side and scooped the Halloween cuffs from under the mattress as fear spread across his face. I hovered over him and locked a cuff on his reluctant left wrist and the other one on my right. He exhaled with relief.

"What did you think I would do? Cuff you up and lock you away forever?" I asked with flirty eyes.

"I wish you would," he said and flipped me over.

I reached over to the iPod stand and pressed play. *On the turning away* floated like smoke in the room. We drowned in each other's eyes for still moments, then attacked one another's lips with the kind of sexual tension that ignites a mid-ocean fire. He slid my strapless bra and tight shorts off with his free hand but left the stockings and the high heels on.

"Is this a statement?" he whispered as he raised his wrist in the air, dragging mine along with the jangle of the chain.

"No, just play." And if I didn't know any better, I'd translate his lopsided smirk into a trace of disappointment.

He slid his fingertips across my knee-highs and my nails dug into his shoulder. He looped his cuffed wrist across my skin, hauling mine along for the ride above my head, down on my neck, straight to my thighs and back around. And every time the metal chain rattled, hinting imprisonment, his tentacles gripped on my flesh and our fervent joyride spiked to neurosis from the rush of the restraint. We rumbled in a furious grind, panting and moaning, our kisses hot and fiery and our bodies melting into a ball of fire. We hit the peak of pleasure locked under the tongue of the cuffs, our minds flying high under the spell of our bliss mixed with the vibe of Pink Floyd.

"I have to get the key for the cuffs," I murmured as we lay on the bed. "And you have to come with me."

"Fuck it. Let's sleep like this."

"I want to shower anyway."

He groaned as he followed to the shower, washed with eyes half-lidded and trailed behind me back to bed.

"Goodnight, baby," he said, kissing me gently. And we kissed and kissed until our minds drifted to sleep with our lips glued together and still handcuffed to each other. I unlocked our wrists in the morning.

Saturday evening, I worked on my blog in bed with the laptop on my thighs, sipping on hot tea.

"Do you have plans for tonight?" Serena asked, leaning against the bedroom door frame.

"No, I'll be done in a minute."

"I'll wait for you in the living room."

I concluded my post, tucked my computer away and glided to the living room to an anxious Serena on the couch and a bottle of unopened red on the coffee table.

"Are we celebrating something?" I asked as I sat next to her.

"I don't know, maybe." I tilted my head. "I have news," she said as she opened the bottle. "Kyan asked me to move in."

"That's great." I sprung my arms her way as she yielded to my embrace. "That's what you wanted, right?" She nodded. "Then why the sad face?"

"We won't be roommates anymore."

"No worries. We can see each other whenever."

"I guess we should transfer this apartment in your name."

"We'll go to the rental office one of these days. When are you moving out?"

"I'd like to do it before the holidays. Can you handle this place on your own? Financially?"

"Yes, my blog is doing well and growing. I'm comfortable."

"Good then."

"I'm sad to lose you as a roommate too but I'm happy for you at the same time. Come here," I said as we leaned into a hug.

"If things go sour, I'll be moving back in," she said in a would-be-threatening tone that didn't sound threatening at all. Then she poured the wine.

"And you're welcome back anytime but you and Kyan will be fine. Cheers."

We chatted the night away and reminisced about the day we met and the strange fact that we never heard from Tania again, the one who introduced us in the first place.

On Monday, Vinson tapped me an invitation to his place. I raced out the door with the same rush to the head as always. I let myself in to the sound of drizzle behind the bathroom door and parked it on the futon. When he padded in with his hair wet and a towel wrapped around his hips, his smile lit the room.

"Hey, doll," he said as he dug a T-shirt and a pair of silver satin pants out of the closet. He slipped into them and kissed me.

"Satin pants? And silver?"

"What's wrong with silver satin pants?"

"Nothing. I didn't picture you in satin pajama pants, that's all."

"Why not?" he asked, his face an inch away from me, his voice cartoonish.

"I don't know. You just don't —"

"I don't what? What?" He tickled me down and across the futon and stopped before I almost slipped into a coma with laughter.

He played a movie we didn't plan to watch and snuggled next to me. We must have had our eyes on the TV for less than sixty seconds before he cupped my chin and spun it his way. He leaned his head in and tested my lips, deeper and deeper into urgent smooches.

"You know what I want to do?" he said. "Kiss you. I want to spend the whole night kissing you. I don't think we gave our kissing mastery the recognition it deserves."

"You're starting to sound like me."

"Nothing wrong with that," he said and kissed me.

We kissed for hours with swollen lips and movie trailers on repeat. I couldn't get enough of his sensual mouth and velvety tongue. His deep whiskey eyes sparkled in the dim light and his face, the most erotic one I'd ever seen. I stopped between kisses to absorb his sensual gaze. I was hypnotized.

We fell asleep coiled around each other, like two snakes in mating season. But only after two febrile sex sessions that were glorious enough to pave down memory lane. We did it again on Wednesday but the weekend turned dry as neither of us signaled the other for no reason in particular.

On Sunday, I drove to The Big Smoke to see Maureen one more time before the winter holidays. We ate at La Rocca and talked boys and Christmas plans before I leaped on the highway and traced my way back home.

Vinson called after his Tuesday pool game but only for small talk before bedtime. The next day, I took a break from the laptop and texted him in the afternoon. "I'm coming over tonight. I want to pamper my prince." It paid off. Not only did he reply with the promise he'd call after work, he kept his word.

As soon as I stepped foot in the door, he sprang at me and cupped my head in a kissing frenzy. Our garments fell on the floor in our insatiable hunger for one another. We tumbled and pulsed and plowed and burned and cradled and cuddled and whispered and unburned. Rewind. Play. Repeat.

"You know why our sex is so good?" he said as he lay on his back satisfied, wearing nothing but a smile.

"Enlighten me."

"It's because we take our time to build it up and build the energy between us and it becomes this intense, amazing intimate relationship." And *relationship* sounded so fresh out of his mouth.

"I agree."

He gazed at me with adoring eyes. "I've never lived anything like this before."

"Me neither."

"And I hope to live it for a long time," he said, stroking my hair.

His words took me to heaven and back and I finally breathed easy. His spills melted my heart. We navigated in the right direction and our soon-to-be-relationship should fall into place. And judging by the connection we had, physically, emotionally and sexually, no other option made sense.

On Friday, Vinson asked me to pick him up from Sloan's house. They'd shared a couple of drinks and he decided to leave his truck there until morning. As I waited in the driveway, Sloan moseyed out to my car window to greet me.

"Why don't you come inside? I'd love to have you over."

"Thanks, Sloan but I'll wait here. Next time for sure."

"I'll tell him to come out." Sloan winked and retraced his steps as Vinson came out with his trademark smile and Peter Pan strut.

I coasted to his rental where we dipped into the futon in each other's arms. The night was to be our last together before my trip to visit my mom for the holidays.

As I stretched on the futon, he enfolded his head in the slope of my shoulder and brushed my body up and down with his palm.

"My baby . . . my baby . . . my baby," he whispered.

I toyed with a lock of his hair and let him do the talking. I'd waited for a confession before I flew away, something he hadn't said before, to nurture my soul on the trip. A breakthrough statement.

"I looove you to baby me," he said, then glanced up at me. Now repeat what you said but without the to-baby-me part, I wished in my mind.

In the morning, we smooched into a spectacle of fireworks again. One for the road to keep us spiritually together. Not that I needed help in that sense but just in case he did.

I drove Vinson back to Sloan's house. Then I idled in the drive-way for our goodbye before spending the next three weeks apart. He kept eye contact brief, his vision an invisible laser through the windshield and a hand on the door handle.

"Do you want me to call you when I'm away?" I asked.

"Why don't I call you?"

"I may have my phone off at times. It's easier if I call you."

"Then I'll leave a message." He forced a smile and kissed me. "Have a great trip," he said and dashed out of the car. As he strode to his truck, he didn't even turn to wave.

This act came after he called me *my baby* three times, spiced with *I love you* and *relationship* in deviated contexts yes, but they still came out of his mouth less than a week apart. Mixed messages again but I refused to dwell on it. I had an exciting trip ahead.

Back at the crib, Serena waited for me with fresh coffee and an anticipated final chit-chat as roommates.

"Thank you for everything you did for me. You welcomed me here without hesitation when you didn't even know me," I said.

"My pleasure. Running the risk of sounding conceited, we can agree that Tania can pick the right friends."

"Just not for herself. But you, my dear Serena Foyle, you're welcome to come over anytime."

"Thanks. I hope you and Vinson will work it out. Maybe he'll move in next."

I slipped a faded smile, then sprinted to my bedroom. I zipped up my suitcase, showered and dolled myself up for the trip. Then I drew Serena into a hug on my way out.

"Happy Holidays. It will be your first one living with Kyan."

"I'm so excited. Enjoy your trip and call me when you get back."

I descended to the parking lot, tossed my luggage in the trunk, my carry-on on the passenger floor and my butt in the driver seat. I dropped my car off at the longterm airport parking and marched into Pearson for my international departure. I'd booked a flight overseas, all the way to the country of sunflower fields, virgin forests and Vlad the Impaler's cradle and throne and where my mom retreated after my father passed away.

My father, a commercial realtor and my mother, an interior decorator were born in Romania. When the real estate firm in the native land delegated my father across the Atlantic to meet with potential investors, he fell for the Western culture and the notion that sharing two worlds would be better than one. They moved to Canada with me when I was still wearing diapers.

I spent my childhood summer vacations and the odd winter one as a voyageur, flying to and from my grandparents in Romania. I'd grown up bilingual and with both cultures under my belt, switching airports during layovers and snoozing in the constricted plane seats during interminable flights in the process.

The European winter was unforgiving while the Canadian weather sang its way into quotidian sunrise with timid flurries. The irony of Mother Nature. Western European countries had been shielded in snow and countless flights were canceled or delayed. Airports shut down one by one and I shuddered at the thought of spending Christmas in a waiting area. TV monitors showed thousands of passengers trapped across European airports with phones glued to their ears and faces on the brink of despair.

My connecting flight from Brussels squeezed its head out of the mess and into the Eastern European skies before an avalanche of snow. I landed in Bucharest sans my luggage but nothing mattered more than crumpling into my mother's arms at destination. I picked up my suitcase the next day, flustered but unscathed.

The winter holidays turned Bucharest into a fairy tale city, a spectacle of light, music and gleaming decorations. I roamed with Mom around town, between the ancient architectural buildings and down the narrow streets. The milder climate sure soothed Mom's stiff joints, the reason why she moved back to the motherland — also Indian summers — because she bounced in and out of shops like a miffed starlet's assistant. We shopped for trendy clothes and lunched at chic cafés, no shortage of either around the city. We sipped on mulled wine at an outdoor concert at the Christmas Market, the atmosphere intoxicated with good vibes.

I checked my phone in hopes that Vinson would care to know about my flight. Canadian TV stations must have reported the weather conditions in Europe. No voicemail, not even a text with Happy Holidays. In a way, his silence didn't surprise me. He didn't bother to ask about the time zone difference before he rushed out of my car. I suspected he wouldn't call but I still checked my phone, hoping he'd prove me wrong.

CHAPTER
2 6

A week after New Year's Day, I landed back on Canadian soil, dead tired and jet lagged. I debated about spending the night at Maureen's or Heather's. I collected their open post-flight invitations for emergency use. But after I exited the terminal, the chilly winter breeze invigorated my bones. And I caught my second wind.

I hopped in my car and jetted northbound to Cape Kay. By the time I made it home, I'd been awake for thirty six hours but I couldn't keep away from Vinson, even if he didn't deserve it. "Welcome back. Having dinner with family. I'll call you after," he wrote seconds after my text.

A smiley face on a Post-it drawn by Serena rested on my bed, now moved to the master bedroom. I unpacked and showered, then sank into the couch she left behind. I replayed in my head the carefree sentiments in Romania with a cup of tea until the phone rumble stirred me into the present.

"Hi, doll. How was your trip?"

"Great. I'll tell you all about it."

"Can't wait. On my way home. You up for a visit?"

I cruised through the fresh snow with my own stomach flurries. He welcomed me with a beaming face and drew me into a lingering hug.

"Did you make it overseas okay?"

"I'm back here. So, obviously yes," I said, sinking into the futon.

"They showed the weather in Europe on TV. I was worried about your flight."

I shot an invisible spear his way. "I believe Alexander Graham Bell invented something called the phone."

He chuckled with concealed guilt. "I'm sorry, doll." Always sorry but not enough to kill the crap.

I fished a gift bag out of my tote and placed it on the coffee table. "I have something for you."

His expression grew tense. "What is it?"

"Relax. It's nothing big, just a couple of souvenirs."

He gave a wary incline of the head while he stared at the gift bag, as if he'd seen the big bad wolf. "It looks big."

I drew a metallic keychain and a black T-shirt out of the bag in slow motion, as if I tried to protect a frightened child's emotions. The keychain dangled the letter V to the side. On the tee, I custom-imprinted in blue letters, *All roads lead to Vinson** on the chest with **Vinson is a trademark owned exclusively by Vinson Donohue Inc.* written in small cursives about an inch above the seam. I produced it at a shop in Bucharest after I tortured my brain an entire night over the deciding catchphrase.

I held the T-shirt against my torso to show it off. "So, what do you think?" He forced a smile and nodded an inaudible yeah.

I hoped he'd find it amusing but it did the exact opposite. I folded the gifts on the coffee table. He roamed to the kitchenette to wash dishes for something to do. I wasn't aware a couple of souvenirs held the meaning of a marriage proposal. He returned on the futon and raised my legs on his lap.

"You don't mind if I watch the last ten minutes of the football game, do you?"

"No, go ahead. I can hang out." He never said a word about the CFL before.

I pretended to watch along while he stared at the TV in a daze, almost using it as an excuse for stewing in absentia of the mind. When we snuck into bed, our sexual tension soared like old times but before we fell asleep, his mind sailed away again.

Overnight, our bodies kept close under the covers but far from glued to each other. And by the time the light of dawn brushed my face, Vinson paced around the room dressed and ready to bolt.

"Morning. You should have woken me up too," I said, sitting up in bed to an abrupt head rush.

"Morning. Stay in. I have to leave for an hour. Go back to sleep."

I sat in bed immobile, confused. I didn't dare to ask where he'd planned to go, unsure he'd give me a straight answer. After he rushed out, I couldn't fall asleep. I tossed and turned about what could've happened while I was away. I didn't even have the chance to tell him about my trip. He didn't care to ask.

A couple of hours later, he ventured back and crawled in next to me. We lay in each other's arms, each drowning in thoughts. After three weeks apart, we should have turned our first night — and morning — into a sexual rampage. But no, none of that, not even close.

Late morning, when we finally escaped the bed, Vinson busied himself around the room while I rested the borrowed T-shirt on the armchair and slipped into my clothes. We strode out of the apartment together but he skipped the goodbye kiss before we claimed our cars.

"Have a good day." He disappeared into his pickup and blasted the engine in a different direction.

The next day, a dreadful cold hit my body. It happened every time I traveled overseas in the winter. The climate differences and my lowered immunity system from the trip exhaustion did the trick. I exchanged a couple of texts with Vinson, in which he casually wished me to get well. No phone call, no visit.

I transferred my clothes to the master bedroom through sneezes and coughs. I moved Serena's old desk and chair from the living room to my old bedroom, which I turned into an office. Then I worked on my blog wrapped in a blanket and sipping on hot tea.

Four days later, on a Tuesday night, I had yet to hear from Vinson, not even a question on my health progress. Only when I texted him, he responded with a phone call.

"Playing pool, doll. Do you want me to call you when I'm done?"

"Yes."

He still asked that question after three months of Tuesday night post-pool rendezvous. He didn't call back. He did the next night when he asked if I'd like to *chill* with him and I accepted. I was dying to be with him.

I drove to his place drowning in anxiety. The sentiment I dreaded, the fear of imminent disruption in our trysts re-nestled inside me and I knocked on his door with my heart hammering at my ribs. He invited me in with a faded smile. We chatted about nonsense and cuddled on the futon but our tender communication had crumbled. No declarations, no compliments and no emotional spills. I didn't force it. I let him be.

On Friday, he called after midnight and I huffed as I picked up.

"I'm leaving a friend's house. Would you like to come over?"

"Yeah." I cursed myself for lacking the strength to say no.

When we embraced on the futon, he ran his fingers through my hair with a stare, as if he yearned to divulge words he wouldn't allow himself to divulge. Between kisses, I dissected his face for a clue as he frowned. His expression turned sensual but I couldn't read it beyond the front. I wanted to crawl inside his head and capture the truth hidden in the brain cells.

We slept in until late morning, then once awake, we smooched into lust. Back to himself, he acted his usual childlike, tossing in bed and calling out, "baby, babyy, babyyy," his way of asking to be babied. I grazed my fingers through his locks, yanked his body against mine and whispered sweet nothings in his ear. We rolled around in bed, giggling like teenagers until the afternoon when I finally heaved out of the sheets and tripped into my clothes.

"Do you want to spend a weekend in bed? Like, the whole weekend to do nothing other than eat, sleep and make love?"

"Sounds good," I said with a smile. I planted a kiss on his throbbing lips and left him in bed.

Our emotional connection resumed to utterly fantastic again and I could've bet a million dollars, he'd call as soon as Monday. He didn't. Nor did he call the day after. Nor the one after that.

Early evening Thursday, my text to Vinson drifted into the cosmic sphere. Later on, I dialed his number and when the ringing sound perpetuated like a broken record, a ball of chill looped from my head to my toes like Six Forty Nine on Saturday night. I didn't need to wait any longer. I'd connected the dots.

By Monday, I keyed out one more pitiful message. "My Vinson, where are you?" I wanted to drill it into my brain that, in fact, he was long gone. When my phone remained stubbornly quiet, an onset of dysphoria crept in my chest.

I'm okay. I'm okay. I'm okay. I'm okay. I took deep breaths to keep myself from slipping into hyperventilation. Then I squeezed my eyes shut as my mutilated soul slid on the path to emotional inferno. His silence numbed my knees like Dilaudid and I collapsed on the floor with my stomach torn into my throat.

Hours later, I crawled into bed and stewed under the covers with a crushed soul and a bleeding heart. My poor attempts at holding my Vin-related emotions in check tumbled like a rock down the steep.

Three days later, I levered my body on the side of the bed to pull myself together. And the more I revived, the more I craved an answer from the man himself, the player of hearts, the king of make believe. When the evening rolled, I stormed to his place. I wanted him to tell me the truth. Tell me why he vanished again. I wanted to hear him say that he didn't care, that he never wanted to see me again and then, I'd accept defeat.

I angled into the driveway next to his truck with my heart pounding out of my chest. The apartment light sparkled through a neglected corner of his covered up window. I rounded the corner and turned the knob with no luck. I banged my anger through but he left me out in the cold. "Coward. I don't want to see you ever again," I texted, then gunned the engine and bawled my eyes off all the way home. I couldn't decide what made me madder — his deserting me or my allowing him to desert me. All over again.

CHAPTER
27

I raced down south through February weather to see Maureen. A snowstorm was announced on this cold Monday morning but I would have driven out of Cape Kay through a blizzard. I had to skip town. Vinson's ghost hung in the air and I couldn't breathe.

Moments after I pulled into La Rocca's parking lot, Maureen's car swung on two wheels around the corner. When she stepped out in black high heeled boots and a long trendy coat, the stone in my heart pulverized and I came alive. She transmitted the loved and cherished sensation with the signature of a best friend.

We dined and yapped the day away, then moved the chatter to her house over a glass of wine. We giggled on the couch over old memories while her daughter was sound asleep in her room and her husband watched sports in the den. Once the dusk squeezed the energy out of our frames, I camped on the couch for the night. And I slept like the little girl upstairs.

In the morning, Maureen cooked breakfast. Coffee and toast did it for me. I couldn't fit anything else in my tormented belly. The weather application on my phone estimated fifteen inches of snow, so I hugged my best friend and took to the highway.

By the time I made it to Cape Kay, the weather tamed up. I'd left the blizzard in my tracks, somewhere south. After I filled my car tank, I paid for the fuel and almost butted heads with Sloan on my way out of the gas station lodge.

"Sloan, sorry, just in a rush to get home."

"Hey, sweetie. No worries. How are you doing?" He gave me a robust hug.

"Good. You?"

"Exhausted."

"Why?"

The glance in Sloan's eyes turned coy. "I partied with Vinson for the last week straight."

"What do you mean? Like, every night?"

"Every night."

I paused to recollect my thoughts. Then, "On Thursday too?"

"We partied at my house and he cabbed it home late that night."

"Are you sure?"

"Yeah. I picked him up early morning in the work van, so we said that since he didn't have his truck, we could have a few drinks at my house. I figured he'd invite you too. Why do you ask?"

"No reason."

"I have to get some sleep. I'll tell Vinson I ran into you."

I settled in the driver seat and blew out my cheeks. I pictured the shock on Vinson's face when he read my coward-calling message while having a good time with friends. I burst into a laugh as I twisted the key in the ignition. He'd probably come to the conclusion that I was insane and chances were, he wanted nothing to do with me. But I had nothing else to lose.

On Saturday afternoon, my face brightened when my phone rattled with Nikki's name as I worked at my desk. I picked up with guilt in my throat. She invited me over on a night when her now live-in boyfriend, a fireplace salesman, traveled out of town on business, even on weekends.

"I'd love to but I wouldn't make the best company right now." Deep down inside, I'd reached a new low.

"What happened?" she asked and I paused. I feared that if I spoke, I'd explode into a torrent of tears. "Girl talk is exactly what you need right now. I'll send you the address. I finally moved in with Brevin."

"Vinson told me he helped you with your stuff. Congratulations."

"Thanks. Now move your butt over here."

I drove to Thunder Hill — why did it have to be the same neighbourhood? — and after she opened the door with a glow on her face, she pulled me into a hug.

"Jesus Christ, I thought you dropped off the face of the earth," she said and pointed to a staircase across the front door. "Up the stairs."

I hurdled up the stairs and scouted around as she closed the door. She'd moved into a bungalow with a gigantic backyard and a jade hued picket fence in a tranquil cul-de-sac. The house was cozy and bore a woman's touch. Her mystic touch. I dipped into the couch, soft as powder.

"Where the hell have you been?" she said with wide open arms as she shimmied into another hug.

"Here but —"

"Busy with life?"

"Some kind of life. But anyways, I have something for you," I said and rooted for the red polka dot shoe out of my tote.

"You have my shoe? No wonder I couldn't find the damn thing. Did Vinson give it to you?"

"Yes, he did. I'm sorry for not bringing it sooner."

"No biggie. I lost it, what, around Halloween? It's not like I would have worn it all this time anyway. But thanks, dude."

She served coffee as the two of us chatted up a storm, forgetting about the time. We caught up on my Vinson troubles — especially the latest — and I'd swallow my tears and she'd throw a pun in the air and we'd burst out with laughter until our stomach muscles twisted in a hurt.

"You're staying the night, right?" she asked.

"No . . . I don't know."

"It's Saturday, what do you have to do? Go home, be alone and miserable? Besides, I'm scared to sleep alone. You're staying."

"Okay, I'm staying."

We listened to music and laughed our way through the night and I didn't remember laughing so much in one night since I met

Vinson. Late into the night, I lay on the long side of the couch and covered myself with a duvet Nikki flipped at me. Then she descended to the semi-basement bedroom.

"Goodnight."

Halfway through the night, I snapped my eyes open as the wooden stairs behind the couch squeaked under human steps. I peeked over the backrest with my heart thudding in my throat.

"Hey, are you asleep?" Nikki whispered.

I exhaled. "Not now I'm not."

"Do you want to sleep in the bedroom with me? I'm scared down there alone."

"Don't worry. The door is locked and I'm up here."

"Tell that to the three-year-old inside me when she sleeps at night." She rushed to the front door. "Now it's locked."

I rolled off the couch and followed her downstairs. We climbed in bed where comfort and warmth lavished.

"I have a habit of sleeping naked. You don't mind, do you?" she said, shoving her clothes from under the covers.

"It's February."

"I've always done it year round. Come on, spoon me and let's go to sleep."

I shifted my eyes at opposite angles in the dark. Then I shimmied behind Nikki, laced an arm around her tiny waist and almost drew circles with my thumb on her ribs. I wore a pair of lace shorts and a white T-shirt, which I wished I had the balls to toss on the floor too. I closed my eyes and drifted to sleep, keeping my body still and my hands glued to her creamy skin.

In the morning, the smell of freshly brewed coffee woke me up. Nikki's steps thumped in the kitchen above. I freshened up in the bathroom at the end of the hall and roamed upstairs.

"Good morning, princess," she said. "How did you sleep?"

"Like a baby. Your bed is comfy."

"Good. We'll do it again soon."

Days of blogging later, the sight of a startling email arrested my eyes on the phone display. "Alexa, please call me as soon as possible. I don't care if it's four a.m.," signed by Zee with a phone number attached. I read it over and over in disbelief. Zeke?

The last time I spoke to Zeke was at the college library, the day I drove to Cape Kay to honour my first date with Vinson, almost a year ago. At first, I ignored his email but two days later, I found myself alone and in complete boredom after I'd finished my online work for the day. I tapped out a one word email. "Hello?" The question mark implied *did you just slide out from a rock you've been hiding under all this time?* "Hi, gorgeous. What are you doing tonight? Let's get together."

I clenched my jaw and cursed at the phone. I couldn't believe the nerve. What made him think I'd jump at the chance to get together a year later? What made him think I wasn't taken? "I think about you every once in a while. You causing any trouble lately?" Zeke emailed again. Bearing in mind the drama during our college friendship, I took it as a joke. "I find myself looking for you at the library. I miss our good times," he bombarded with another. "What good times? All we did was play cat and mouse," I rebuffed with a spew of chagrin. "But it wouldn't have been the same without you."

We emailed back and forth on shared memories and wound up laughing about how silly we'd been most of the time at the college. He was gearing up for his upcoming graduation in a couple of months and I updated him on my move to Cape Kay.

The next day, he hit me with an elated email about his move into the same student house on Sycamore Drive, where I briefly stayed at back in September before I withdrew from Brimley. That part stunned me. He mentioned my name to the landlord out of pure enthusiasm and that's when the clue surfaced. "I'm in the same room you rented. The first bedroom on the left." I couldn't help it. "That's it." We hadn't talked in almost a year and we still had something in common. During Brimley days, we shared an unworldly connection, one Zeke failed to acknowledge. And now he insisted to let him know whenever I'd pass through Brenton City again. "It's doubtful," I texted. I passed through Brenton City whenever I hooked up with Maureen down south but he didn't have to know that.

On Valentine's Day, my stupid self still hoped for a miracle from Vinson. A message, a phone call, a surprise visit, anything would do. My sentiments were set in stone and I couldn't shake them. There was always the what-if question racing through my stubborn mind. I had used so many what-ifs when it came to Vinson, I exhausted my lifetime supply.

A week later, I woke up to find an email from Zeke received at three sixteen a.m. "I need you so bad, Alexa. Please come see me tomorrow." Zee, the one with flesh made out of pride, never pleaded. He'd rather die a slow death than show — what he'd consider to be — a sign of weakness. How bad did he have it for him to beg?

"What do you want from me, Ezekiel?" I finally wrote. "No, I'm still Zeke . . . Zee for you and I miss you like crazy." "I thought you said you think of me once in a while." "That's because I didn't want to sound creepy but besides school, thinking about you is all I do these days." "Too bad. You're a year too late." "I'm sorry, so sorry for all the pain I've caused you. I was being stupid. Can't you give us another chance?" I jerked my head away from the phone. "The answer is no." He shot email after email with apologies I trashed one after the other and ignored him in the end. But our conversation came as vindication to my soul. Vindication for the heartache, mind games and emotional joyride he'd put me through at Brimley and I'm not going to lie, it felt fucking good.

CHAPTER
2 8

I kicked off March with an acceptance to the Nursing School at the university in Cape Kay and drew a mental picture of the good aspects in my life. Future university student, beauty blogger, entrepreneur. My heart finally smiled.

Meanwhile, Zeke besought me over and over to visit him in Brenton City because he hadn't acquired a full driving license yet, so he couldn't drive on the highway alone. To think that during Brimley era, all I had to do to make him chase me was turn him down whenever he called or even better, ignore him altogether, angered my wits more than it should.

But by mid-March, I skipped town and stopped by Brimley on my way down south. Zeke's newfound attitude moved me and for the sake of gloating, I decided to give him a shout.

Once inside the college, I mouthed, I fucking love this school with every step I took on the corridors. Then I scanned the library for Zeke, a one-eighty of the former epicenter of my soul. I e-mailed him from my phone to announce my arrival onto the school grounds. By the time he responded, his text caught me behind the wheel seconds before peeling away from campus. "Leaving home and on my way to see you." "Sorry but I left Brimley already. I'll be busy for an hour. I'll call you when I'm done." It would take longer to lunch with Maureen but who cared? How many times didn't I wait for his messages? I waited for hours, days, weeks, months.

I slid southbound to The 6ix and joined Maureen at La Rocca and every time we dunked into the high-backed booths with pre-gossip giggles, I thought that fewer things in life could beat these glorious moments.

I journeyed back to Brenton City and stopped at a coffee shop in town for a solitary latte and a self-debate on whether to call Zeke or not. Since our text swap, an hour had turned into four but my mental argument oscillated according to mood not time. Mood — undecided.

When I finally shrugged an email his way, nothing came back. I gulped the last drops of my latte and scurried to a gas station. I stuffed my tank with gas and hopped on the northbound lane. Half an hour into my drive, a red flickering light broadcast a new text on the passenger seat.

I angled on the paved shoulder and Zeke's response flashed before my eyes. "Sorry I didn't answer sooner. I was in the kitchen cooking dinner." "How domestic of you." "I cooked for us. I hoped you'd come over." Zeke took the time to cook dinner for me? My heart would have danced around had he invited me over for dinner a year prior. "It's most important that I see you and please don't say you left town," another email popped on my phone. "Sorry but yes, I'm on the highway." I tossed the phone on the passenger seat and rumbled the car back on the road.

Ten minutes into the drive, my mind took me to the off-ramp. I pulled over at a rest stop to ruminate over Zeke's words. "Please, I'm begging you to stop and call me. Even if it's for five minutes." I arched my neck against the headrest to decide if his demeanour was real. Then I pushed the gas pedal out of the rest stop and southbound on the highway.

Back in Brenton City, I veered into the student house driveway with faded butterflies. I knocked on the door and Zeke opened it.

"You came."

We froze into stones with eyes on one another and a whirlwind of flashbacks poured through my brain.

"Hi." He looked taller, grown up.

"Come here." He took my hand and hauled me into the house, straight into a violent hug. I leaned back but he drew me into his arms again, then shoved the door shut.

"I can't believe I'm here," I said, scouting the house.

"I can't believe you're here either . . . in the flesh."

"Where is your room?" I dashed across the living room and up to the first bedroom on the left side of the corridor. I clogged my legs in the doorway.

"That's the one." Hard to believe six months after I evaded this room, Zeke tailed as the new renter.

I tiptoed in. The same furniture had been moved around the room with masculine belongings scattered over them. I planted one of Zeke's collection caps on my head. Then I sat on the bed and toyed with the cap's visor on my forehead.

"You're graduating this year."

"Yeah."

"Are you excited?" I bounced my butt on the bed.

"Yeah."

"You don't sound too sure."

"I am and I'm not 'cause I'll be out there trying to make a living."

"I'm not worried about you."

"You see, once I graduate, I'll be . . .," and as his voice trailed off, I shifted into analysis about the novelty of the situation. Then Zeke dipped his palm into the mattress next to my thigh. "So, am I sleeping in the same bed, you did?"

I scanned the bed through the sprinkled clothes. "It looks like it's the same one. But I only stayed here briefly."

"It still means the world to me."

He peeled the clothes off the bed and arranged them in the closet. Halfway through the stack, he chucked them on the floor. Then he glided closer and cupped my head.

"I can't believe you're here. I thought I'd never see you again," he said with the same adoring eyes he did when we first met by the lockers. "I looked for you at the library and got worried when I didn't see you anymore."

I slanted my head, like a dog trying to make sense of his master's words. "Zeke —"

"Zee."

"Zee, I waited for you to talk to me for over a year when we were at school together."

"And I'm sorry. I'm terribly sorry about how I made you feel."

"Why now?"

"I missed you, plain and simple. I missed you so much. I had to see you and be with you." He slung his arms around to hug me but I pushed them to the side.

"What if I am involved with someone else?"

He squeezed through my knees with hopeful eyes. "Are you?"

I glanced away in silence. Yes would be a lie but I refused to say no. I crossed my arms. I would've given my life to hear these words at Brimley. He undid my arms and leaned to kiss me. The lips I adored in college. He slid his hands below my waist and tugged at my T-shirt. I angled my head away as sorrow clouded his eyes.

"Why not?"

"Because, Zee. How long has it been?" And it wasn't like we were a good match in sex anyway.

He cupped my chin. "Come on, I missed you. I want to make you mine-all-mine."

"What's the point, Zee? It's been so long —"

"Which is why it's exactly the point. It's been too long." He whispered in my ear and kissed my neck.

I pulled away. "Whatever happened to What's Her Name?"

He shrugged his shoulders. "We finally got together but after a while, I realized the one I truly wanted was you."

"Translation — she dumped your ass and you ran to me for an ego boost."

"No, nothing like that." He grazed his thumb over my bottom lip and down my chin. "It turned out she was no match to your heart, your beauty and your brains."

I slid off the bed. "I should go."

"I'd like to take you out to dinner."

"Isn't that supposed to come before sex?" I figured I'd thrown in a joke about our brief but emotionally dignified sexcapades.

"I want us to do it right this time."

"All right. You probably have homework to do."

"Can you drop me off at school?"

I took my tote and jacket off the bed. "Sure, come on."

On the way to Brimley, he pointed out the lingering similarities and coincidences that don't ever seem to stop. He beamed as he talked about us in a frame of a new beginning. Our bright future together.

I rolled to a stop by the campus barrier as Zeke's face turned solemn.

"When do I get to see you again?"

"I don't know."

"But soon, right?"

"Right," I said and joy seared through his eyes. I didn't know what else to say.

He hugged me tight and shuffled out, holding the car door open. "Drive safe and text me your new number."

I nodded with a courteous smile, my sentiments for him dead and gone. I waved goodbye and he vanished inside campus where I closed the final chapter on the story of Zee and me.

CHAPTER

29

Mom frisbeed a plane ticket my way and flew me to Romania before I had the chance to say no. Not that I would. "Your ticket's in the mail. I mean, email. I'll be cooking your favourites," she said on the phone. Eager to obey the woman who gave me life, I packed up my bags and gunned it to the airport. Long flights, layovers, airplane coffee. But who cared? I could use a change of air and Easter dishes cooked by Mom.

Two weeks later, I returned to Cape Kay pounds heavier and loving life again. The morning after my landing, I jerked the sheets to the side and levered out of bed. I skipped to the kitchen, poured the fine coffee grounds into the filter, water in the reservoir and called Nikki.

"Where have you been?"

"Romania."

"What do you mean, you've been in Romania?"

"You know me and my flights on a whim."

The only time Nikki had been out of Cape Kay was on a journey to Toronto she'd planned ahead for months and from which she recoiled back home at supersonic speed. "Too crowded, too many skyscrapers, insane traffic." She found my instant trips to Romania as something from a fantasy world. Unreal, undoable. But for me, the story of my life.

"Come to my house. My boyfriend's at work."

By the time I dressed up, the coffee maker squeezed the brew in the pot. I turned it off and dashed out the door. I'd heat it up later.

"Let's go for breakfast," Nikki said from the doorway. "You want to?"

"Yes, I'm starving."

"You're all smiles. Did you see Vinson last night?"

"I landed last night. And I'm over it."

She squinted her eyes in disbelief but nothing could spoil my refreshed April mood. Not even Kara's presence in the driveway.

"Awesome, the more the merrier," I said.

"What happened to you?" Kara asked, her tone wary.

"Come on guys, can't I be happy for no reason?"

"It must be the European air. She just flew back from Romania," Nikki said.

"Where the hell is Romania?" Kara asked.

"It's where Dracula was born and vampires are real," Nikki said. Kara frowned and I simpered.

"Point is, traveling makes me happy. Let's go," I said.

"Go where?" Kara said.

"Breakfast," Nikki said.

"I already had breakfast," Kara said.

"You can at least have a coffee. Get in the car."

The sisters eyeballed each other, stunned by my newfound — and so untypical of me — bossiness. But they conformed.

We drove to Sammy's Diner, a breakfast place around the corner from Nikki's house. During our feast, Vinson's name remained unmentioned and I didn't care to ask.

Post-breakfast, Nikki and I traced back to her house while her sister claimed the serving bar at The Tavern. We yapped and laughed until our jaws hurt.

"You're staying for dinner, right? Brevin will be home too. I'll make mushroom and basil pasta, especially for you."

"I'll help you."

CHAPTER
30

Despite a May rainy day, Nikki invited me to The Tavern for a drink and surefire glee. Chatting over an alcohol-free cocktail at the bar came as Nikki's brilliant idea of killing a boring Monday in good company. An hour of giggles later, I put on my jacket in preparation to leave when she hit me with newsflash.

"You'd better sit down. Vinson walked in."

"Fuck."

"You mean that in a good way, right?" She peeked over my head. "He's with a friend but it's not Sloan. They stopped at a table."

I eased back into the seat with tingles in my legs facing Nikki. I refused to turn around with my panicked face and give Vinson the satisfaction. She strolled over to take the order as I sat still as a lighthouse until she returned.

"I have to go."

"No, don't. He'll think you're leaving because of him."

"That is exactly why I'm leaving. Give me a hug."

Nikki paddled to the crack of the serving bar, draped her arms around me, held tight and spun me around to position my face in Vinson's direction. I hadn't seen him in four months. He'd grown his locks down the nape of his neck again. We locked eyes and a smile lit on his face, enough to spark a sea of flames in my heart. I spun us back around.

"What did you do that for?"

"Don't tell me you didn't enjoy it," she said and I grinned. "That's what I thought."

I dashed out of the bar without looking back and when I arrived home, a text from Nikki urged me to call her.

"You should have gone over to say hello," she said.

"Not a chance."

"He asked about you."

"Then why didn't he come over to say hello?"

"Shy maybe, I don't know but he asked why you left."

"And what did you answer?"

"I said to him, 'what do you expect her to do, stay? You can't get close to her and disappear. Twice. You can't do that to people.'"

"And?"

"He gave the guilty face."

Only fate's sick sense of humour would bring Vinson and me in the same room, right after I swore I finally recouped. You never expect to run into someone who hurt you on a rainy Monday night at the town's local pub.

Nikki called me to her house on a Friday night after Brevin left town for a family visit. She stayed in Cape Kay in the event that Kara required the extra pair of hands at the bar. We dissected Vinson's ways, flipped them up and around to explain his eternal mixed messages. We didn't find a logical explanation or a longterm solution but we still had fun blabbering about it.

In the morning, I sped home for a shower and a change of clothes, then bounced back to Nikki's and parked it on the couch. Early evening, her phone buzz sliced my words mid-sentence.

"It's my sister. She wants me to help at The Tavern." I rose up and fixed my clothes. "Come with me," she said.

"No, I'm going home."

"Oh, come on. I'll only be there for a couple of hours while it's busy. You can sit with me at the serving bar."

"A couple of hours? It's Victoria Day weekend. Plus, I don't want to run into Vinson again. It'll be awkward."

"That is the very reason why you should come." I crinkled my face. "Once I'm done, we'll come back here." I glanced away. "You know I'm scared to sleep alone, don't you let me sleep alone."

"Okay, I'll come but if Vinson shows up, I'm out of there."

Nikki dangled the keys on our way to the front door. "That's what I don't get about you. You want to be with him but you won't stay to talk to him."

"That's because I don't want to take the first step. I've done it so many times, I'm tired of it. And if I don't, he won't and it'll only be this weird vibe between us."

"I hope he's there," she said and I glowered. "Fine, I hope he's not there. Better?"

The Tavern hummed with music from the parking lot. We marched to the serving bar where Kara welcomed us with a forced smile. The room was packed and the air was sweaty and cluttered.

"Glad you could join me," Kara snapped at Nikki, then turned to me. "Guess who's here?" And an abrupt surge of panic lanced from my stomach to my throat. She jerked her head across the bar. I turned in slow motion, as if I feared punishment. Vinson & Co stood by the deck, mingling and laughing in all their grandeur.

Vinson had a good reason to party — not that he needed one — because on Tuesday coming up, he'll have turned twenty eight. He radiated energy, his body steering and spinning around like a whirligig. He was a one man show, a great comedian. More often than not, his entire persona came as an act and at times, I was un-sure which part of him was real and which one was play.

He pretended to meet my eyes by chance and held my gaze for a lingering moment. I broke eye contact first but his gape already rocked me over inside. I was doomed for life and without escape from his sorcery. He was the air I breathed. He was my drug to which I had no antidote.

Nikki leaned over the granite counter. "I hope you're not leaving again."

"Why couldn't you let me go home?"

"So you can go to sleep? I have a feeling that by the end of the night, you'll thank me." Vinson chuckled from the crowd, perhaps at my uneasy stance.

"Why don't you go over? What did you say once? That waiting for him was like waiting for winter? Don't know why you'd say that. I love winter," she said between serving beer bottles.

Okay, Vinson. Here's your get-out-of-jail-free card but only because it's your pre-birthday weekend. I waded through the crowd in his direction, his eyes fixated on my face.

He bowed his head with a smile. "Hi, doll."

The crowd pushed me into his body. He caught me in his arms but I pulled back.

"You're something else, you know that?" I said.

"About that night . . . it was a misunderstanding, Usually when I don't call, it's for a reason and you went all freaking out on me and I didn't know what to do."

"You call and straighten it out, that's what you do, even if it's the next day," I said, searching for remorse in his expression and I found a trace.

"I still love you to death. I still think you're an awesome girl. No hard feelings here."

Sloan stood in the corner of my eye. I nodded a hello and he winked.

"Come here." Vinson drew me into a hug and I inhaled his scent with my eyes closed. "It's good to see you," he said as he ran a gentle hand on my back. The breeze of his voice in my ear fondled my insides.

"Good to see you too."

We stood in the middle of the crowd, taking in the touch of our bodies and the sight of our eyes.

"Any special plans for the rest of the long weekend?" he asked.

I couldn't decide if he cared to find out, tried to be polite or made conversation to avoid uncomfortable silence in a noisy crowd.

"Shouldn't I be asking you that? Your birthday is coming up. Happy birthday."

"Thank you. But I asked first."

"I'm sleeping over at Nikki's tonight and maybe tomorrow. I don't know yet."

"I'm having dinner at my parents' house tomorrow after which, I don't know either."

"I should go back to Nikki," I said. But I wished he'd ask me to stay.

He drew me into another hug. "OK. We'll talk later."

Talk later in Vinson's lingo could mean talk the next day or talk a year later or talk never, which was why I didn't ratify. I made my way back to the serving bar.

Nikki leaned over. "So?" I shrugged my shoulders and crinkled my nose. "Want to go? Back to my house?"

"Please."

A week later, a thunderstorm announced its onset on a cool vapid night. The thunder struck lightning bolts, penetrating the infuriated sky. And before I switched my mind off Vinson, my phone quivered on the coffee table. I glided away from the window to the name on the display.

"Hey, doll. What are you doing on this stormy night?"

"Watching the thunder, you should try it sometimes."

"Do you want to watch it together?"

"Are you inviting me over to your place or should we meet on a deserted field for that?"

"I am inviting you over. Would you do me the honour?"

"In that case, I would."

"I moved into a new apartment. I'll text you the address."

"Again?"

"Yes. Be careful driving."

I preferred the old one. We'd collected a fair share of memories in that tiny bachelor. I raced to my car marinating in enthusiasm. The rain poured in by buckets but I would've driven to see him through a cyclone, much less through thunder and rain.

I parked my car next to his truck and jumped out, holding the phone to my ear with Vinson at the other end.

"Look up," he said. I scanned the two storey building for his shadow.

He stood sky high on top of the exterior stairs draping the wall and waved at me with the same golden smile, I'd recognize from miles away. I wanted to fly Superman style to the second floor but instead, I climbed up cool as ever on the slippery metal stairs. Shirtless in the rain, he wore a Raiders cap with hair locks sticking out the back. Before I reached the landing, he stretched his hand out and I latched on to safety. How could I still be mad at this charming gentleman? He was my greatest weakness of all.

"Glad you made it okay," he said as the rain drops bounced off his lips. He ushered me inside the apartment, locked the door and loomed close for a hug. "Come on, let's get comfy."

He led me by the hand to the living room, then fled to the bathroom to dry up.

"You need a towel?"

"No."

"Drink?" I nodded. "Dr Pepper okay?"

"Dr Pepper's fine."

"So, what do you think about this apartment?"

"It's much bigger."

He'd rented a two bedroom apartment with a friend I hadn't met and apart from being messy, it came as bright and spacious. His roommate had gone to work for the evening shift.

Vinson joined me on the couch with a beer for himself and a smile in pretense that nothing worth talking about happened between us lately. As if he hadn't vanished again, leaving my heart in pieces. He lifted my legs over his knees, dragged his torso closer and dropped his head on my chest.

"I just want to sit like this for a minute," he said.

I wondered if he missed the way I pampered him, toyed with his hair and baby-talked to him. I stroked his hair and he closed his eyes. I wished I could peer through his thoughts. He hardly shared anymore and that part hung like a stone in my heart.

Moments later, he reached for the remote and pointed it toward the media station. *On the turning away* filled the room and he shot me the seductive stare. I lowered my head and kissed him and this time, I closed my eyes.

"Do you know how many times I listened to this song on my iPod? This song is all you now," I said as I opened my eyes.

He straightened his posture and shifted his gaze from my eyes to my lips. "Still the same kissable lips," he said, brushing his mouth over mine. "I love kissing you."

"Then why do you always run away?"

"I . . . I guess I have issues."

"What kind of issues?"

"Issues."

"Can I help?" A moment of silence. "I'm here for you Vinson."

He pressed his finger on my lips. "I know."

I angled away. "I think that's the problem."

"What?"

"That you know."

"You just told me."

"You've always known, you ass." His face mimicked mine into a serious expression. "We have to talk about what happened. The night I drove to your place uninvited, we have to talk about it."

"We talked about it at The Tavern," he said.

"We didn't talk-talk about it. You just excused yourself."

"I was in the shower and by the time I came out and saw your messages, I didn't know what to do. I'm sorry." There he was doing it again.

"Wait, you were at home?" He nodded and rubbed his chin.

Sloan told me a different version at the gas station, said that he'd partied with Vinson at his own house that night. I bet Vinson didn't even remember where he'd gone or what he did. He figured, he'd throw in the shower lie. Short and sweet. Quick escape.

"That's not the issue Vinson. The issue is that you can't keep disappearing on me and coming back into my life whenever you please, expecting me to be there."

"I'm sorry. I won't do it again." He planted a kiss on my lips to further seduce me and stop the oh-so-pointless conversation, as far as he was concerned.

"I mean it. We have to communicate. Are you familiar with the term *communication*? No matter what it is, just tell me and I'll understand. Don't just evaporate on me because one day, I won't be there anymore."

"OK, I won't. I promise." He inched closer for another kiss.

I jerked my head away. "You're not listening."

"Yes, I am. I heard everything you said."

"You heard it but you're not processing it. You automatically agree with everything I say to get off the subject as fast as possible. I'm serious Vinson. I can't play this game anymore."

"Got it. No more games. Can we enjoy our night together now?" he said, replaying his favourite song. His mouth popped empty promises like a magician's hand popping coins and I'd spoken my words in vain.

He tucked my hair behind my ear and brushed his fingertips on my cheeks. Then he wriggled his hand into mine and shimmied off the couch, silently inviting me to the bedroom. When I jerked my hand in hesitation, he turned and blazed his mystic eyes into mine. No need for that trick, I'd lost my soul in his wild eyes forever ago. I drew in a deep breath and followed him in like an idiot.

CHAPTER
31

Fourteen days after our thunderstorm rendezvous, Vinson texted to ask how I've been. Everything we talked about — I talked about — skidded straight to his brain recycling bin. "Great," I keyed back. He played the I've-been-busy-working card and informed me that he might work an early day on Thursday. I didn't ask for an explanation for his two-week hop nor did I suggest a get-together. "Let Thursday come and we'll take it from there."

Thursday came and went without his call. I never understood the reason why he'd call and make the plan himself when he couldn't keep his word. His call, his plan, his deceit. Every time. He even lacked the decency to text me an excuse, like he promised he would. I handled my frustration in hush.

In mid-June, Nikki and I pulled an all-nighter at her house. We settled on the patio sofa facing the backyard next to the outdoor fireplace to scare off the summer bugs. We sipped on chilled white wine and yapped the night away with music in the background.

Halfway through the night, I stepped inside the house for a jug of ice cubes to add to the bucket cradling the wine bottle. A red light flickered on my phone with two texts. In the first, Vinson excused himself for the promised Thursday, reasoning that the day at work ran longer than he thought and had the audacity to ask if I had plans for the night. "Hope you're not upset with me," popped ten minutes after the first. I thanked the mighty forces I'd left my phone in the house. They spared me the temptation to respond.

The next night, Vinson called around midnight. I'd deserted my phone on silent mode and out of sight while I worked on my beauty blog and an hour later, the red light gleamed again. He babbled to call him back, something out of his character. "I never leave voicemail. It's a waste of my time," he once said and I guessed, his voice message translated to making an effort. I toyed with the phone in my hand before pressing the call button with immediate regret. When my call fizzed answerless, my regret deepened times tenfold. Half an hour later, after I'd slid under the duvet, he returned the call. I let it ring. Fuck you and your late night visits, pal.

Days later, I shifted into a flat mental state. I'd worked long hours all week, constructing posts for my blog and brainstorming ways to boost the sales at Heather's spa through my site — dear sweet commission, fly my way and land in my pocket — and by Saturday evening, I collapsed on the couch exhausted and lonely.

When Vinson texted at seven p.m., I read his message three times over. His early hour text came as a shock, a good shock, finally. I wanted to give him a chance to see what he made of the night, so I replied with a casual hello. He called cheerful as ever.

"Hey, doll. What are you doing?" he asked with a semi-shaky voice, unsure of what to expect.

"You know, weekend plans and stuff."

"Would you like to come out for drinks with me and my room-mate or maybe come to our place for drinks and a laugh or two?"

"Suppose I could."

"I'll call you back in an hour to let you know what's going on."

"All right." Wait, I thought we knew what was going on.

The fucker didn't call back. He stood me up but it'd be his last.

On Monday, after tumbling through the weekend alone, I dashed to Nikki's house for a sleepover. When Vinson called around nine p.m., interrupting Nikki's speech on the benefits of aged white wine mid-sentence, I urged her to continue.

"Aren't you going to answer?"

"No."

"That's my girl. Where were we?"

CHAPTER
3 2

On Canada Day, I honoured Nikki's invitation for a celebration at her house with bells on. Sofa on the deck, outdoor fireplace, a bottle of chilled white wine, laughter galore. One too many wine glasses later, we held hands with arms crossed and danced in a circle barefoot in the grass until we rattled the mosquitoes into mad-attack. They ate us alive, bug spray and all.

The next day, she worked at The Tavern and insisted I kept her company, at least until everyone herded back in town from camp and the place boomed with social butterflies again.

By the time Nikki filled me in on Vinson's presence, his profile had already flashed on the mirrored wall behind the serving bar. He'd pranced inside in a spectacular entrance with his convoy and I rolled my eyes. His confidence oscillated from skyrocketing in the company of his entourage to underground level when alone with me. He gazed at the nape of my neck but as soon as I peeped sideways, he shifted his eyes like a pre-programmed android.

I plunked my butt on a bar stool and giggled with Nikki as I sipped on my soft minty cocktail with my don't-know-don't-care mask on. Vinson loomed toward the bar while I pretended to be unaware of his existence. He spilled out the order for his group, then turned to me.

"Hi, doll."

"Alexa. My name's Alexa," I said and turned my head back without a word. Nikki angled away to prepare the drinks, tittering under her breath.

"You mad at me?"

"What do you think?" I said, facing the serving bar.

"Why are you mad at me?"

"You stood me up twice and that's only lately. I'm tired of it."

He jittered from one foot to another. "I stood you up? When?"

"Let me hit replay, in case you forgot. You called me on Saturday last week, made plans and never called back. The same thing a couple of weeks before that."

"Yeah but sometimes plans change and other times I'm not sure what I'm doing until the last minute."

"If that's the case, don't call me." He gazed at me as I corner-eyed his chest rising and compressing with hasty breaths. "I told you before, I'm not the kind of girl you stand up or forget to call."

"Then come to me and say something, yell at me, give me shit but don't ignore me," he said, his face flushed.

"What's the matter Vinson? You don't like being ignored?"

"No, ignoring sucks."

"Now you know how I feel all the time. You've been ignoring me time and time again for a year and a half and I ignore you once and you don't like it?"

"You've ignored me more than once," he said.

"You have to ignore him longer than he ignores you," Nikki once told me and damn, she was right. Giving him a mouthful of his own game tasted like powdered sugar on chicory. And maybe, just maybe, he acknowledged for once — not to me but to himself — what he'd done wrong.

I peered at the side of my shoulder and met Vinson's gaze. He'd worked up the courage to lace an arm on the small of my back and frissons flashed up my spine.

"I want to bury the hatchet," he said.

"There's nothing to bury, except for my feelings for you."

"No, please. Don't ever do that."

Nikki slammed the order on the counter. "There you go." No matter how good of a friend she'd been to Vinson, she'd had enough of his gibberish too.

"Don't you have friends waiting for you?" I said.

"Can we go to your place tonight?"

"No, of course not. I can't believe you have the nerve to ask me that."

"Why not? Don't you miss us?"

"Whatever I miss, it's not in you anymore."

"Try me out."

"Why?"

"Because I miss it too."

"Liar."

"No, I miss it for real," he said with begging eyes.

"Do you even know what the word *real* means?" His body stiffened, hand off the small of my back. "And don't say you'll come over, if you know it's not going to happen."

"Then I'll have to surprise you but I have to go home first."

"I already know how this story ends."

"I've been out and about all day. I need to shower and change. I'll meet you at your place."

Nikki gave a doubtful expression as he carried the drinks to his group and gulped his in two minutes straight. Then he winked at me on his way out.

"Have fun tonight. But if he doesn't show, he's going to have to deal with me," she said as I hugged her goodbye.

I paced through my apartment, as if stepping on nails in my wait for Vinson, uncertain he'd show up until he called.

"I'm four minutes away."

I breathed a sigh of relief but I could only be a hundred percent sure he'd show up, the moment I'd make visual contact with his body in close proximity. I stood by the window as he parked his truck, leaped out and cut across the parking lot. He strutted to the entrance door, five floors down below.

When I swung the door open, he stood tall with arms wide open, as if waiting to be praised for keeping his word. "Ta-daaa."

He kissed me on our way to the living room. We crashed on the couch and shared current events. I didn't have much to share but of course, he did. He was a man of the world. He belonged anywhere and everywhere. My mind flew off as he dribbled on funny stories about himself and his friends but even that kind of blubber runs out of fillers and pads a silent moment with a kiss.

"I missed you."

"I've heard that before."

"It's because it's true." He glanced toward the bedroom, then at me with sensual eyes. "Why don't you let me prove it to you?"

"That's not how you prove it to me, Vinson. Proving your feelings to me is an entirely different ballgame," I said and his expression turned sour. "But I'll go for the fun now and the rest later," I said and his face brightened like the sun.

We raced to the bedroom holding hands and jumped on the bed, kissing like mad.

"Wait. If we're going to do it, we're going to do it right," I said.

I shimmied off the bed, lowered the lights and pressed play on my iPod sitting on the docking station. Pink Floyd, *On the turning away* came through. The thing about Vinson, I never knew when I'd have him alone again, so I aimed to make it memorable enough for him to come back.

He raised his torso on his elbows. "You know, it doesn't get any better than this." Then why do you keep running away, you idiot?

I crept on top of him and we smooched uncontrollably. The thirst for the each other was still fresh, unaltered by the time. Our rhythm, our touch, our vibe still the same and all in unison.

We rolled between the sheets with our lips glued and burnished, fingers through our hair strands, legs intertwined in bare plunder. As I lay beneath his naked frame, I held his head above mine and gaped into his eyes. I had to ensure the moment was real.

"It's still amazing between us," he purred.

"That's why we do it once every four months?" I whispered, swallowing my tears.

"Come here, baby." He caressed my lips as his tongue coiled his name on the roof of my mouth.

When the light of dawn grazed our faces, we flipped another crazed fondling session to boot the day. And before he stepped out the door on his way to work, grin on his face, hands touchy and lips kissy, that same burning question flashed in my head — when will I see him again?

Three days later, I texted him to say hello. We exchanged boring texts and wished each other goodnight with empty messages and without an ounce of meat in them, just dreary as hell.

Three more days later, on a beautiful Sunday, I'd finished my errands and prepared a dish of spinach pasta, my specialty now. I invited him over with a text for a taste of my cooking to which he replied, "I'll take a rain check. I want to stay in and play vids." I scowled at the phone, baffled and benumb with disgust. How could he turn down my dinner invitation in favour of video games and tell me about it like it's no big deal? He could. And he did.

In the days following, I'd slipped back into melancho-mode and couldn't take the torture anymore. Waiting and waiting for a call to arrive was like waiting for snow in the Sahara.

One night, I took a giant sip of red, banged the wine glass on the coffee table and keyed a message to the one who'd played with my emotions, my sanity and my life. "I can't do this anymore. I will always love you." The three magic words had to be told before our charade was over. "What is this message about? I have a feeling it's a glass of wine talking. I'll call you tomorrow," read his text two hours later. Even if he was right about the wine, my soul winced in sobriety and my mind pounded with lucidity. And I meant every word.

He didn't call the next day.

CHAPTER
3 3

I nestled in solitaire with my wits immersed in my beauty blog.
I'd expanded to lifestyle and healthy habits and wrote for hours
on end, pure therapy. My social life revolved around phone chats
with Mom and Maureen. On her birthday, I skyped with Maureen
to send her my wishes and virtual hugs. She had a romantic night
ahead planned by hubby with dinner and a room for two at a hotel
in Mont-Tremblant.

I hardly ventured outside my apartment anymore. I made short
runs for food and necessities and raced back. I needed to nurture
my soul back to life. I fought the Vinson-withdrawals with everything I could and hoped that one day I'd be freed from addiction.

On a fateful Saturday halfway through August, Nikki rang my
phone to ensure I still breathed.

"I haven't heard from you in three weeks. I was worried."

"I kept under the radar to spare myself the emotional hassle."

"And I thought Vinson didn't let you come up for air."

"On the contrary."

"But he showed up at your place that night after The Tavern,
right?"

"He did but I lost him again, which explains my hiding."

"Time to come out and spread your wings."

"Where to?"

"If I tell you, will you still come?"

"Probably not but tell me anyway."

"We're celebrating The Tavern's three year anniversary. Everyone
in town will be there —"

"Which is why I'm not coming."

"Are you going to lock yourself in the house forever? Give me a break. You're coming."

"I'm not."

"He probably won't even be there. It's invitations only," she said.

"And he didn't get one?"

"He doesn't need one. Besides, it's our big night of the year and I'd like you to be there with me."

"I'm not sure it's a good idea. I'm trying to heal my wounds."

"You need to come out and socialize, live your life. That's how your wounds will heal. Get dressed. Be at my house in an hour. We'll go in my truck. My boyfriend's out for a pre-party drink with the boys. He'll meet us there."

An hour later, I knocked on Nikki's door. But I shouldn't have.

"That's my girl." She scanned me up and down. "You look fresh."

I wore a pair of cobalt-blue Capri jeans, a black silk blouse with ruffled sleeves and Romanian made indigo wedges.

"It will take a hell of a lot more pep talk for this party than complimenting me into high confidence," I said.

"Come on in. Coffees are on the table."

I sipped on the brew hunched over the coffee table with my legs pressed together.

"Dude, stop fretting," Nikki said.

"I'm not."

"You are and you need to loosen up, like, right now. We're going to a party not a schooling exam."

"I wish it was an exam."

Two hours later, we ambled inside The Tavern where familiar faces bombarded us with nods and loose hugs. Indeed, the event was a VIP party where everyone who was anyone in town attended. I expected to run into Tania but no sign of her.

"Kara and I tried but she wasn't available. We hired someone else to put it together." Nikki circled her eyes around the bar. "She did a good job too."

I jabbed a boomerang scan at the bar. Balloons in the colours of Skittles, confetti poppers, champagne flutes, tasting trays with baked goodies and dangling gold and white paper lanterns out on the deck.

"I'd say so," I said as I took in Vinson's absence.

"Brevin's waiting for us."

I followed Nikki to a group of partiers at the end of the serving bar where Brevin waved through the crowd to catch our attention.

"What took you guys so long? I thought you'd be the first ones here," he said.

She gave him a smirk. "Girl stuff."

Brevin bought a round of drinks, my usual soft drink for starters. The night was young and I wanted to hang out sober for now. I pretended to take part in the cluster's chatter while everyone stood close together and clung to the serving bar. "Yes." "No." "Wow." "That's great."

Nikki spun to me with a shiny piece in her hand. "Kara handed me a shot of tequila. It's for you."

"What? No, I'm nervous enough as it is." I still couldn't escape the needles and butterflies mixed into one cake of despair in my gut. After all, Vinson could show up any minute.

"Have one. It will put you in a good mood. Grab it before some-one spills it on your outfit. Or mine." She shifted her eyes to her sister. "Make that two."

Kara glided over with another shot and banged it on the bar with a plastic smile. I couldn't decide if she shunned Nikki's bond with me or held a grudge for being stuck behind the bar while her sister was having a good time. But then, why would she offer me tequila?

"Cheers," Nikki said and we licked the salt off the back of each other's hand, guzzled down the shots and bit the lemons, scrunched up faces and all. A flaming glow lanced down my throat to my stomach and ten seconds later, the needles succumbed and my butterflies turned into invincible dragons.

I leaned close to Nikki's ear as she joked with Brevin and friends. "What are the chances that —"

"That he'll show up? I thought you didn't want that."

"One word — freaking tequila."

Nikki giggled. "That's two words."

"Whatever," I said as Vinson's bubbly head gripped on my double take from across the room. "Fuck, he's here."

"You want another shot?"

"No."

"Kara, two more shots," she yelled out but her sister shuffled out cocktails and beers at the other end. Brevin boosted Nikki over the serving bar and the tomboy trapped in a dazzling woman's body fetched two tequilas in five seconds straight.

"Down it," she said.

"No. I won't be able to walk out of here."

"You'll be fine. Down it." We gulped the happy potions and slammed them on the granite.

I turned my face in Vinson's direction as my insides bubbled into a sizzling superpower that shot through my veins and straight to my brain. I snaked my way through the mass of bodies and hooked his arm out of a midst of group chatter. The crowd propelled us into the perfect nearby corner where I pressed on his chest and pinned him against the wall. And all this transpired in slow motion in my head.

"Hi," I said, blazing fire through my eyes.

"How are you?" he asked, uneasy but attempting to stay cool.

"What's going on with us?"

"Us?"

"There used to be us, remember?

"Alexa, you know I'm a wild child, you know how I am and right now, I can't give you a relationship." His words cut through my heart, thin even slices of thudding muscle, one carve at a time.

I bore my eyes into his and asked him with the saddest voice I'd ever heard myself speak. "Are we done?"

"I guess. You told me to move on and I did." And the only time he followed my instructions had to be when I ended it over a text after a glass of wine, only to end my misery of infinite waiting.

I fought my tears at the back of my throat. "Are you back with your ex?"

"Fuck no."

"Is there someone else?"

"No."

"Then what's the problem, Vinson?"

"You told me to leave you alone. Isn't that what you wanted?"

"No, that's not what I wanted and you know that."

"What *do* you want?"

"I want *you*. I want to be with you. I'm in love with you. I don't know what you did to me but I'm in love with you and there's nothing I can do about it." Somehow my desperation fought its way out through my lungs and I searched his face for an emotion.

A vague smile fissured in the left corner of his mouth. "I can't give you a relationship right now. I'm sorry, I just can't."

"Have I ever pushed for a relationship?" I did want a relationship but apparently this notion was forbidden.

"So, what do you want to do?"

"I'm not saying let's have a relationship but what we had between September and December was perfect. Why can't we go back to that?" I had no idea I could sink to the bottom of my pride tank until the moment I recognized that I begged him to be my fuck friend again, just so he'd stay in my life. "We could be so happy together but you won't let it happen," I screamed.

"You're right. I won't."

I loomed my head an inch away from his face. "See, that's your problem right there. You don't want to be happy."

"I'm not going to stand here and argue with you about this."

I pushed him back against the wall as heated blood rushed to my stomach. "Are you willing to lose us? How would you feel if I went on and dated someone else?"

"I don't how I would feel. I don't know what I would think. I don't know what I want."

I softened my voice, swallowed my tears. "You don't care at all?"

"I care, of course I care. But I don't know what to say to you, Alexa. Right now, I'd like to have a drink with my friends," he said and angled away with a whiff of disdain.

I gripped on his wrist and snapped him back in place. "Look me in the eyes and tell me right now that you don't want me and then, I can move on."

I had to finish what I'd started. I had to hear these words freshly baked out of his mouth, so I could finally end my suffering and move on with my life.

He glimpsed at the floor, then at me. "I can't tell you that."

"Why? Why? If you don't want me, you have to let me go. Please, if you ever cared about me at all, let me go. You can't expect me to wait for you forever." I pleaded with tears rolling down my face and for a moment, sadness clouded his eyes. But only for a moment.

"I don't know what to tell you right now. We'll talk about this later but right now, I'd like to join my friends." He glared at my hand locked around his wrist. "Do you mind?" I unlocked my grip, after which he turned his back on me and squandered back to his rubbernecking friends.

I careened to the exit door with Nikki catching up behind.

"I'm leaving."

"No, you are absolutely not leaving," she said as she grabbed my arm but I swung it back.

"I have to get out of here. I can't breathe."

I banged out the back door and threw myself at Nikki. I bawled in her arms, like the world was coming to an end. My world has come to an end and I didn't want to exist anymore.

"Can I use your phone? My battery is dead," I said.

"You're not going to call him."

"I want to call a cab. I'll pick up my car from your house later."

"Sure but don't leave, you're fine now. Come back inside."

"I'm not fine and there's no way I'm going back in."

The door screeched open with Kara's shadow in the exit light.

"What the hell happened?"

"Nothing," Nikki said.

"Don't tell me you'll let that idiot ruin your night," Kara said. She stared at me with — what I could make through the misty night and the fog of my tears — disgust.

"It's more than that. You don't know the depth of the story," Nikki said.

"All I have to say is . . . he's not worth it," Kara said.

"He's worth it to her," Nikki snapped. "Can you call a cab when you get back in?"

Kara smashed the door behind her while Nikki slung an arm around my shoulder. "Are you going to be okay?"

"Yeah. I have to be," I mumbled.

"I have tons of work when we close, otherwise I'd follow you home. My sister would freak if I left her alone for the after-party clean up."

"No, it's okay. I need be alone anyway."

"Call me in the morning?" I nodded. "I love you."

"I love you too," I whispered as the cab rolled to a stop.

I scrambled into the back seat and waved to Nikki, who raised her thumb and pinkie finger, the call-me sign with her hand.

I stumbled inside the apartment and dropped on the bathroom floor with my head in the toilet, puking my guts out along with the two shots of tequila and my broken heart. I left the lights off, only a faded glimmer from the parking lot lamppost squeezed through the window. I couldn't bare my reflection in the mirror. I couldn't bare the illumination of my pain. I hurled myself to bed and buried my head in the pillow as tears let loose until I had tears no more.

I booked a flight first thing in the morning, courtesy of Air Miles' mountain supply since childhood. I had to get out of town fast. And I didn't want to just get out of town. I wanted to get out of the country, change continents, change constellations, if I could. But first, I cabbed it to Nikki's house to pick up my car.

"Brevin and I could've brought your car later on. Come in. We'll have coffee." I stepped inside and dropped on the couch, one leg out and ready to go. Nikki headed to the kitchen. "You should've stayed," she said on her way back, planting the tray on the coffee table.

I stretched my hand out and hauled a cup to my mouth. "After the conversation I had with Vinson? Hell no."

"Brevin invited everyone to our house after the party."

"Everyone?"

"Everyone we know, like, Vinson and his group."

"It would've been awkward."

"But you guys could have talked things out."

"There's nothing left to talk about. It's done."

"I talked to him about you. He said he couldn't give you a relationship right now but he said, he wished he could. I told him that even if you guys don't get into a relationship, you should at least stay friends."

"His *can't* excuse is crap. If a guy wants to be with you, he'll be with you. I was too blind to see that from the get-go."

"He did say that he gets along really well with you, so that's a good thing."

"And what am I supposed to do with that? Add it to my collection of V-bullshit? I have a stack of them in my back pocket. It's over. I'm tired of waiting."

"It's not over. You guys will talk again."

I checked my phone for the time. "I have to go pack. I'm leaving town tomorrow."

"Where to?"

"Romania."

"Dude, you're not leaving town. You're leaving the country."

"Something like that."

"Only you would run across the world after a fight with Vinson."

"I'm not running. I need a break and this is how I take breaks."

"That's funny. When I take a break, I go out for a smoke."

"I'll call you when I get back."

At the front door, we embraced in a hug. Then I climbed into the driver seat under Nikki's wary expression. She waved from the doorway as I backed out of the driveway also unsure that running was the best option. But then I decided that it was.

The next day, I bolted to the highway, dropped my car off at the longterm airport parking and boarded the first plane out with phone buds clinging to my ears. I collapsed into an aisle seat as I painted the latest events into a short story frame for Maureen.

"I understand your departure. You need a different environment right now," she said.

Maureen understood the meaning of far and away trips to find the inner self. Her Greek parents moved to Canada before she'd been born and she also grew up on the plane, swinging back and forth to and from the family's native land vacations.

"I'll email you the rest of the story from Romania."

"Don't forget to come back."

CHAPTER
34

The day after my arrival, I unpacked in a blue funk over my return while the sound of enthusiasm in Mom's voice still echoed in my brain. "Mom, I'm calling from Schiphol," my Royal Dutch layover on my way to R.O. and she screamed with joy, then ordered me to hang up, so she could start to cook before my landing in B.U.

I pulled my mind back to The Great White North where I suspended my garments in the closet, dousing in jet lag as my phone rumbled. I picked it up in slow-mo.

"You're back. I tried you every day for the past week but your phone was off," said Nikki. "I know, roaming charges and shit. You up for a visit?" Her question sounded like Vinson's and I almost said no, but then I remembered I didn't want to be alone and unpacking was a painful process at the moment.

"I'll see you soon."

When Nikki wrenched the door open, we threw ourselves in each other's arms, then skipped up the stairs into the living room.

"I went for a quick drive to Timmies to buy coffees after I called you," she said as I sank into the couch. "I figured you missed it." I once told her I took a thirty-three-ounce can of Tim Hortons coffee with me on every trip overseas. Except for the last one when I spun across like a tornado.

I fished two pairs of shoes out of my tote. "Since we're talking surprise . . ." I flung a pair of turquoise wedges with ankle straps and a pair of low-cut beige high-heel boots next to her.

"You bought me shoes? I thought you'd forget." She threw her arms around my neck. "You always wear extravagant shoes," she said when we first met. "Where do you find them?" "Europe," I said and she shifted her eyes between my pupils. "Could you ever bring me a pair?" Of course I could. "Yes."

"Do you like them?" I asked now.

"I love them," she said as she held them in mid-air. "These are a work of art. We need to celebrate." She strutted to the kitchen and back with a bottle of Merlot. "You're sleeping over, right? It's only the two of us tonight."

"Yes. Now open the wine and tell me what's new."

On Tuesday after Labour Day, I turned up at the University of Northern Ontario campus with poise, embracing the student role as good medicine for the morale. I'd slipped the student card in my back pocket and bang, I had superpowers. I was back on track and in a place where life made sense again. I pranced to class with purpose and goals.

First day classes kept short and sweet with professors combing through the syllabus out loud. At least they skipped the part where I'd have to turn to the student next to me and introduce myself. Or worse, stand up and introduce myself to class. Painful. My classmates knew each other already, so I eased into a lonely seat.

And leave it to me to spoil the novelty of the university experience. As I ventured through the hallways, my inflated enthusiasm gradually swooshed out like the air of a pricked balloon. The library extended on two floors but it only donned eighty computers. Brimley had two hundred and fifty. The cafeteria held a football field sized sitting area but it resembled an old warehouse. Brimley's was modern with electrical outlets built-in the tables. Off-hours classrooms were locked, so I couldn't settle into one and study should the library become rowdy. And the quiet study rooms bore no computers. I didn't carry my laptop to school. The textbooks weighed a ton on their own.

The university campus aligned the lakeshore and dispersed an idealistic look with sunsets glittering in the still water and greenery along the pathways. Then it dawned on me that I'd have to walk to class from building to building in cryogenic winter mornings. At the end of my first day, I cruised home in apathy.

Two weeks later, I still missed the friendships I formed at Brimley, the closeness with my classmates and teachers. "In university, you're on your own," I recalled hearing through the grapevine. I'd go to class, I'd sit down, I'd take notes, I'd go home.

On a given Wednesday afternoon, I coasted from school, shambled into my apartment and tossed my bag on the study room floor. I fell on the couch soaking in sorrow when Nikki's call came to the rescue with an invitation to her house. She always called at the perfect time.

I charged out the door and I couldn't remember the last time I blissfully drove through the pouring rain. Actually, I could. The torrent drenched the air in grey mist and diminished the visibility to a blur. I'd planned to stop at the convenience store by Nikki's house for snacks but a closer shop squeezed its head through the haze at a red light. I crossed the junction on green and veered into the parking lot on the left side of the road. No cars in sight, except for a massive pickup truck parked a step away from the store's entrance. A good idea. I planted my car nose-to-nose with the truck. I shut the engine's mouth as my eyes drifted above the dashboard and through the windshield at the flowing numbers and letters on the license plate.

I sprung into the store and the moment I stepped inside, my brain caught up with the last three letters on the truck's teeth. I never remembered the numbers but always the letters, the last three on the license plate. I gazed up with my heart in the shape of a firebomb and there he was, standing at the cashier waiting for his change. He stared with lips parted and eyes the size of lemons.

"H-hey," Vinson stuttered. I gave a mere nod. My speech was disabled as much as his.

"Next," the clerk called, interrupting our staring gala. Vinson picked his change off the counter while he attempted to say, have a good day to the clerk but swallowed his words halfway through. He brushed the air off my shoulder on the way out. I blinked when his scent snaked through my nostrils and inside my skeleton, rattling my emotions into a gleam of doodling hearts.

"Miss, can I help you?" The clerk's face unclouded my vision.

"I'll pick something off the racks." I dissipated between the aisles as the truck rumbled into the distance.

I retreated to my car, tossed the snacks on the passenger seat and gave myself a minute to breathe. I cackled as I reeled the ignition. I'd never seen Vinson so tensed before. Maybe he feared I'd pull off a scene but I'd never repeat it. It was done and dealt with but his ravished expression came as rare as genuine black pearls and I'm not going to lie, I enjoyed it.

On the down side, he missed a chance to kiss and make up under the pouring rain. It could've been dramatic and romantic at the same time. If he only waited for me to come out of the store, we'd argue for a few minutes, then he'd confess he couldn't live without me and I'd throw myself in his arms and we'd kiss in the rain. Then we'd drive to his place to dry off and make love to a happily ever after.

I breezed to Nikki's house with my mind lost in the encounter. We laughed about the story over sizzling coffee. Three days later, I celebrated my birthday at Nikki's. Just the two of us and it turned out a blast. We yapped on the deck next to the fireplace over red wine and upbeat tunes under the fall moon.

CHAPTER
35

Meanwhile at school, it was back to the grind and far from easy but I skated along with my academic developments. I took pride in the science woman I'd become but I still waited for the university itself to grow on me. I did relish the lectures, gradually bonded with peers and embraced a sense of belonging. Back-to-back classes could be exhausting and tedious but I enjoyed sharing breathing space with like-minded people.

One day on break week — or reading week as they called it at Brimley, that mid-semester week when you get to breathe off the books, even though it's instated for reading academic material — I invited Nikki to my place for breakfast after her boyfriend skipped town on business. Then we bounced to her house to spend the night. She served her signature mushroom pasta with Sauvignon Blanc and a hot case of the giggles.

A knock at the door tapped halfway through our dissection of my story with Vinson, which usually came as dessert. Kara stepped in beaming with optimism, her face bright in comparison to her standoffish demeanor and I braced myself for a budding disguise.

"So, if you're both here, who's working The Tavern?" I asked.

"We hired a bar-back," Kara said.

"A bar-back?"

"A bartender's assistant, she's new. We sometimes let her work the bar for a couple of hours on slow days. We'll see how she does. I was bored stiff and wanted to get away for a bit. Come to think of it, let's go out for a drink."

"Yes," Nikki-the-extrovert agreed.

"No, I . . . I don't want to go out. I want to stay in and hang out and share stories all night," I said.

"Isn't that all you guys do every time you get together?"

"Yeah and I enjoy it. I like the intimacy. I hate crowded places," I said, shifting my eyes to Nikki, "you know that."

"My sister's right. Let's go out. It's been a while anyway."

"And you know how my last festivity ended. Besides, it's only Tuesday." Tuesday, a magic word once upon a time.

"That won't happen again. You said it yourself," Nikki said.

"Who cares if it's Tuesday?" Kara said as she fished her whistling phone out of her purse.

I shuffled to the kitchen with a pout to help Nikki with the dishes.

"No need. I'll put them in the dishwasher," she said.

"Yes, Vinson. I'd like those movies back by tonight. You've had them long enough," Kara said on the phone in the living room.

I jerked my head in Kara's direction and back to Nikki within a split second. "Is she talking to Vinson?"

"It sounds like she is."

"I'll drop by to pick them up," Kara said on the phone. Her conversation with Vinson had nothing to do with me but my heart pounded through my ribs, the moment she spat out his name. "Okay, let's go," Kara said to us.

"Where?" I asked.

"I have to pick up the movies Vinson borrowed from me a while back. He's playing pool at The Billiard Club. We'll go there first."

"Nice plans but I'm not going," I said.

Nikki evil-eyed me. "Yes, you are."

"No, I'm not."

I dreaded going anywhere, let alone to a place where Vinson had the chance to ignore me. I refused to give him the satisfaction of thinking that I came out of my way to score a glimpse of him. He flattered himself enough times already.

"I'm sure you want to see him," Nikki said.

"I do but not like this. We don't even have a thing anymore. He'll think I'm chasing after him."

"No, he won't, because you're with us," Kara said.

"And that exonerates me from being lame?"

"You can come with us or you can wait here," Nikki said.

I couldn't drive home after sipping on post-dinner wine and I didn't want to stay at Nikki's all by myself for God-knows-how-long.

I gritted my teeth. "I'll come with you but I'll wait in the car."

Kara rolled her eyes. "Wait in the car? You should walk in with us, like normal people."

I stumbled in the back seat of Kara's SUV. "I'm not normal people." I sat on mute behind the driver seat the entire way.

We swerved into the parking lot at The Billiard Club where Kara parked and rang Vinson's phone. A couple of words later, she peered over her shoulder and I followed her gaze through the side tinted window. He hung over the railway at the top of the stairs at the side of the building and waved at the car.

"He's coming to us," Kara said and my heart boomed like crazy.

He descended the stairs, two steps at a time and strutted toward the car. Nikki rolled down the passenger window as he approached her side.

"Where the hell have you been?" Nikki asked her famous line, lightly slapping his face, his head barely visible behind hers.

"Around," he said. His face may have been out of my view but the sound of his voice rolled my emotions in a tumble, like the frielationship we'd been through for a year and a half.

He leaned inside the vehicle to hug Nikki and wedged his head between the front seats, inches away from me. We locked eyes for a sheer three seconds and it was like fire in the heart. I stopped breathing and exhaled when his head drew away.

He exchanged words with the sisters, none of which my brain registered, then he handed the movies and sprinted away. I found it unexplainable why this mere encounter had startled me more than the one at the convenience store. His eyes pierced through the envelope of my soul and stirred my sentiments for him like my mom's Kitchen Aid mixer.

"You okay?" Nikki asked. I half-nodded.

Back in Nikki's driveway, we hopped out sans her sister.

"I have to check on the bar-back and close the bar," Kara said, immobile in the driver seat.

"Thanks for tonight," I said.

She bowed her head. "Have a good night, both of you." I never knew she could be human.

I trailed Nikki inside the house and chortled under my breath. There I was with my girlfriend and her sister in the car, two of Vinson's closest fem-friends, who cheered on my could-be-would-be-should-be relationship with him and yet, Vinson and I were not on speaking terms. Comical to the grotesque.

CHAPTER
3 6

Nikki's birthday landed on the first weekend of November. She threw a bantam bash at her house with Brevin, myself and a friend of Brevin's, the latter as a filler, not as my potential something. I presumed her sister worked the bar but I still couldn't care enough to ask. We cheered with wine and gags well into the night and fractured our necks with laughter and mouthfuls of birthday cake.

Three weeks later, I slouched in boredom during a lecture on nutrition when my phone gleamed with Nikki's name on silent mode. After class, I played the voicemail as I took the stairs to the main floor. The dreading wait for the crammed elevator exceeded my patience level, which was limited by birth anyway. "Leave New Year's Eve open. We've been invited to a private party. Guess where? Vinson's house. He told me to invite you."

I rushed home and returned the call.

"What do you mean, *we've* been invited?" I asked, my voice wary.

"Dude, he told me to invite you to his house."

"His house? He lived in an apartment the last time I —"

"Long story short — he owned a house which he moved out of after his last relationship went sour, before you. Court papers came and went and he moved back in. With Sloan Bonaventure as a roommate. And they're throwing a party on New Year's Eve and he invited us both. Yay."

"I thought Sloan had his own house."

"It was a rental."

"But I'm not even on speaking terms with Vinson. The guy could barely say 'hey' at the convenience store but now he invites me to his house on New Year's?"

"I thought you'd be happy," she said. "The other day, he came by The Tavern for a quick beer and we talked about you. He admitted screwing up with you, his exact words, and thought he could fix it on New Year's Eve. What more do you want?"

"Oh, I don't know, sending flowers, picking up the phone to invite me himself and begging for forgiveness? That could work."

"I agree with you but considering it's Vinson we're talking about, it's a promising perspective."

"I don't know. I'm hopeless."

"You're not hopeless, you're hopeful, even I know that. I asked him if he was sure about inviting you and he replied with 'please do'. You're welcome," she said.

"Thank you, my awesome girlfriend. It's on."

"That's more like it. My pleasure."

I let myself fall on the couch at a loss of words. Confusion, welcome back. Why didn't he pick up the phone and call now? If he wanted to fix our vibe, why wait until New Year's Eve?

CHAPTER
37

B y the first week of December, school had drained me sense-less. Exhausted from tests, projects, assignments and clinical practice, I could hardly find the energy to work on my blog. I had final exams coming up left and right. I had my nose in textbooks every minute of every day and sometimes at night.

But I pulled through to the end of the semester and exam time and mid-December caught me school-free and gratified. I had the first semester at UNO under my belt and I beamed with pride inside. The best part — I had time to blog, relax, socialize and most of all, sleep. The worst part — I had all the spare time in the world to ruminate about Vinson.

I pondered in my naivety if he'd send out a sign before the apparent private party. Crazy but I still waited for his call. I swore to myself so many times, I'd finally gotten over him but who was I kidding? Almost two years had passed since we first met and I still hadn't found a way. Not by a long shot.

On Christmas Eve, I exchanged gifts with Nikki at her house. We bought each other identical pink pajamas and socks with rac-coon faces imprinted on and — as corny as it sounds — we loved the idea. The day before, we took to shopping for our Christmas presents. When we roamed inside a store the size of a plane hangar, we split in opposite directions. We caught ourselves looming to one side, eyeing the same pajamas. We snatched them on the spot.

On Christmas Day, my first to spend it alone, I settled on the couch at my place with the TV on for company and yapped with my mom and Maureen on the phone. Still no sign of Vinson.

On New Year's Eve, Nikki called. "Sorry dude, Vinson's private party plans fell through."

"Why?"

"Brevin and I decided to stay home. Do you want to come to our house for the night?"

They had their reasons for the switch but I sailed with the plans. No point in asking information I wasn't meant to know.

I took over a bottle of gold tequila. We socialized in four, the same clique from Nikki's birthday. We diced riddles and puns over dinner and drinks and close to midnight, we played word games, listening to music. After all, I may have been spared a potential throwback to the fiends from spending the night at Vinson's.

Happy New Year 2012.

CHAPTER
38

On New Year's Day, we sipped on coffee and munched on breakfast to shunt the headaches from Nikki's homemade double-sized tequila shots. I stumbled home and crashed on the couch to wear off the hangover with mint tea and bad TV.

Three days later, I dreaded going back to school. I needed more time to unwind. I contemplated on skipping the first day of classes but at the last minute, I dragged myself to campus. I caught my wind back in Psychology, a full year course, the lecture held in the auditorium. I mean, if one doesn't get an appetite for school sitting in a majestic university amphitheater, one never will.

My spare time turned scarce again and Nikki grew unimpressed. Between classes and clinical practice, homework and studying, insert blogging and I couldn't produce a split moment to mingle with friends. I declined invitation after invitation to Nikki's house and her patience degenerated to indignation.

"I'd love to see you but I have tons of work," I said, on the phone.

"Is this what our friendship has been demoted to? A phone friendship?"

"I mostly have a phone friendship with my best friend from elementary and nothing's changed after all these years."

"You should know that I'm a physical person. I like my friends within reach," she said, her voice grave.

"I understand but —"

"Never mind. I'll call my sister."

CHAPTER
39

S ometime at the end of February, I snapped my eyes open at dawn with my soul ravaged. Vinson had visited me in my dreams. We smooched around the bed, heated and unguarded, like we did in our better days. I jerked up to the sitting position and scouted the room for his head flaring through the bedroom door, my dream so vivid.

I couldn't concentrate on anything else all day. I couldn't even study. The way he gazed at me in my sleep mesmerized me all over again. He'd slipped back on my mind along with questions that tormented me since day one. Would I ever see him again? Was he thinking about me now? Was he ever? He'd left an imprint on my soul. And he didn't even allow me to move on in my dreams.

CHAPTER
40

Four months later, the summer arrived with the first year of university under my belt and still on the Dean's List.

On a Sunday morning, I met Nikki for breakfast at Sammy's Diner in Thunder Hill. She'd planned a trip out of town to meet Brevin's parents and she wanted the two of us to make up for good luck. We took turns to apologize over coffee. I did for neglecting our friendship during school and she did for losing patience with me. Then we swayed back to her house for a window yap until her boyfriend returned from errands.

"I'll be meeting them for the first time," she said.

"I couldn't be happier for you. I'm announcing myself as one of the bridesmaids."

"That's a given. It will happen for you too."

"So, when's the wedding?"

"Wait, we're not even engaged yet. But you and I said we'd have our weddings together."

"We did but you'd be waiting to have yours for a long time."

A door slam echoed in the living room. Kara walked in, holding random coffees on a takeout tray. "

"Mmm, I love ready-made coffee," Nikki said, winking at me.

"We already had coffee."

"You can never have too much coffee," Kara snapped back, planting the tray on the coffee table. She sank into the couch, scanning Nikki's turquoise dress to match the wedges I'd brought for her from Romania. "Going out of town?"

Nikki ruffled her jet-black hair, uneasy with anticipation of her sister's next comment.

"It's meet-the-parents day, remember?"

"Be careful. They might like you too much," Kara said.

"Parents happen to like me a great deal, which is more than I can say for you missy," Nikki said and shot upright to the kitchen.

Kara spun her head in my direction, sending instant jitters down my legs. "And you? What are you doing for the rest of the day?" I shrugged my shoulders. "Do you want to go to dinner? I don't have plans either."

"Uhm —"

"I'll make the reservation."

A heavenly call on Kara's phone disturbed the awkward coercion and she stepped on the deck to take it. Nikki trooped back to me.

"Did my sister ask you to join her for dinner?"

"Yes and I don't know what we could possibly talk about at a restaurant."

"You should go. She's not as bad as she wants to come across."

"She left me no choice," I whispered, my tone satirical.

"Good. It beats sitting at home."

"Sloan and Vinson are coming over," Kara said as she pranced back in, phone in hand.

Nikki nudged my elbow. "See? It'll happen for you too."

"Sloan, as in Vinson's friend and Vinson, as in Sloan's friend?"

"Do we know any others by those names?" Kara said.

"Take it easy, sis. She's been in school for almost a year. She just came out of the cave."

"That's okay. I'm just . . . surprised. Does he know I'm here?"

"Yes, I told him."

The three of us moved camp on the deck sofa with chilled beer cans dripping sweat on the table to enjoy the beaming sun rays. June had the perfect weather conditions in Cape Kay. Warm enough to enjoy the outdoors but not hot enough to run for shade. The sunlit morning predicted a bright day with clear skies and suddenly the world turned pink and shiny. Nikki kept the front door unlocked during the day — and sometimes at night —

and when the boys arrived, they stumbled in noisy as ever, infusing the living room with tickled testosterone.

Vinson's voice rushed to my ears, like the blood in my veins.

"Ta-daaa," he said as he trampled on the deck, arms spread open, smoky sunglasses on his nose.

Sloan tailed behind. "Hi, girls." We all nodded and he gave each one of us a hug. Vinson held back.

The boys dropped into the patio chairs Nikki had aligned for them before she added two more beers to the table. Vinson's eye trajectory remained undetected. His face volleyed in different directions, angles slightly off my peripheral vision.

The deck soon breezed with laughter while Vinson slipped into the clown role, center of attention as always while Sloan inserted puns between his best friend's facial expressions. As the social banter filled the air, the portion of tension drifted away and the ambiance curved into relaxing and comfortable.

At first, Vinson and I weaved our words into the group chatter. But sooner than later, we shared direct thoughts like traffic on a two way road emerging from rush hour, at which point my butterflies kicked the bucket. Kind of.

"What are you guys doing later today?" Sloan asked.

"Going out of town with Brev," Nikki said with a beaming face.

"We're dinning out," Kara said, jerking her head my way. "Where do you want to go?" she asked and I blew out my cheeks.

The boys glimpsed at each other, then Vinson spoke. "Do you guys want company?"

Kara peeked sideways and my corner lip quirked up. "Yes."

I couldn't decide what shocked me more — Kara granting me the honour of visual confirmation or the picture of Vinson and me having dinner with friends. As I processed the would-be rest of the day, Brevin charged into the house. "Babe? Ready to go?"

Kara leaned close to my ear. "I'm heading home to change. Come to my place in an hour. I'll text you the address."

"But it's too early for dinner."

"We can do something before dinner." She winked, then she rose from the sofa.

"I'm leaving too," I said. Nikki escorted me to the door while her sister dashed to her car. "Have a great trip to your future in-laws. I'm sure they'll love you."

"Thanks, dude." She waited until the boys squeezed behind me and out the door. "I'm happy you and Vinson can socialize again. Today is an awesome day."

"You're my lucky charm," I said and wrapped my arms around her five feet four inch porcelain frame.

"Nikki," Brevin called out, tapping his foot on the floor at the speed of an angry hammer.

"I'm out. Enjoy your trip."

"Thanks. And do me a favour, punch Vinson for me if he screws up with you again, will you?" Brevin said.

"And another punch from me to snap him out of his immaturity," Nikki added.

"Consider it done," I said and rushed out the door.

I gunned it home and changed my attire to simple but elegant. I donned a black summer dress with straps, mid-length, bouffant and pliable and black wedges. Before I banged out the door, I splashed a touch of makeup to complete the dinner ensemble.

When I strode inside Kara's narrow but chic apartment, she and Vinson had engaged in an avid discussion by the kitchen counter. It sounded like business talk but his presence stunned me. Forever late, he'd returned to the meeting place first. He now sported knee-length beige cargos and a yellow T-shirt. Not too fancy for dinner but whatever.

I claimed a seat by the kitchen counter as Kara fished glasses out of a cupboard.

"Where's Sloan?" I asked in her direction.

"He's coming. He had to make a quick stop somewhere," Vinson jumped for the answer. The door flung open and Sloan bustled in. "There he is."

We yapped over lemonade while I tried to digest the momentum. After all the drama between Vinson and me, here we were, in the same room, mingling with friends like no big deal. I had trouble framing the normality of the scenario into our story. I wondered if I should be happy or worried.

The four of us decamped in two cars. I hopped in mine with Kara while the boys did in Sloan's metallic grey with black lining pickup. I hoped for Fusion on The Bounty but the crowd decided on a pizza joint. As we herded inside the restaurant, a dynamite convoy, the boys stumbled upon compadres and we regrouped at their table, dynamite no more. The crowd ballooned beyond my introvert taste but I had no choice, except to go along. Unless I wanted to go home and sulk on the couch on this fine late after- noon, which I didn't.

I eased into a chair with Kara on my right while Vinson sank in on my left, his knee brushing mine on his way down. I pretended oblivion but the butterflies awoke and tickled my gut.

"Do you think it's going to rain?" he asked, slanting his face at the clear blue sky, not a damn cloud in sight.

"I'm no weather woman," I said as greetings swirled around the table. Kara knew everyone short of two people. I knew no one, except for the three.

"I can see some clouds up there," Vinson said. I bet you can.

"Kara, is your bar-back working at The Tavern?" I asked.

"Why? You want to go there?"

"No, just curious."

She loomed closer. "You're sitting next to Vinson and you're asking me about The Tavern?"

"Just making conversation and he's the one who sat next to me."

Vinson's bare knee tapped mine again, his way of diverting my focus back to him and testing the air for my reaction.

"Isn't it strange? The two of us having dinner with friends?" he said. His knee stayed glued to mine this time.

"Sort of but not really," I said and his face grew somber.

This expression had gone down in the history of us as an answer he should have masticated to pieces, instead of shoving it out at me. Months ago when we were steady and nestled on his futon, I mentioned the word *frielationship* and he said, "we're more than friends, like, kind of together," and when my face brightened, he added, "well, sort of but not really."

I munched on a slice of pizza and slurped on iced tea while Kara and Sloan made plans for the four of us to go boating on the lake.

"Are you guys aware that I'm wearing sandals and a dress?"

"We said boating not swimming," Kara said. Back to the bitch version of herself.

Vinson dropped a hand on my leg. "That's okay. You'll be the sexy girl on the boat." I slipped a faded smile as Kara evil-eyed him. "We should take one car," he added.

"Good idea. We'll take mine," Sloan said, dropping a couple of bills on the table.

Vinson mounted a couple more on top. "Shall we?"

We broke away from the tabled group and headed to the parking lot. Kara paddled ahead with Sloan in a flirtatious body language while Vinson lingered next to me.

"I'll bring you back to your car. I promise," he said with a sparkle in his eyes. Then he tapped the back of his shoulder.

"You want me to jump on your back, so you can carry me to Sloan's truck?"

"Why not?"

"No, thanks. I can walk with my own two feet."

"Why don't you want me to carry you?"

"Because, no."

He raced behind me and lifted me in his arms, the way a groom carries his bride inside the matrimonial suite for the first time.

"Damn it, Vinson. Put me down."

"No."

"Okay. Don't put me down then. Fuck." And fuck the day you stormed into my life and turned it upside down, fuckboy.

When we reached Sloan's truck five steps away, Vinson slipped my body out of his arms and into the back seat and climbed in beside me. Kara joined Sloan in the front.

We listened to rock music and talked random crap on the drive. I sided along for good sport. Vinson scooted to the middle of the back seat and dropped his forearm on my leg as he chattered to the front seats and me occasionally. The blaring music made way for his whispers in my ear and whispering in my ear made way for his arm around my shoulder.

Sloan trundled to a stop on the lakeshore gravel and we scattered out to the marina. A couple on an anchored boat, more friends of friends, I presumed, waved at us. The couple expected us, Vinson & Co's entourage unlimited in numbers.

Vinson leaped inside the boat, then held out his hand for mine, true gentleman at heart but sometimes the gentleman disappeared, not the case today. The moment I lowered my foot onto the deck, the marvel of the facts sank into my brain. I'd have given years off my life for such normality in the past and now boom, I woke up in the morning and hours later, I boated with Vinson and friends.

After semi-awkward introductions, we sailed across the glistening water, basking in the sun. We disembarked on an island shore where a Sea-Doo afloat waited for us. Sloan and Kara, friends for a long time but in courtship as of late, mounted on the Sea-Doo and wandered into the horizon.

Vinson and I joined the boat owners for babble on the deck, bottles of ice cold beer in everyone's hands, except for mine. Mere words about the weather later, the gab centered on me, the new one in the crowd and I prayed to the mighty forces not to get grilled with questions. I've always dreaded those interview style conversations when meeting new people where I'm bombarded with queries about my likes and wants and dreams and aspirations and whether I'm secretly a vampire or not. I don't unravel my life story in half an hour to people whose names I forget within two seconds of meeting them.

Fortunately for me, the yap stayed on the light side, "Do you live in town?", "Where did you buy your shoes?" — I could handle that — after which the masculine half of the couple decided it was time for another sail. I like people who know what they want out of life. The man sailed the boat while his doting girlfriend held on to his waist from behind. The picture perfect of a retirees commercial, except for the age.

Vinson and I sprawled on the cushioned seats at the back and admired the town in the distance with its fumes and traffic without talking much at first, either because the wind flipped our hairs inside our mouths — his hair had grown mid-length by now — or not finding the right words. We sat up and leaned close to share our impressions on the million dollar mansions along the shore, a way to kill the taciturn vibe. Our heads grazed as we pointed and hummed, "Yeah, I like the one on the right," and "Whoa, check out the one to the left". A circle around the island later, we returned to the point of origin.

"I have to bring more friends off the main shore, so I'll drop the two of you off," the helmsman said and Vinson eyeballed me.

"You're not leaving us here, are you?" I asked, jolting upright. Then it dawned on me — holy crap, great idea. Sloan and Kara were still lost in their aquatic adventure. What more could I ask for than to be abandoned on an island with Vinson, uncomfortable silence or not? "I mean, not that it's a bad idea."

"OK. Let's go," Vinson said, then hopped off and offered me his hand. Before I slipped my hand into his, I took off my wedges. I sprang off the boat and into the tepid sand as I held on to him with one hand and my sandal laces with the other.

The boat sailed away and here we were dumped on an island, the first time we'd been alone in months. Eight months had passed since our brief gaze in the car when he dropped off Kara's movies and a blend of anguish and inner delight swooshed to the pit of my gut.

Vinson dragged his feet to a tree trunk discarded in the sand. I dipped mine into the cool water and squished the wet sand between my toes. I kicked the sand on my way to the tree trunk under his stare and dropped next to him. I still kept a glimpse of hope. I wished that by the evening's end, we'd recapture a particle of the connection we once shared. Kept my fingers crossed.

We faced the flaming sunset as it spread its wings across the lake and bounce its glow off the water. The sun settled down and if the panorama unveiling its splendor before our eyes could not bring a crack of old emotions out of our throats, nothing ever could. This was it. Our last chance to rekindle.

Vinson turned his face to me. "Look at that, you and me, alone on an island. Who would have thought?"

I'd already thought of that, you twerp. "I was going to say the same thing. Look at the sunset, isn't it beautiful?" Not that I came up with something cleverer. Or original.

"Yes, it is beautiful." And we'd become the official definition of lame. Before I forked out another crippled observation about the scenery, his tongue played hoops in my mouth, awkward moment sealed with a kiss.

"Make me understand . . . make me understand why we didn't work out," I said.

In the eleventh hour, I tried to find a solution to the puzzle but he gave a dreading whiff instead. I rose upright, away from his plastic arms and took two steps in the sand. He followed behind, yanked me back, laced my loose arms around his hips and raked his fingers through my hair.

We stood in the sand glued to each other and kissed in the sundown gleams. In the right context, what could be more romantic? But the real love story, the most important piece of the puzzle was missing. We'd lost it somewhere along the way long time ago. I wondered if he'd cuddle in this moment with anyone else — might as well take advantage of the sunset — as long as they bore a pair of tits.

He wriggled his hand into mine and tugged me back to the tree trunk, sat down and tapped for me to sit on his lap. I did.

"Oh, Vinson."

He buried his head in my chest like a child and I kissed the top of his head, caressed the silk of his hair. What was it with these noncommittal freaks — insert Zee's picture — begging to be doted on? I held a steady ninety percent in Psychology, recited it in my sleep and chewed it for breakfast but I could never find the secret keyhole to these guys. I checked their backs but nothing there.

"I'm glad we're friends again," I said. The silence had turned dense and it needed a spatter.

He straightened his posture and kissed the back of my hand. "Me too, doll. Me too." He pulled me into claim, a superficial one until further notice, and kissed me with lips made of sugar.

The Sea-Doo roared in the close distance and grew louder by the second. Kara waved a hand as she and Sloan approached the island. A hundred feet away, the boat sailed in our direction, bringing more friends of friends, girls screaming at the top of their lungs, as if the ferry was on the leg of sinking. Great.

The boat and the Sea-Doo anchored ashore as the newcomers jumped off and everyone gathered in a crowd. No introductions this time because the new girls didn't give a shit who was who and who did what. They just wanted to rumble.

As the evening settled in, the boys built a bonfire. Cold beer and bursts of sharp laughter looped around the fire. Vinson broke away toward the new arrivals. I camped outside the circle next to Kara on a nearby boulder as Vinson shone in the center of attention again. The perpetual entertainer never lets down his crowd, except for the person who loves him the most.

After dark, when the beer-well dried, the boys put out the fire. Then we squeezed on the boat and sailed to the main shore. The four of us crossed over first with the helmsman and his girlfriend. The boat sailor would then return to the island for the next round of passengers, the ones I didn't care about. But Vinson might.

"My house guys. The party continues at my house. I'll meet y'all there," the helmsman said as we hopped onto the marina board.

We piled in Sloan's truck and Kara rode in the back with me. Not sure who changed the rules or if the rules changed themselves but it came as a good idea anyway. I shot her the I-don't-want-to-go-to-this-guy's-house look, snapped my eyebrows to underline my want and she shrugged her shoulders. What could she do?

We parked in the driveway in our wait for the rest of the gang to arrive along with the host, listening to low radio music, not a word said out loud. Twenty lousy minutes later, everyone scattered across the helmsman's living room, yapping and laughing. I dipped into the lazyboy — lucky I scooped it up first — and reclined. I drifted into my own silence while everyone mingled and sometimes I murmured gibberish to Kara, who sat in a stiff chair next to me.

After pizza arrived, the chatter dimmed but once consumed, the commotion ascended to mayhem. Everyone screamed at each other with enthusiasm as stinging laughter serrated my ear drums. Vinson scrunched up his face, so the bratty chicks could laugh, a chain reaction going spiral. And all I could think of was my car waiting for me in a hollow parking lot.

Close to the end of the night, Vinson winked at me from across the room where he seated himself, so the rowdy bimbos could have a clear picture of him. He mouthed, "Are you okay?" to which I nodded, "Yes," and that was the extent of our interaction at the house party. I struggled with my sanity in the midst of the uproar.

We vacated the insane asylum around four a.m. and I took in the serene nocturnal breeze. I rushed my sandy feet in Sloan's truck, wedges dangling in my right hand and surprise-surprise, Vinson compressed in the back seat with me. I creased my forehead and he loomed close to steal a kiss, still checking if I'm under his hook. I turned my head to glance out the window and he kissed the air. He took it in stride as Sloan and Kara climbed in the front, then joined the after-party banter with music in the background all the way back.

Sloan rounded the truck in the pizza joint parking lot, a couple of empty spots away from my car. Vinson leaped out and held my hand as I stepped onto the pavement.

"I had a good time tonight. I'll see you soon," he said.

"Goodnight." He planted a kiss goodbye on my lips before I had the chance to turn my head.

I pulled away unimpressed, gave Sloan a friendly hug and strode to my car. Kara joined me moments after giving her share of hugs and goodnights. Before Sloan revved the engine away, Vinson blew a kiss my way from the rolled-down window. I let it squirm to the ground and stomped on it with my car wheels on the way out of the parking lot.

"Do you want to talk about it?" Kara asked on the drive home.

"Talk about what?"

"Tonight. I thought you might want to talk about tonight at my place. But let's do coffees first."

I changed the route via first open coffee drive-thru on the way to her place.

"What do you think about today?" she asked once we took our seats at the kitchen counter.

"Not sure what to think."

"Why? What's wrong?"

"I don't know. When we were alone on the island, affection came out of his pores but back in the group, he hardly acknowledged my presence," I said as I craned the coffee cup to my lips.

"Yeah but that's Vinson. He has the attention span of a two-year-old."

"I'm serious. It's like, he's two different people."

"That's because sometimes, he is. But I thought his behaviour to you was genuine tonight."

"Really?"

"Yes. I think it was a promising restart for the two of you."

"He could've fooled me."

Nikki texted one afternoon. "I'm downstairs with Sloan. We're waiting for you." Sloan's monster — black linings and all — idled downstairs deafening my neighbours to death.

Dressed and ready to go, I snagged the keys and my tote and descended with a frown. Nikki sat in the passenger seat with her side of the pickup toward the building's front door and waited for me with the door open.

"I thought we were spending the night at your place."

"We are but we're going to the lake first," Nikki said.

"Again?"

I flicked a hello at Sloan, then forced my eyes in a straight gaze to keep them from swirling around inside the car in search for Vinson. Two weekends had passed without a word from him and I wished words were made out of cardboard, so I could make him swallow them whole.

"It's again for you but it's not again for me. I heard you guys had a blast. I want some of that too."

"They can speak for themselves," I mumbled under my breath as I scrambled into the back. "The lake it is. And you can tell me about your visit with the in-laws."

She peeked over her shoulder. "I'll save the details for later but long story short, they loved me."

"I told you they would."

We gravel-parked at the lake and the same story unfolded but without Vinson, the boat and the screaming nuggets. Nikki and I took turns riding with Sloan on the Sea-Doo circling the island, the lonely tree trunk in the sand setting off flashbacks but not for long. The lake adventure came short and sweet this time around, much to my delight.

Sloan swerved the truck on the road, then took turns familiar to the ones leading to my place.

"Sloan, I'm not going home. I'm spending the night at Nikki's."

"I'm driving to my place, sweetie. I need to change my clothes and I'll join you two for a while."

"Your place as in Vinson's house?"

"You're cool with that, right?" He slipped a brotherly smile in the rear view mirror.

"Why wouldn't I be?" I leaned against the back of the seat and swallowed my abrupt anguish.

Sloan parked in the driveway behind Vinson's truck, which gave me the jitters. I gasped in awe at how close Vinson lived from my apartment. A two-minute drive, not to mention the house was located on the road I took to and back from school. I must have driven by this house a hundred times, unaware who hid inside.

A humble house but cute enough for two, should a woman add a lively touch and switch the exterior wall paint to a warm hue, instead of the gloomy grey. I trailed my friends inside the house through an emotional pole vault jump.

Once in the living room, humble didn't suit the house but rather neglected, uncared for, the furniture bland, the walls too. Clothes were scattered everywhere, empty boxes of pizza piled on the counter, dirty dishes mounted in the sink. I didn't recall Vinson's place this messy when he lived in the bachelor.

"Sorry for the mess," Sloan said, his expression demure.

"Where's Vinson?" Nikki asked.

"Out but I don't know where," he said.

"What do you mean 'you don't know'? Aren't you roommates and best friends?" she asked as I inspected Vinson's family photos on a side table.

In a photograph, a teenage Vinson with hair down to his waist wore a Pink Floyd T-shirt flanked by mama and papa. In another, he posed with his two sisters and a birthday cake. "To our wonderful brother who is one of a kind," they wrote at the bottom. He sure is. In a third, he held on to a brown ball with CFL initials, next to a couple of friends who held beers in mid-air. I guess he liked football after all.

"He doesn't always tell me where he's going or when he's coming back," Sloan said. Then the justification stopped. He could've winked Nikki into silence for all I knew.

I couldn't escape the irony. My first visit to Vinson's house — the actual house, not some rented basement apartment he fell behind on rent every month just because he kept forgetting to write a damn check — took place in his absence. How bizarre! Despite my inner torment, I wished my first visit to his house transpired with the two of us play-fighting and ordering pizza and exhausting our senses over multiple fornications. Basically, a repeat of our rendezvous at the rented basement apartment he fell behind on rent every month just because he kept forgetting to write a damn check.

"I'll be back," Sloan said and dissipated into what I guessed was his bedroom.

Nikki and I waited on the couch.

"I'd say things are evolving," she said.

"Sure they are, except he's not here."

"Can you look at the positive side for once? You're sitting on his couch."

"He doesn't even know I'm here. I'm actually being realistic for once."

"I'm ready," Sloan said, back in the living room, tugging at the cufflinks on his blue shirt.

"Going on a date?" Nikki asked as we stood up.

"No. I wanted to look sharp."

"Kara won't be at my place tonight."

"I know."

Layers deep down inside beyond realistic thinking, I still hoped down to the last step out the door that Vinson would show up, his face would brighten up about my visit and I'd jump in his arms with joy. Then I'd slap his left cheek for failing to invite me over myself. I descended the front stairs in dejection.

At Nikki's, us girls sipped on iced tea with music in the background while Sloan cracked jokes on an assembly line, beer bottle in hand. I slipped forced smiles and pretended the visit at Vinson's had little to no effect on me. But it had. Like nothing else.

Sloan shifted his eyes to me, then shimmied over from the far side of the couch. He hailed one arm around my shoulder and I slanted my head to follow his hand in surprise.

"I've had enough of this charade. Someone has to tell you."

"Tell me what?"

"I won't beat around the bush. Move on, Alexa. You're a great girl and I'm telling you as a friend to move on. He's not good enough for you. You deserve so much better."

Acid soared like a fountain from my gut to my throat. "But Sloan," I said, scooting away as his arm fell to the side, "when we're together, he acts like he wants to be with me but when we're not, on to the flip side."

"He's my best friend and we talk." He sighed. "I can tell you many stories but trust me, you don't want to know." His gaze pronounced silent condolences and I might as well have been attending a funeral. My own, because my heart seized. Then he awoke my heart with a tap on my back. "Do yourself a favour and move on. That's all I'm saying."

"Thanks, Sloan. Now she'll take off," Nikki said, returning from the kitchen.

Sloan's intention to spare me the lingering pain with words I'd known all along still came as a big blow. I bobbed my head like a dashboard doll while my heart chambers drowned in agony.

"I . . ." I shot straight for the door with Nikki chasing behind.

"Dude, you can't go. You're pale as a ghost." The alphabet turned into slush on my tongue and I forgot to speak. "You can't be alone right now. Come inside." I shook my head as my eyes flooded with tears. "Listen, why don't you give Sloan a chance?" she asked, casually, as if she'd suggested a stroll in the park. I crumpled my face, as if trying to understand someone who spoke Sanskrit. "He always told me, he'd go for you in two seconds straight."

"What?"

"I said, why —"

"I thought he was going for Kara."

"You'd be his first choice." I jerked my head back in confusion. "Don't get me wrong, I want you to be with Vinson but he's never around. Sloan would be glued to you twenty four seven."

"I have to go," I muttered and angled away.

"Call me later?"

I staggered on the sidewalk in a daze, eyes fixated in mid-air, my heart inflicted with pain, my soul hollow like an empty bottle. I waved a cab down and stared out the window like a zombie on the ride. And all the way home, Sloan's words echoed in my head over and over again, chopping my heart into fragments of nothing.

CHAPTER
41

Early July caught me driving to The 6ix for a dazzling summer lunch with Maureen. Her husband planned to whisk her to a secluded cabin, days later on her birthday. We spent half a day together, sipping on light cocktails on the patio at La Rocca and marinating in a healthy dose of optimism.

Returning to Cape Kay, I inevitably passed Vinson's house on my way home. I rolled to a stop at a red light before my wheels would hug the right corner that edged the road snaking to my zip code. Music resonated in my earphones and my finger tapped to the beat on the steering wheel.

Sloan's frame stung the corner of my eye from the top of a staircase outside a bar across the road. He gestured to company sitting on the steps behind the banister. I yanked the earbuds out of my ears and glanced at the light. Still red.

"Sloan, Sloan," I yelled and waved with my arm out the window. He only meant well after all.

He waved back, then Vinson jolted up from behind the wooden rail. I hardened my face and snapped my arm back in.

Vinson beckoned. "Alexa, why don't you come in for a drink?"

He held my gaze — but I didn't flinch — until a horn from behind startled me back into motion. I stamped on the pedal around the corner and flipped him the finger in my head.

CHAPTER
4 2

A lightning bolt lanced through the August sky in a spectacle of light, set to drench the town in drizzle. The show came as a nocturnal delight after a long day of juggling letters off the keyboard. The thunderstorm reminded me of my rendezvous with Vinson in his minuscule bachelor when he was human and funny and loving and kind.

The phone buzz pulled my mind back. I glided to the coffee table and cast an eye on the display. Nikki. Phone to my ear without a word.

"I have to tell you something but please, don't hold it against me," she said. Whatever it was, it didn't sound good.

"What is it?"

"I think you know."

"What do I know?"

"You know."

I huffed. "If this is about Vinson, I don't —"

"Yes, it is."

"What? What is it?"

"I'm scared to tell you." Only one thing in the world Nikki was terrified to confess.

"Is Vinson in a relationship?"

"Yeah," she said and I sensed the blood dripping away from my face. Drip-drip-drip.

I eased into the couch with my legs numb from the knees up and my heartbeat in my throat.

"Is it with someone I know?" I muttered.

"Yeah."

The cell phone trembled in my hand. "Who is it?"

"It's my sister." In an instant, I recalled Kara's car in Vinson's driveway more than once. Nothing uncanny crossed my mind at the time, except for two longtime friends hanging out. But now, the final piece of the puzzle clicked into its shape. "But please, don't hold it against me. I'm not my sister," she added.

"But I thought she was my friend. How can she do that to me?"

"I don't know how it happened but it did. They are together again."

"What do you mean, 'again'?"

"They . . . sort of have history together."

I fell against the back of the couch as my heart turned to stone.

"What kind of . . .?" And a spark dawned on my face. "Is she his ex . . . like, *the* ex? The one he broke up with six months before he met me?" And I didn't wait for the answer. "Why didn't anyone tell me? Why didn't *you* tell me?"

"I . . . I thought that if I told you, I'd ruin things between you two even more. You were so in love with him and I did want you guys to wind up together."

I shifted my eyes sideways on the wall, anger infusing in the seams of my stomach.

"But she encouraged me and even helped me get together with him."

"That was her way of playing him, making him think she doesn't care. I didn't even realize this until lately."

"What about Sloan? I thought she liked Sloan."

She released a big puff. "Her way of making Vinson jealous. Sloan and Kara played second fiddle to each other on purpose. I told you, Sloan wanted you from the beginning."

"My God," I said and swallowed hard, my throat dry as the desert. "I've been living a lie all this time."

"Not entirely. I've always been your friend. And I would never do that to you."

"You should've told me the truth."

"I thought it was over between them and it was, for the longest time. And then, I thought he'd brush her off if she tried anything and you guys would be together in the end."

"He never loved me."

"He did. I know he did."

"Then why is he with her now?"

"That's what Brevin and I are trying to figure out."

I rearranged my thoughts but no matter how many times I did it, they lined up the same way. And I cringed with disgust.

"How long?"

"Them two? About a month or so."

"About a month? That's around the time I saw him with Sloan in front of a bar on my way into town. He called out for me to join them for a drink."

"Really?"

"I don't get it. The guy has commitment phobia."

"She wants to move in with him. Again. But for whatever's worth, I don't think they're going to last." I dropped the phone on the couch with Nikki's words reverberating into the room. "They broke up once before . . . Hello . . . Dude, are you okay? Hello?"

I soared off the couch with a frozen heart from the double betrayal. Double, triple, I'd lost count on the rogues. My blood swished through my veins dead cold, my lips frosty, my eyes glacial and wide open.

The room spun around me as I stood in the dark with my insides crumbling. I flew down the hallway and snatched my car keys and my tote. I threw my coat over my pajamas and stormed out the door. I had to get out of Dodge. Away from this town and never to return.

As I charged out of the lobby, the wind tossed me to the ground, my hair to high heavens and my keys through my fingers. I scouted the grid in the moonlight and crawled on the soaked cement to reach for the keys. I limped up, unlocked the car door, swung it open and dragged the defeated version of myself in the driver seat.

I turned the keys and *On the turning away* exploded mid-song from the speakers. And no more holding back the tears. I punched the steering wheel and wailed and wailed with my heart ripped into shreds and my gut turned into soup.

I squealed away from the parking lot, *On the turning away* pre-set on repeat. I took the dark-dark road away from home, cutting corners on two wheels. The tires slid on the moistened road, throwing rainwater off the ground. The wiper blades squeaked against the glass in vain, the windshield thicker and thicker with pouring rain. At the crossroads — the same one Vinson beckoned me for a drink — I veered to the left and the tires skidded out of control. The car lifted its nose, then the body and spun in the air with me clasping on to the steering wheel, rotating like an aerobatic aircraft before a deafening sound rammed the tail of my car into the crepuscule. Crash.

The darkness turned into light as I drifted into a high beam ceiling church. Humans crowded the chamber, some familiar and others not. I pranced down the aisle, my dress immaculate, a perfect pick. My heart smiled, my soul roared. The guests scanned my bridal aura of incandescent emotion with glorifying delight.

Mom gaped on from the first row with tears of joy. Vinson smiled with adoring eyes from the mouth of the altar, draped in a tuxedo, his hair sleek like satin and parted on one side. Sloan stood as best man followed by friends whose names I never remembered. From the left flank of the aisle, Maureen, Serena, Heather, Tania and Nikki shot encouraging squints my way. The bridesmaids wore fuchsia dresses and commended my steps on the corridor of bliss. Except for Kara at the back of the line dressed in jet-black.

The groom held his hand for mine. I slipped my palm into his as we united at the altar.

"I'd been waiting for this moment all of my life," he said and I embraced my dream come true.

We voyaged into each other's eyes as we spoke our eternity vows.

"I love you."

"I love you more."

"I love you the most."

We locked lips and sealed the deal. I shut my eyes to taste his kiss, honeysuckle and mint, deep in my bones, deep in my brain.

I snapped my eyes open as ambulance sirens grew nearer by the second. The world hung belly up as rain drops clashed on the windshield and the gloom pressed on my soul. I unbuckled the seat belt, dropped and turned slow as a serpent until my eyes aligned with the horizon. I tilted my head in the cracked rear view mirror, my face purple and bloody. Specks of raw flesh on my arms shone in the dark and only then, my body ached with every inch.

I kicked the car door open and comminuted windows crumbled to the ground. I crawled out and away, chasing the fumes of a pickup truck rolled on its cheek with the windshield shattered and the wheels gyrating like French roulette. And the closer I loomed, the more I trembled with fear. Fear I dreaded to fear. His chin was dunked into his chest, his body belted into the seat.

I extended my hand, shaky and mortal through the windshield frame and brushed the dashboard to flip his hair away. Away from his forehead, away from his face. As my fingertips swam through, my chest rose out of composure and my pulse hastened in fright. I tucked the hazelnut strands behind his ear and gasped in anguish. Tiny pieces of broken glass slithered from his locks as he craned his head up with blood dripping down his temples and one eye swollen shut.

I cupped his head in my hands. "Stay still. Stay still. Help is on the way . . ." I choked on my words and tears mixed with a tint of revenge.

He parted his bloody lips as his tongue — a velvety one, the one I played with for hours on end and marked its territory inside my mouth — found its way into muttered speech.

"I . . . w . . . coming . . . t . . . see . . . you."

"Shhh, don't speak."

I lay still halfway through the windshield frame, nestling his head in my chest as my tears drenched his hair, loose over my forearm.

"I . . .," Vinson mouthed and his tongue twisted into the letter L up at the roof of his mouth. Then his eyelids sealed over the distended, uneven pupils drowned in sorrow and his head dropped in my hands like a dying butterfly.

ACKNOWLEDGMENTS

Forever grateful to Maria for your eternal support and words of wisdom each and every time I needed a strong shoulder to lean on and those times came in high numbers. You are my rock and my optimistic bubble. You motivate me to become a better person every day. You've taught me so much about friendships and life in general. And you gave me that extra kick to write my first book. Your existence brightens my life.

Deep thanks to my mother for putting up with my tantrums and mood swings during the writing process, especially when dead ends in disguise ate at my soul from the inside out. I am indebted to you for your patience and understanding in those times of script crisis and not only. Thank you for your kind words and dedication from the time I was born to infinity.

To my dad, you are and will be forever an inspiration for me. I know you're watching from high heavens with your protective armour over me.

Thank you to my partner in crime, Harley. You patiently stood by me every single day and encouraged me with your beautiful bright eyes and kind heart. You are my prince and always will be. I love you to the moon and back.

Last but not least, a warm thank you to my wonderful readers. You have my deepest gratitude for taking a chance on me as a first time author and for perpetuating the art of reading. I hope you enjoy this dramatic tale of friendship, love and heartbreak. Some of you may even relate to this story. This book is for you and anyone else who wants to read it.

ABOUT THE AUTHOR

E. E. Robens is a Canadian-Romanian writer who embraces life on both sides of the Atlantic. She is equally fascinated by state-of-the-art libraries and minimalist interiors. She graduated from university with a degree in the medical field but took to writing to fulfill a long-awaited dream. *Spellbound* is her first novel.

www.ingramcontent.com/pod-product-compliance
Lightning Source LLC
Chambersburg PA
CBHW051940240626
47153CB00005B/1566